Derivatives Demystified

Wiley Finance Series

Derivatives Demystified

A Step-by-Step Guide to Forwards, Futures,
Swaps and Options

Andrew M. Chisholm

John Wiley & Sons, Ltd

Other Wiley Editorial Offices

John Wiley & Sons Inc., 111 River Street, Hoboken, NJ 07030, USA

Jossey-Bass, 989 Market Street, San Francisco, CA 94103-1741, USA

Wiley-VCH Verlag GmbH, Boschstr. 12, D-69469 Weinheim, Germany

John Wiley & Sons Australia Ltd, 33 Park Road, Milton, Queensland 4064, Australia

John Wiley & Sons (Asia) Pte Ltd, 2 Clementi Loop #02-01, Jin Xing Distripark, Singapore 129809

John Wiley & Sons Canada Ltd, 22 Worcester Road, Etobicoke, Ontario, Canada M9W 1L1

Wiley also publishes its books in a variety of electronic formats. Some content that appears
in print may not be available in electronic books.

Library of Congress Cataloging-in-Publication Data

Chisholm, Andrew, 1952–
Derivatives demystified : a step-by-step guide to forwards, futures, swaps & options / Andrew M. Chisholm.
    p.   cm.
Includes bibliographical references and index.
ISBN 0-470-09382-X (alk. paper)
1. Derivative securities.   I. Title.
HG6024.A3C487   2004
332.64'57–dc22   2004002791

British Library Cataloguing in Publication Data

A catalogue record for this book is available from the British Library

ISBN 10: 0-470-09382-X (pb)
ISBN 13: 978-0470-09382-5 (pb)

Typeset in 10/12pt Times by TechBooks, New Delhi, India
Printed and bound in Great Britain by MPG Limited, Bodmin, Cornwall
This book is printed on acid-free paper responsibly manufactured from sustainable forestry
in which at least two trees are planted for each one used for paper production.

For Margaret and Sheila

Contents

Preface

This book is based on a series of seminars delivered over a period of many years to people working in the global financial markets. The material has expanded and evolved over that time. Participation on the seminars has covered the widest possible spectrum in terms of age, background and seniority, ranging all the way from new graduate entrants to the financial services industry up to very senior managing directors. What all these many and varied individuals had in common was a strong desire to understand how derivative products are used in practice, without becoming too involved in the more complex mathematics of the subject.

The seminars (and this book) originated from the conviction that bankers, fund managers and other professionals in the modern financial markets must have a grasp of derivative products. In fact the target audience broadened out over the years to include technology specialists, operations experts, finance professionals working in the corporate environment and their business advisers. It is estimated that over 90% of the world's largest 500 companies now use derivatives to help to manage their exposures to the risks arising from factors such as currency fluctuations, interest rate changes and unstable commodity prices.

Derivatives are everywhere in the modern world, but sometimes are not easily detected except by those in the know. If you have the option to extend a loan or redeem a mortgage early, then you have a derivative product. If a company has the opportunity to increase its production facilities or exploit some new technology, then it has what is known in the world of derivatives as a *real option*. This has a value, and given certain assumptions its value can be measured.

It is my view that with a little application anyone can achieve a working knowledge of the key derivative products. It is not widely appreciated that many people in the financial markets who handle derivatives regularly are not specialists in higher mathematics. Nor is it important for them to be so, but they do need to understand how the products can be used in practice to create risk management, investment and trading solutions that are appropriate for particular organizations in certain market circumstances. The real strength of derivatives is that they offer a new set of tools with which to solve real-world problems. They are not a substitute for thought or creativity; quite the reverse. Human beings have to analyse the problems and learn how to use the appropriate tools to design the best possible solutions.

A number of excellent textbooks are available that take a quantitative approach to this subject and explain in detail the pricing models used to value derivative products. At the end of this book there is a list of further reading for those who wish to delve more deeply into this subject.

There is also an appendix covering some of the basic financial calculations, and although this material provides a useful background to the main text, it is not absolutely essential reading. The primary objective of this book is to help readers to develop a solid working knowledge of the key derivative products through a range of practical examples, case studies and illustrations, using the minimum amount of mathematics.

It is important, however, not to gloss over the significant developments that have occurred in the derivatives industry in recent years. Without this background it is difficult to appreciate how derivatives are radically changing the way risk is managed and investments are structured. For this reason the book includes details of what are sometimes known as 'exotic options' – products with arcane names such as barriers, cliquets and choosers. It is perfectly possible to achieve a respectable understanding of such products without knowing how the pricing models are constructed, and I hope to show that the effort is well worth while. There are also discussions of highly versatile new instruments called credit default swaps, and a final chapter is devoted to the creation of structured securities using standard and exotic derivative products.

The book is constructed as follows. Chapter 1 provides additional background about the derivatives industry and explains the basic building blocks used to create a myriad of derivatives solutions and structured products. Chapters 2 and 3 consider forward contracts, including forwards on shares, currencies and interest rates. Chapters 4 and 5 discuss futures contracts, which are the exchange-traded relatives of forwards. They explore futures on commodities, bonds, interest rates, equity indices and individual shares. Chapters 6 and 7 concern a key product in modern finance, the swap transaction. The focus is on real-world applications of interest rate, cross-currency, equity and credit default swaps.

Chapter 8 begins the discussion on option contracts by introducing the fundamentals of the subject. Some readers may already be familiar with this material although the chapter provides a useful platform of knowledge for the later development. Chapter 9 provides a wide range of examples of the practical applications of options in hedging and risk management. The discussion is not confined to standard or 'plain vanilla' options but explores some of the newer products created in recent years. Chapter 10 covers exchange-traded equity options, on single shares and on indices, while Chapters 11 and 12 consider the applications of currency and interest rate contracts, including products such as caps, floors, collars and swaptions.

Chapters 13 and 14 outline the basic concepts involved in option valuation and risk management, but the treatment here is intuitive rather than mathematical. They explain the idea of the expected payout of an option; and introduce the industry standard Black–Scholes option pricing model and its sensitivities, the so-called 'Greeks': delta, gamma, theta, vega and rho. Later, in Appendix A, there is an explanation of how the model can be set up on a simple Excel spreadsheet. Chapters 15 and 16 build on this discussion to consider how option traders manage the risks on their positions; and some key trading applications of options, including volatility trades and certain applications of non-standard or 'exotic' contracts, are presented. These chapters are especially aimed at people who are likely to be involved with options from a dealer's perspective rather than that of the 'end-users' who are simply using options to manage risk or enhance investment returns.

Chapter 17 explores convertible and exchangeable bonds – securities whose returns are linked to the value of a share or a portfolio of shares. Chapter 18 contains an extended case study on structuring new types of investment products using standard and exotic options, and concludes with a discussion on a process known as securitization – one of the most significant developments in modern finance. The chapter also presents an example of how credit default swaps are being used to create new families of securities. For those who wish to explore the mathematical aspect of the subject, Appendix A gives a brief review of the fundamental financial calculations that form the background to derivative products. Appendix B contains an extensive glossary of the terms used in the industry, and Appendix C gives some suggestions for further reading, together with a list of useful websites.

In writing this book, I have benefited enormously from the ideas, comments and suggestions made by many seminar participants over the years. I also owe a debt of gratitude to all the derivatives market practitioners who have deepened my understanding of the subject by allowing me to observe how they work and by sparing the time to discuss their activities. My hope is that some portion of their creativity and enthusiasm is transferred to the book, although, of course, I take full responsibility for all errors or omissions in the finished product. Finally, I give special thanks to Sir George Mathewson and John Davie who (no doubt inadvertently) started me off on this road so many years ago.

The Market Background

DERIVATIVES BUILDING BLOCKS

A derivative is an asset whose value is derived from the value of some other asset, known as the *underlying*. Imagine that you have signed a legal contract that, with the payment of a premium, gives you the option to buy a fixed quantity of gold at a fixed price of $100 at any time in the next three months. The gold is currently worth $90 in the world market. The option is a derivative and the underlying is gold. If the value of gold increases, then so does the value of the option, because it gives you the right (but not the obligation) to buy the metal at a predetermined price.

For example, suppose that the market price of gold rose sharply in the weeks after signing the deal and the quantity specified in the contract was now worth $150. Then you could if you wished exercise (take up) the option, buy the gold for $100, and immediately sell it on to a dealer for $150. The option contract has become a rather valuable item. Suppose, instead, that the price of gold had collapsed, and the quantity specified in the contract was only worth $50. The option would then be virtually worthless, and it is unlikely that it would ever be exercised.

Derivatives are based on a very wide range of underlying assets. This includes metals such as gold and silver; commodities such as wheat and orange juice; energy resources such as oil and gas; and financial assets such as shares, bonds and foreign currencies. In all cases, the link between the derivative and the underlying commodity or financial asset is one of value. An option to buy a share at a fixed price is a derivative of the underlying share because if the share price increases then so too does the value of the option.

In the modern world there is a huge variety of different derivative products. These are traded on organized exchanges or agreed directly in the so-called over-the-counter (OTC) market, where deals are contracted over the telephone or through electronic media. The good news is that the more complex structures are constructed from some simple building blocks – forwards and futures; swaps; and options – which are defined below.

Forwards. A forward contract is a contractual agreement made directly between two parties. One party agrees to buy a commodity or a financial asset on a date in the future at a fixed price. The other side agrees to deliver that commodity or asset at the predetermined price. There is no element of optionality about the deal. Both sides are obliged to go through with the contract, which is a legal and binding commitment, irrespective of the value of the commodity or asset at the point of delivery. Since forwards are negotiated directly between two parties, the terms and conditions of a contract can be customized. However, there is a risk that one side might default on its obligations.

Futures. A futures contract is essentially the same as a forward, except that the deal is made through an organized and regulated exchange rather than being negotiated directly between two parties. One side agrees to deliver a commodity or asset on a future date (or within a range of dates) at a fixed price, and the other party agrees to take delivery. The contract is a legal and binding commitment. There are three key differences between forwards and futures. Firstly, a futures contract is guaranteed against default. Secondly, futures are standardized, in order to promote active trading. Thirdly, they are settled on a daily basis. The settlement process is explained in detail in later chapters.

Swaps. A swap is an agreement made between two parties to exchange payments on regular future dates, where the payment legs are calculated on a different basis. As swaps are OTC deals, there is a risk that one side or the other might default on its obligations. Swaps are used to manage or hedge the risks associated with volatile interest rates, currency exchange rates, commodity prices and share prices. A typical example occurs when a company has borrowed money from a bank at a variable rate and is exposed to an increase in interest rates; by entering into a swap the company can fix its cost of funding. (Although it is often considered as one of the most basic types of derivative product, a swap is actually composed of a series of forward contracts.)

Options. A call option gives the holder the right to buy an underlying asset by a certain date at a fixed price. A put option conveys the right to sell an underlying asset by a certain date at a fixed price. The purchaser of an option has to pay an initial sum of money called the premium to the seller or writer of the contract. This is because the option provides flexibility; it need never be exercised (taken up). Options are either negotiated between two parties in the OTC market, one of which is normally a specialist dealer, or freely traded on organized exchanges. Traded options are generally standardized products, though some exchanges have introduced contracts with some features that can be customized.

MARKET PARTICIPANTS

Derivatives have a very wide range of applications in business as well as in finance. There are four main participants in the derivatives market: dealers, hedgers, speculators and arbitrageurs. The same individuals and organizations may play different roles in different market circumstances. There are also large numbers of individuals and organizations supporting the market in various ways.

- *Dealers.* Derivative contracts are bought and sold by dealers who work for major banks and securities houses. Some contracts are traded on exchanges, others are OTC transactions. In a large investment bank the derivatives operation is now a highly specialized affair. Marketing and sales staff speak to clients about their requirements. Experts help to assemble solutions to those problems using combinations of forwards, swaps and options. Any risks that the bank assumes as a result of providing tailored products for clients is managed by the traders who run the bank's derivatives books. Meantime, risk managers keep an eye on the overall level of risk the bank is running, and mathematicians – known as 'quants' – devise the tools required to price new products.
- *Hedgers.* Corporations, investing institutions, banks and governments all use derivative products to hedge or reduce their exposures to market variables such as interest rates, share values, bond prices, currency exchange rates and commodity prices. The classic example is the farmer who sells futures contracts to lock into a price for delivering a crop on a future date. The buyer might be a food-processing company which wishes to fix a price for taking delivery of the crop in the future, or a speculator. Another typical case is that of a company due to receive a payment in a foreign currency on a future date. It enters into a forward

transaction with a bank agreeing to sell the foreign currency and receive a predetermined quantity of domestic currency. Or it buys an option which gives it the right but not the obligation to sell the foreign currency at a set exchange rate.

- *Speculators.* Derivatives are very well suited to speculating on the prices of commodities and financial assets and on key market variables such as interest rates, stock market indices and currency exchange rates. Generally speaking, it is much less expensive to create a speculative position using derivatives than by actually trading the underlying commodity or asset. As a result, the potential returns are that much greater. A classic application is the trader who believes that increasing demand or reduced production is likely to boost the market price of a commodity. As it would be too expensive to buy and store the physical commodity, the trader buys an exchange-traded futures contract, agreeing to take delivery on a future date at a fixed price. If the commodity price increases, the value of the contract will also rise and can then be sold back into the market at a profit.
- *Arbitrageurs.* An arbitrage is a deal that produces risk-free profits by exploiting a mispricing in the market. A simple example occurs when a trader can purchase an asset cheaply in one location and simultaneously arrange to sell it in another at a higher price. Such opportunities are unlikely to persist for very long, since arbitrageurs would rush in to buy the asset in the 'cheap' location, thus closing the pricing gap. In the derivatives business arbitrage opportunities typically arise because a product can be assembled in different ways out of different building blocks. If it is possible to sell a product for more than it costs to buy the constituent parts, then a risk-free profit can be generated. In practice the presence of transaction costs often means that only the larger market players can benefit from such opportunities.

There are, in addition, many individuals and organizations who support the derivatives market and help to ensure orderly and efficient dealings. For example, those who are not members of a futures and options exchange have to employ a broker to transact or 'fill' their orders on the market. A broker acts as an agent and takes an agreed fee or commission. Trading in derivatives generally is overseen and monitored by government-appointed regulatory organizations. For example, the Commodity Futures Trading Commission (CFTC) was created by Congress in 1974 as an independent agency to regulate commodity futures and options markets in the USA.

Market participants have also set up their own support and self-regulatory organizations such as the International Swaps and Derivatives Association (ISDA) and the US-based National Futures Association (NFA). Trade prices on exchanges are reported and distributed around the world by electronic news services such as Reuters and Bloomberg. Information technology companies provide essential infrastructure for the market, including systems designed to value derivative products, to distribute dealer quotations and to record and settle trades.

ORIGINS AND DEVELOPMENT OF DERIVATIVES

The history of derivatives goes back a very long way. In Book One of *Politics*, Aristotle recounts a story about the Greek philosopher Thales who concluded (by means of astronomical observations) that there would be a bumper crop of olives in the coming year. Thales took out what amounted to option contracts by placing deposits on a large number of olive presses, and when the harvest was ready he was able to rent the presses out at a substantial profit. Some argued that this proves that philosophers can easily make money if they choose to, but they are actually interested in higher things. Aristotle was less than impressed. He thought the scheme was based on cornering or monopolizing the market for olive presses rather than any particularly brilliant insight into the prospects for the olive harvest.

Forwards and futures are equally ancient. In medieval times sellers of goods at European fairs signed contracts promising delivery on future dates. Commodity futures can be traced back to rice trading in Osaka in the 1600s. Feudal lords collected their taxes in the form of rice, which they sold in Osaka for cash. Successful bidders were issued with vouchers that were freely transferable. Eventually it became possible to trade standardized contracts on rice, similar to modern futures, by putting down a deposit that was a relatively small fraction of the value of the underlying rice. The market attracted speculators and also hedgers seeking to manage the risks associated with fluctuations in the market value of the rice crop.

The tulip mania in sixteenth-century Holland, which saw bulbs being bought and sold in Amsterdam at hugely inflated prices, also brought about trading in tulip forwards and options, but the bubble finally burst spectacularly in 1637. Derivatives on shares were being dealt on the Amsterdam Stock Exchange by the seventeenth century. At first all deals on the exchange were made for immediate delivery, but soon traders could deal in call and put options which provided the right to buy or to sell shares on future dates at predetermined prices.

London superseded Amsterdam as Europe's main financial centre, and derivative contracts started to trade in the London market. The development was at times controversial. In the 1820s problems arose on the London Stock Exchange over trading in call and put options. Some members condemned the practice outright. Others argued that dealings in options greatly increased the volume of transactions on the exchange, and strongly resisted any attempts at interference. The committee of the exchange tried to ban options, but was eventually forced to back down when it became clear that some members felt so strongly about the matter that they were prepared to subscribe funds to found a rival exchange. Meantime in the USA, stock options were being traded as early as the 1790s, very soon after the foundation of the New York Stock Exchange.

The Chicago Board of Trade (CBOT) was founded in 1848 by 82 Chicago merchants. The earliest forward contract (on corn) was traded in 1851 and the practice rapidly gained in popularity. In 1865, following a number of defaults on forward deals, the CBOT formalized grain trading by developing standardized agreements called 'futures contracts'. The exchange required buyers and sellers operating in its grain markets to deposit collateral called 'margin' against their contractual obligations. Futures trading later attracted speculators as well as food producers and food-processing companies. Trading volumes expanded in the late nineteenth and early twentieth centuries as new exchanges were formed, including the New York Cotton Exchange in 1870 and Chicago Mercantile Exchange (CME) in 1919. It became possible to trade futures contracts based on a wide range of underlying commodities and (later) metals.

Futures on financial assets are more recent in origin. CME launched futures contracts on seven foreign currencies in 1972, which were the world's first contracts not to be based on a physical commodity. In 1975 the CBOT launched futures on US Treasury bonds, and in 1982 it created exchange-traded options on bond futures. In 1981 CME introduced a Eurodollar futures contract based on short-term US dollar interest rates, a key hedging tool for banks and traders. It is settled in cash rather than through the physical delivery of a financial asset.

In 1973 the Chicago Board Options Exchange (CBOE) started up, founded by members of the CBOT. It revolutionized stock option trading by creating standardized contracts listed on a regulated exchange. Before that, stock options in the USA were traded in informal over-the-counter markets. The CBOE first introduced calls on 16 underlying shares and later in 1977 launched put option contracts. Within a few years option trading had become so popular that other exchanges began to create their own contracts. In 1983 the CBOE introduced options on stock market indices, including the S&P 500. By extreme good fortune, just as the CBOE was starting up, the industry-standard option pricing model developed by Fischer Black, Myron Scholes and Robert Merton was published. For the first time it was possible to value options on a common and consistent basis.

Meanwhile in Europe in 1982 the London International Financial Futures and Options Exchange (LIFFE) was set up as a marketplace for trading financial futures and options. After the 1996 merger with the London Commodity Exchange it also began to offer a range of commodity futures contracts. The purchase of LIFFE by Euronext was completed in 2002. Euronext.liffe is now an international business comprising the Amsterdam, Brussels, Lisbon and Paris derivatives markets in addition to LIFFE.

LIFFE's great rival in Europe is Eurex, which was created in 1998 through the merger of DTB (Deutsche Terminbörse) and SOFFEX (Swiss Options and Financial Futures Exchange). Eurex is the world's leading futures and options market for euro-denominated derivative instruments. It is also now the largest exchange in the world, measured by trading volume – over 1 billion contracts were traded in 2003, with the highest turnover achieved by contracts on German government bonds. In that year 640.2 million contracts were traded on CME with an underlying value of $333.7 trillion. Eurex has global ambitions and launched a fully electronic futures and options exchange in the USA in February 2004.

As the exchanges have continued to expand their activities, over-the-counter trading in forwards, swaps and options has experienced an explosion of growth in the past twenty years or so. The first proper interest rate swap was agreed as late as 1982. The statistics in the next section show just how rapidly the market has grown from small beginnings. It is now possible to trade futures contracts on swaps on a number of exchanges, and to arrange a third-party guarantee against the possible risk of default on swap contracts. In the OTC markets dealers offer an array of more complex derivatives, including later-generation option products with exotic-sounding names such as barriers, cliquets, choosers and digitals.

At many times in its long history the derivatives business has unfortunately been associated in the public mind with financial disasters and scandals. The collapse of Barings Bank in 1995 as a result of speculative trading on (among other things) futures contracts on the Japanese stock market by Nick Leeson is very well documented. But there are other examples, some involving still larger sums of money. In September 1998 the US Federal Reserve was forced to organize a $3.625 billion bail-out for the Long-Term Capital Management hedge fund because of trading losses, including those on complex derivatives deals. In 2002 the US division of Allied Irish Banks lost around $700 million from currency-based deals made by John Rusnack. The counter-argument is that many such stories concern poor risk-control and bad management practices rather than anything that is specifically about derivatives. After all, over the years financial institutions have lost billions of dollars on activities as mundane as lending money to governments and trading bonds.

The real strength of derivative products is that they permit the efficient management and transference of risk. A farmer who is exposed to changes in the market price of a crop can hedge by entering into an appropriate derivative contract. The risk can then be assumed by a trader or speculator who is prepared to live with uncertainty in return for the prospect of achieving an attractive return. A bank with a book of corporate loans can use derivatives to protect itself against default on those loans. The risk is taken on by another party in return for suitable compensation. Many such applications of derivatives are used every day of the week in the modern world.

The economist and Nobel Laureate Kenneth Arrow once speculated about the possibility of a risk-sharing institution that was prepared to insure against any size and any type of risk. He described this as a 'complete market' and argued that it would increase economic prosperity since people would be more prepared to engage in risk-taking activities. It could also serve to improve the quality of our predictions of future events such as natural and man-made catastrophes. With all its imperfections, and without ever reaching the ideal state postulated by Kenneth Arrow, the modern derivatives market does provide a global network for the intelligent assessment, management and distribution of risk on a truly industrial scale.

THE MODERN OTC DERIVATIVES MARKET

The data in Table 1.1 indicate the vast size of the global OTC derivatives market at the end of 2001 and 2002 (see also Figure 1.1). The values in the table are in billions of US dollars. The notional amounts involved are enormous – for example, the total amount outstanding on interest rates swaps at the end of 2002 was $79 trillion. However, these figures can be misleading since, with many contracts (such as interest rate swaps), the notional amount is never actually exchanged and exists simply to calculate payments due to one party or another. The market value of interest rate swaps outstanding at end-2002 was $3.86 trillion, which is still a huge number and indicates that this is by far the largest single product group in the OTC derivatives market.

Next, in Table 1.2 the global OTC foreign exchange derivatives market is broken down by currency. This involves counting both sides of a foreign exchange deal so that the individual

Table 1.1 The global OTC derivatives market. Amounts outstanding in billions of US dollars

	Notional amounts ($ billion)		Gross market values ($ billion)	
	At end-December 2001	At end-December 2002	At end-December 2001	At end-December 2002
Grand total	111 178	141 737	3 788	6 361
Foreign exchange contracts	16 748	18 469	779	881
Forwards	10 336	10 723	374	468
Cross-currency swaps	3 942	4 509	335	337
Options	2 470	3 238	70	76
Interest rate contracts	77 568	101 699	2 210	4 267
Forwards	7 737	8 792	19	22
Swaps	58 897	79 161	1 969	3 864
Options	10 933	13 746	222	381
Equity-linked contracts	1 881	2 309	205	255
Forwards and swaps	320	364	58	61
Options	1 561	1 944	147	194
Commodity contracts	598	923	75	85
Gold	231	315	20	28
Other commodities	367	608	55	57
Other OTC contracts	14 384	18 337	519	871

Source: BIS Derivatives Market Statistics

Table 1.2   The global OTC foreign exchange derivatives market. Amounts outstanding in billions of US dollars

	Notional amounts ($ billion)		Gross market values ($ billion)	
	At end-December 2001	At end-December 2002	At end-December 2001	At end-December 2002
All currencies	16 748	18 469	779	881
US dollar	15 410	16 509	704	813
Euro	6 368	7 819	266	429
Japanese yen	4 178	4 800	313	189
Pound sterling	2 315	2 462	69	98
Swiss franc	800	936	28	49
Canadian dollar	593	701	25	22
Swedish krona	551	708	18	31
Other	3 281	3 003	135	131

Source: BIS Derivatives Market Statistics

currency values sum to 200% of the totals at the top of the table. It is clear that the US dollar still predominates. Deals involving the US dollar grew by over 7% between end-December 2001 and end-December 2002 measured in terms of notional amounts outstanding. However, deals involving the euro, the new European single currency, grew by about 23% over the same time period and using the same measure.

Finally, in Table 1.3 the global OTC single-currency interest rate derivatives market is broken down by currency. The figures illustrate the rapid growth of deals in euros in recent years.

Since these statistics were issued, the global OTC derivatives market has continued to grow strongly. According to the BIS the total notional amount outstanding at end-June 2003 was $169.7 trillion, a 20% increase from end-December 2002. Over the same period gross market values grew by 24% to $7.9 trillion. Interest rate swaps maintained their position as the largest single group of products, with $95 trillion in notional amounts outstanding at end-June 2003.

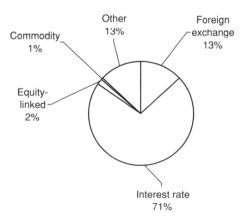

Figure 1.1   Global OTC derivatives by asset class. Based on notional amounts outstanding at end-year 2002
Source: BIS Derivatives Market Statistics

Table 1.3   The global OTC single-currency interest rate derivatives market. Amounts outstanding in billions of US dollars

	Notional amounts ($ billion)		Gross market values ($ billion)	
	At end-December 2001	At end-December 2002	At end-December 2001	At end-December 2002
Total contracts	77 568	101 699	2 210	4 267
US dollar	27 427	34 400	952	1 917
Euro	26 230	38 429	677	1 499
Japanese yen	11 799	14 691	304	379
Pound sterling	6 216	7 442	148	252
Swiss franc	1 362	1 726	21	71
Canadian dollar	781	828	29	31
Swedish krona	1 057	1 094	16	26
Other	2 696	3 089	63	92

Source: BIS Derivatives Market Statistics

EXCHANGE-TRADED FUTURES AND OPTIONS

Following a period of stagnation, trading in exchange-traded derivatives started to expand again in the first years of the new millennium. Much of the increased activity was in interest rate futures and options, which are used extensively by banks and by OTC derivatives dealers seeking to hedge against or take advantage of changes in short- and long-term market interest rates.

Table 1.4 shows the notional amount of exchange-traded financial futures and options contracts outstanding at the end of 2001 and 2002, and the trading turnover during those years. One noticeable fact is the relatively small size of the currency segment, which is much smaller than the OTC foreign exchange derivatives market. During this period the exchanges continued to introduce a range of new equity-based contracts, primarily on stock market indices, which contributed to the overall growth in turnover.

In the first half of 2003 the exchanges globally posted a 61% increase in notional amounts outstanding, compared to 20% in the OTC derivatives market. Trading in interest rate products

Table 1.4   Financial futures and options traded on organized exchanges. Notional principals in billions of US dollar

	Amounts outstanding ($ billion)		Turnover ($ billion)	
	At end-December 2001	At end-December 2002	2001	2002
Total futures	9 673	10 332	446 360	501 918
Interest rate futures	9 265	9 951	420 934	472 201
Currency futures	66	47	2 499	2 513
Equity index futures	342	334	22 927	27 204
Total options	14 126	13 542	148 548	191 622
Interest rate options	12 493	11 760	122 766	154 510
Currency options	27	27	356	423
Equity index options	1 605	1 755	25 426	36 689

Source: BIS Derivatives Market Statistics

was up sharply, showing a rise of 65% over the period. Trading in equity index contracts in the USA was boosted by the successful launch of an 'e-mini^{TM}' futures contract on the S&P 500 index by CME, designed for electronic trading and targeted primarily at the retail market.

CHAPTER SUMMARY

A derivative is a product whose value depends on some other underlying asset such as a commodity or a share or a bond or a foreign currency. Contracts are either traded on organized exchanges or agreed directly between two parties in the over-the-counter (OTC) market. Exchange-traded contracts are generally standardized but carry the guarantee of the clearing house associated with the exchange.

There are three main types of derivative product: forwards and futures; swaps; and options. A forward is an agreement between two parties to deliver an asset in the future at a predetermined price. Futures are the exchange-traded equivalent. A swap is an agreement between two parties to exchange payments on regular dates for an agreed period of time. Each payment leg is calculated on a different basis. In a standard or 'plain vanilla' interest rate swap one leg is based on a fixed rate of interest and the other on a variable or floating rate of interest. A swap is composed of a series of forward contracts. The holder of an option has the right but not the obligation to buy (call) or to sell (put) an asset at a pre-set price. The other side of the transaction is taken by the seller or writer of the option contract. Derivatives are used to manage risk, to speculate on the prices of assets and to construct risk-free or arbitrage transactions. The notional value of derivatives contracts outstanding globally at present amounts to trillions of US dollars.

2

Equity and Currency Forwards

INTRODUCTION

A forward contract is an agreement made directly between two parties to buy and to sell a commodity or financial asset:

- on a specific date in the future;
- at a fixed price that is agreed at the outset between the two parties.

Forwards are bilateral over the counter (OTC) transactions, and at least one of the two parties concerned is normally a bank or some other financial institution. OTC transactions are used extensively by corporations, traders and investing institutions who are looking for a deal that is tailored to meet their specific requirements. Futures are similar in their economic effects but are standardized contracts traded on organized and regulated exchanges (see Chapters 4 and 5). Forwards involve counterparty risk – the risk that the other party to the deal may default on its contractual obligations.

Suppose that a trader agrees today to buy a share in one year's time at a fixed price of $100. This is a forward purchase of the share, also called a *long forward position*. The graph in Figure 2.1 shows the trader's potential profits and losses on the deal for a range of possible share values at the point of delivery. For example, if the share is worth $150 in one year's time, then the trader buys it through the forward contract and can sell it immediately, achieving a $50 profit. However, if the share is only worth $50 in one year's time, then the trader is still obliged to buy it for $100. The loss in that instance is $50.

The other party to the transaction – the counterparty – has agreed to sell the share to the trader in one year's time for a fixed price of $100. This is a forward sale, also called a *short forward position*. If the share is trading below $100 at the point of delivery then the counterparty will make money on the deal – he or she can buy it for less than $100 and then deliver it via the forward contract and receive exactly $100. On the other hand, if the share is worth more than $100 in one year's time then the counterparty will lose money on the forward deal. Figure 2.2 illustrates the profit and loss profile of the short forward position at the point of delivery.

THE FORWARD PRICE

A forward contract involves the two parties agreeing to buy and to sell an asset on a future date at a fixed price. This rather begs the question: how can they possibly agree on what is a fair or reasonable price for delivery on some date in the future? The standard answer is provided by what is known in the world of derivatives as a *cash-and-carry* calculation. This methodology is based on the assumption that arbitrage opportunities should not be available in an active and efficient market. An arbitrage is a set of transactions in which risk-free profits are achieved, because assets are being mispriced in the market. Some traders refer to this type of opportunity as a 'free lunch'.

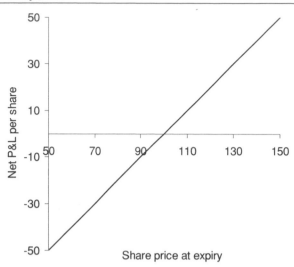

Figure 2.1   Share bought forward at $100: profit/loss at point of delivery

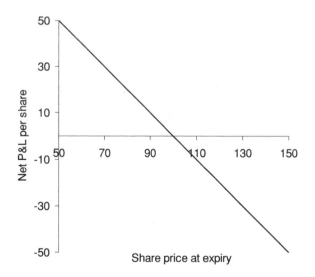

Figure 2.2   Share sold forward at $100: profit/loss at delivery

To illustrate the methodology, let us suppose that a share is trading at $10 in the cash market – the market for buying and selling securities for 'spot' or immediate delivery. We are contacted by a client who would like to buy the share in exactly one year at a predetermined price. How can we determine a fair price for this forward contract? We could take a view on the level at which the share is most likely to be trading at the point of delivery, perhaps by contacting a sample of research analysts or by inspecting charts of the recent price performance of the share and forecasting future movements. The problem is that this is all highly speculative. If we get it wrong and set the forward price – the price at which we will sell the share to the client after one year – at too low a level, the deal could result in substantial losses.

Is there a way of establishing a fair price for the forward contract *without* having to take this risk? The simple answer is 'yes'. We borrow $10 and buy the share in the cash or spot

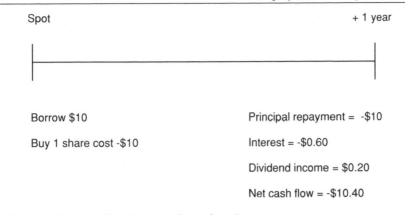

Figure 2.3   Cash flows resulting from carrying a share for one year

market, then hold or 'carry' it for one year so that it is available for delivery to our client at that point. Suppose that the one-year interest rate is 6% p.a. and that the share is expected to pay a dividend of $0.20 during the year ahead. In one year's time we will have to repay the $10 borrowed plus $0.60 interest, though the funding cost is partially offset by the $0.20 dividend received. Figure 2.3 shows the cash flows that result from 'carrying' the position in the share in order to deliver it in one year's time to our client.

The net cash flow in one year's time arising from carrying the share is minus $10.40. Therefore, just to break even on the transaction, we will have to charge the client at least $10.40 to deliver the share through the forward contract. Thus $10.40 is the fair or theoretical forward price established through a cash-and-carry calculation.

Components of the forward price

The theoretical forward price of $10.40 that we calculated has two components: the cost of buying the share in the spot market, and the net cost of carrying it for delivery to our client in one year's time. The carry cost in turn has two components: the funding charge (interest payable) minus the dividends received on the share.

Break-even forward price = Cash + Net cost of carry
$10.40   = $10 + ($0.60 − $0.20)

Net cost of carry = Funding cost − Dividend income
$0.40   = $0.60 − $0.20

Properly speaking, the net cost of carry is likely to be slightly less than this because the dividend payment received during the course of the year can be re-invested. Ignoring this factor, however, suppose that we could actually enter into a forward contract with a client today in which we agree to sell the client the share in one year's time at a fixed price of (say) $10.50. We promptly agree the deal and at the same time we:

- borrow $10 and buy the share in the cash market;
- hold the share for one year, earning a dividend of $0.20.

After one year we repay the principal plus interest on the loan of $10.60.

Adding back the dividend receipt, the net cash flow is minus $10.40. If we are locked into a forward contract in which we can definitely sell the share in one year's time and receive

$10.50 from our client, we will make a profit of 10 cents per share. In theory this is risk-free (it is an arbitrage profit) although in practice there may be some concern over whether our counterparty on the forward contract might default on the deal. If we can insure ourselves against this eventuality at a cost of less than 10 cents, then we really have achieved an arbitrage profit.

In the real world, 'free lunches' of this nature should not persist for very long. Traders would rush in to sell the share forward for $10.50, simultaneously buying it in the cash market for $10 funded by borrowings. The effect would be to push the forward price back towards a level at which the arbitrage opportunity disappears (it may also pull up the cash price of the share). What keeps the forward price 'honest', i.e. at or around the fair value calculated by the cash-and-carry method (in this example $10.40), is the potential for arbitrage profits.

If the forward price in the market is *below* fair value, traders will buy forward contracts and short the share. In practice, shorting is achieved by borrowing the share with a promise to return it to the original owner at a later date; it is then sold on the cash market and the proceeds deposited in the money market to earn interest. The effect of traders buying forward contracts and shorting the underlying will be to pull the forward price back up towards its theoretical or fair value.

In reality the forward price of a financial asset such as a share or a bond can diverge to some extent from the theoretical value established using the simple cash-and-carry method, before arbitrage becomes possible. Transaction costs enter into the equation. Buying and holding a share or a bond involves the payment of brokerage and other fees. Maintaining a short position involves borrowing the asset and paying fees to the lender.

How does the cash-and-carry method work with forward contracts on *non-financial* assets? It is commonly applied to gold and silver, which are held for investment purposes. However, the method has to be treated with extreme caution in the case of commodities, which are assets that are held primarily for the purposes of consumption.

With some commodities (such as fresh fruit) it simply does not apply at all, since storage for delivery on a future date is not a practical proposition. In other cases it is of limited application. Oil is a case in point. Quite often the spot price of oil is actually higher than the forward or futures price in the market, although the simple cash-and-carry method suggests that the situation should be the complete reverse. One explanation is that large consumers are prepared to pay a premium to buy oil in the spot market, so that they can hold it in inventory and ensure continuity of supply.

Forward price and expected payout

It is customary to think of the forward price of an asset as the *expected* future spot price on the delivery date. In other words, the forward price is seen as a prediction of what the price of the asset will actually be in the future, based on all the available evidence at the time the forward is agreed (and subject to later revision based on new evidence).

There is at least one reason to believe this proposition: if forward prices were biased or skewed in some way it would be possible to construct profitable trading strategies. Suppose that forward prices in the market have a systematic tendency to underestimate the actual spot prices on future dates. Then a trader who consistently bought forward contracts would tend to make money on deals more often than he or she lost money. In some ways this seems unlikely although, following arguments proposed by the economist John Maynard Keynes, it has been suggested that this phenomenon actually does exist and the ensuing profits serve to attract speculators into the market. There has been a great deal of empirical investigation into whether or not forward and futures prices are in fact biased in some way, although overall the results are still inconclusive.

If we assume that the forward price of an asset is the expected spot price on the future delivery date, this has important implications. It is an expectation based on the currently available evidence. As a forward contract moves towards the point of delivery new information will be received, changing the expectation. If this is random information, some of it will be 'good news' for the price of the underlying asset and some 'bad news'. There is thus a chance that at the point of delivery the underlying will actually be above the value that was expected when the forward contract was initially agreed, but there is also a chance that it will be below that value. If the new information is indeed random we could say that there is a 50:50 chance that the spot price will be above (or below) that initially expected value. Therefore the chance of making or losing money on a forward contract is about 50:50 and the average payout from the deal is approximately zero.

This result is actually suggested by in Figures 1.1 and 1.2. The forward delivery price in this example was $100. Assume that this is the expected spot price at the point of delivery and that there is a 50:50 chance that the underlying will be above (or below) that value when delivery takes place. Then the buyer of the forward has a 50% chance of making money on the deal and a 50% chance of losing. The buyer's average payout (averaging out the potential profits and loses) is zero.

The seller of the forward also has an average payout of zero. It follows from this that neither party should pay a premium to the other at the outset to enter into the forward contract, since there is no initial advantage to either side. Note that the situation is completely different with options. The buyer of an option pays premium to the seller precisely because he or she *does* have an initial advantage – the right to exercise the contract in favourable circumstances but otherwise to let it expire.

FOREIGN EXCHANGE FORWARDS

A spot foreign exchange (FX) deal is an agreement between two parties to exchange two currencies at an fixed rate in (normally) two business days' time. The notable exception is for deals involving the US dollar and the Canadian dollar, in which case the spot date is one business day after the trade has been agreed. The day when the two currencies are actually exchanged is called the *value date*. A spot deal is said by traders and other market participants to be 'for value spot'. An *outright forward* foreign exchange deal is:

a firm and binding commitment between two parties . . .
to exchange two currencies . . .
at an agreed rate . . .
on a future value date that is later than spot.

The two currencies are not actually exchanged until the value date is reached, but the rate is agreed on the trade date. Outright forwards are used extensively by companies that have to make payments or are due to receive cash flows in foreign currencies on future dates. A company can agree a forward deal with a bank and lock into a known foreign exchange rate, thus eliminating the risk of losses resulting from adverse foreign exchange rate fluctuations. The other side of the coin, of course, is that the contract must be honoured even if the company could subsequently obtain a better exchange rate in the spot market. In effect the company surrenders any potential gains resulting from favourable movements in currency exchange rates in return for certainty.

As we will see, the outright forward exchange rates quoted by banks are determined by the spot rate and the relative interest rates in the two currencies. Traders sometimes talk about this in terms of the relative *carry cost* of holding positions in the two currencies. In effect, the forward FX rate is established through a hedging or arbitrage argument – what it would cost a bank to hedge or cover the risks involved in entering into an outright forward deal. If a forward rate moves out of alignment with its fair or theoretical value, then this creates the potential for a risk-free or arbitrage profit.

MANAGING CURRENCY RISK

This section illustrates the practical applications of outright forwards with a short example. The case considers a US company that has exported goods to its client, an importer in the UK. The British firm will pay for the goods in pounds sterling; the agreed sum is £10 million; and the payment is due in two months' time.

The current spot rate is £/$ 1.5, which means that one pound buys 1.5 US dollars. If the invoice was due for immediate settlement, then the US company could sell the £10 million on the spot foreign exchange market and receive in return $15 million. However the payment is due in the future. If the pound weakens over the next two months, the US firm will end up with fewer dollars, potentially eliminating its profit margin from the export transaction. To complete the picture, we will suppose that the company incurs total costs of $13.5 million on the deal and aims to achieve a margin over those costs of at least 10%.

Table 2.1 shows a range of possible £/$ spot rates in two months' time, when the US firm will be paid the £10 million. The second column calculates the amount of dollars the company would receive for selling those pounds at that spot rate. The third column shows its profit or loss on the export transaction assuming that its dollar costs on the deal are $13.5 million. The final column calculates the margin achieved over the dollar costs.

If the spot exchange rate in two months' time is 1.5 then the US exporter will receive $15 million from selling the £10 million paid by its client. The profit in dollars is $1.5 million and the margin achieved (over the dollar costs incurred) is 11%. On the other hand, if the spot rate turns out to be 1.4 then the company will receive only $14 million for selling the pounds;

Table 2.1   Profit and profit margin for different spot exchange rates

Spot rate	Received ($)	Profit or loss ($)	Margin over cost (%)
1.0	10 000 000	−3 500 000	−26
1.1	11 000 000	−2 500 000	−19
1.2	12 000 000	−1 500 000	−11
1.3	13 000 000	−500 000	−4
1.4	14 000 000	500 000	4
1.5	15 000 000	1 500 000	11
1.6	16 000 000	2 500 000	19
1.7	17 000 000	3 500 000	26
1.8	18 000 000	4 500 000	33
1.9	19 000 000	5 500 000	41
2.0	20 000 000	6 500 000	48

the profit is $500 000 but the margin is well below target at approximately 4%. This could have a serious impact on the profitability of the business – and the future prospects of the senior management!

There is a chance, of course, that the pound might strengthen over the next two months. If it firms up to 1.6 dollars then the US exporter's profit margin is a healthy 19%. The management might be tempted by this thought, but if so they are simply speculating on foreign exchange rates. Does the company have any special expertise in forecasting currency movements? Many firms believe that they do not, and actively hedge out their foreign currency exposures. The next section explores how the US exporter could manage its currency risks by using an outright forward foreign exchange deal.

HEDGING WITH FX FORWARDS

The US company approaches its relationship bankers and enters into a two-month outright forward FX deal. The agreed rate of exchange is £/$ 1.4926. The deal is constructed such that in two months' time:

the company will pay the £10 million to the bank ...
and will receive in return $14.926 million.

The currency amounts are fixed, regardless of what the spot rate in the market happens to be at the point of exchange. The forward contract is a legal and binding obligation and must be fulfilled by both parties to the agreement. Table 2.2 compares the results for the US company of hedging its currency exposure using the FX forward and of leaving the risk uncovered. Column (1) shows a range of possible spot rates in two months' time. Column (2) indicates what would happen if the company left its currency exposure unhedged; it calculates the dollars received from selling the £10 million due at that point at the spot rate. Column (3) shows that if the forward deal is agreed at a rate of £/$ 1.4926 the US company will always receive exactly $14.926 million. Column (4) calculates the difference between columns (2) and (3); for example, if the spot rate in two months is at parity, the company would lose $4.926 million as a result of *not* having entered into the forward FX deal.

Table 2.2   Dollars received by US exporter unhedged and hedged

(1) Spot rate	(2) Received at spot rate ($)	(3) Received at forward rate ($)	(4) Difference ($)
1.0	10 000 000	14 926 000	−4 926 000
1.1	11 000 000	14 926 000	−3 926 000
1.2	12 000 000	14 926 000	−2 926 000
1.3	13 000 000	14 926 000	−1 926 000
1.4	14 000 000	14 926 000	−926 000
1.5	15 000 000	14 926 000	74 000
1.6	16 000 000	14 926 000	1 074 000
1.7	17 000 000	14 926 000	2 074 000
1.8	18 000 000	14 926 000	3 074 000
1.9	19 000 000	14 926 000	4 074 000
2.0	20 000 000	14 926 000	5 074 000

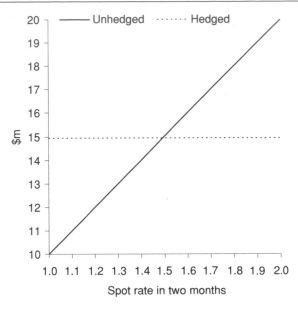

Figure 2.4   Dollars received hedged and unhedged

The results from the table are shown in Figure 2.4. The dotted line in the graph shows the fixed amount of dollars the exporter will receive if it enters into the outright forward FX transaction. The solid line is the quantity of dollars it will receive if it leaves the currency exposure unhedged. If it agrees to sell the pounds forward to its bank at a rate of 1.4926, the US company will receive exactly $14.926 million in return. Its total costs from the export transaction amount to $13.5 million, so it would achieve a margin over cost of 10.6%, comfortably over its target rate of 10%. The hedge has achieved its purpose.

THE FORWARD FX RATE

The theoretical or fair rate for entering into an outright forward foreign exchange deal is established by the spot exchange rate and the interest rates on the two currencies involved. In fact, it is a cash-and-carry calculation. In the previous section the US company hedged its currency exposure by selling pounds for dollars at a forward exchange rate of 1.4926. Is this a fair rate or not? To help to answer this question, let us suppose that we have some additional market information.

- £/$ spot foreign exchange rate = 1.5
- US dollar interest rate = 3% p.a. = 0.5% for two months
- Sterling interest rate = 6% p.a. = 1% for two months.

To simplify matters we will assume here that there are no 'spreads' in the market, that the interest rates for borrowing and lending funds are exactly the same, and that the spot exchange rates for buying and for selling pounds are exactly the same. In practice money dealers charge a spread between their borrowing and lending rates, and currency traders quote a spread between their buy (bid) and sell (offer or ask) rates. According to the data available, one pound equals 1.5 US dollars on the spot FX market. Pounds can be invested for two months at an interest rate of 1% for the period. Dollars can be invested at a period rate of 0.5%. Figure 2.5

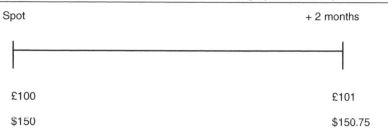

Figure 2.5   Results of investing pounds and dollars for two months

illustrates the results of investing £100 and $150 respectively for two months at those interest rates.

In the spot market £100 equals $150. However £100 invested today would grow to £101 in two months' time. $150 would grow at a somewhat slower rate because the dollar interest rate is lower. In two months it would be worth $150.75. This tells us the value of a pound against the US dollar in two months' time.

$$£101 = \$150.75$$
$$\text{So: } £1 = 150.75/101 = \$1.4926$$

This is the fair or theoretical two-month forward exchange rate. Forward deals agreed in the market must be contracted at or around this level otherwise arbitrage opportunities are created. To see why this is the case, suppose that dealers are actually prepared to enter into forward FX deals in which the two currencies will be exchanged in two months' time at a different rate, say at the current spot rate of £1 = $1.5. Then an arbitrageur could step in and set up the following deals today.

- Borrow $150 for two months at a period interest rate of 0.5%.
- Sell the $150 in the spot foreign exchange market and receive £100.
- Deposit the £100 for two months at a period interest rate of 1%. At maturity the sterling deposit, including interest, will have grown to £101.

At the same time, the arbitrageur would enter into an outright forward FX contract agreeing to sell the £101 due in two months' time for dollars at a rate of £/$ 1.5. After two months the arbitrageur unwinds all the transactions as follows.

- Repay the $150 borrowed plus interest, which equals $150.75.
- Receive back the £100 deposited, which with 1% interest equals £101.
- Sell the £101 for dollars under the terms of the forward contract and receive 101 × 1.5 = $151.5.

As a result the arbitrageur will make a risk-free profit of $151.5 – $150.75 = $0.75, irrespective of what has happened to exchange rates in the meantime. If the transaction was based on $15 million rather than $150, then the profit would be $75,000. This profit is generated on the assumption that pounds can be sold for delivery in two months' time at a rate of £1 = $1.5. If the rate was £1 = $1.4926 then the arbitrage profit disappears (give or take some rounding in the figures). This simple example demonstrates why forward FX deals are transacted at or around the theoretical fair value. If they are not, then traders will quickly rush in to create arbitrage deals, and the actual market rate will move back towards its theoretical or equilibrium value. In practice, dealing spreads and transaction costs complicate the story a little but the general principle still holds.

FORWARD POINTS

In the example worked through above it is noticeable that the theoretical forward FX rate of 1.4926 is lower than the spot rate of 1.5. Market practitioners would say that the pound is at a *discount* relative to the dollar for delivery in two months. In other words, it buys fewer US dollars compared to the spot rate. This results from the different interest rates in the two currencies. The sterling rate was assumed to be 6% p.a. and the dollar rate 3% p.a. The situation can be explained in economic terms. There are a number of reasons why investors might demand a higher return for holding sterling compared to US dollar investments, and two main possibilities may be:

- Sterling-denominated assets are riskier.
- Investors believe that the real value of sterling assets will be eroded at a faster rate because the pound has a higher rate of inflation compared to the US dollar.

There could be other reasons. For example, international investors might place a lower level of trust in the conduct of monetary policy in the UK. It is clear, however, that inflation and concerns about inflation are major factors. If investors anticipate that the pound will suffer from higher inflation than the US dollar they will demand higher returns on sterling-denominated assets in compensation. Also, the pound will trade at a discount against the dollar for forward delivery as its real value in terms of purchasing power is eroding at a faster rate. Market practitioners often quote currency forwards in terms of the discount or premium in forward points compared to the spot rate. For example:

Spot rate = 1.5000
Forward rate = 1.4926
Forward points = −0.0074 (discount)

This is a discount of 74 points, where one point represents $0.0001; therefore, 74 points equals $0.0074 per pound sterling.

FX SWAPS

An FX swap is the combination of a foreign exchange deal (normally for value spot) and a later-dated outright forward deal in the opposite direction. Both deals are made with the same counterparty and one of the currency amounts in the deal is normally kept constant. If the first leg of the swap is for a value date later than spot, then the transaction is called a *forward-forward* swap. The following example of an FX swap transaction uses the same spot rate and interest rates from previous sections.

£/$ spot rate = 1.5
Sterling two-month interest rate = 6% p.a.
US dollar two-month interest rate = 3% p.a.
£/$ two-month forward rate = 1.4926

Imagine that a customer contracts a bank and agrees an FX swap transaction with the following terms:

- *Spot leg*. The customer sells the bank £10 million and receives in return $15 million (at the spot rate).

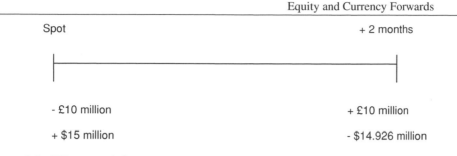

Figure 2.6   FX swap cash flows

- *Forward leg.* In two months' time the customer is repaid the £10 million by the bank and pays in return $14.926 million (at the two-month forward exchange rate).

The customer only pays back $14.926 million on the forward leg, despite having received $15 million spot. The difference between the two amounts is $74 000. Why is there a difference? It is determined by the interest rate differential between the two currencies. For the period of the FX swap the customer is moving out of a higher return currency (the pound) and into a lower return currency (the dollar) and must be compensated. In effect, the $74 000 is the cost of the interest rate differential between the two currencies expressed in US dollars (the sterling amount is kept constant in the deal). The cash flows resulting from the FX swap transaction viewed from the customer's perspective are illustrated in Figure 2.6.

By comparison, if a client enters into an FX swap with a bank and moves from a lower to a higher interest rate currency, it will pay back *more* of that higher rate currency on the forward leg than it receives on the spot leg of the swap (assuming the lower interest rate currency amount is held constant). In this case the client would have to compensate the bank for receiving the benefit of moving into the higher interest currency for the lifetime of the FX swap transaction.

APPLICATIONS OF FX SWAPS

Pension fund managers can use an FX swap to transfer cash into a foreign currency for a predetermined period of time, to increase diversification and boost returns by investing in foreign shares and bonds. The foreign currency purchased on the spot leg of the swap will be exchanged back into domestic currency at a fixed rate on the forward leg of the swap. This helps to manage the currency risks associated with purchasing overseas assets.

FX swaps are also used by banks to manage cash flows resulting from currency and money market transactions. For example, the swap illustrated in Figure 2.6 might be entered into by a commercial bank which has to pay $15 million spot. It notices that it is also receiving £10 million on that day. Rather than borrowing the dollars, it sells its excess pounds for dollars in the spot leg of the FX swap, thereby covering its cash flows on the spot date. The result of the FX swap is to move the bank's sterling and dollar positions forward in time by two months, without actually having to borrow or lend out funds on the money market.

The effect is illustrated in Figure 2.7. This can be a very efficient technique since, unlike borrowing and lending money, the FX swap does not use the bank's balance sheet. It is structured as a spot deal combined with a commitment to re-exchange the two currencies in two months' time.

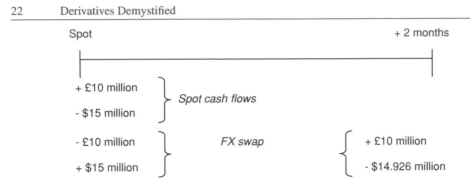

Figure 2.7   Using an FX swap to manage cash flows

CHAPTER SUMMARY

A forward contract is an agreement between two parties to deliver a commodity or a financial asset on a future date at a predetermined price. In many cases the fair or theoretical forward price can be determined through a cash-and-carry calculation. This is based on what it would cost the seller of the forward to cover his or her risks on the deal by buying the asset in the cash market and holding or carrying it to deliver on the date specified in the forward contract. If it is possible to buy or a sell a forward contract at a price other than the fair price then (subject to transaction costs) it may be possible to construct profitable arbitrage transactions. At a fair value the average or expected payout from a forward is zero, therefore, unlike an option, neither party to the deal owes the other an initial premium. With certain assets such as perishable commodities that cannot be stored or shorted the cash-and-carry method does not apply.

Outright forward foreign exchange deals are extensively used by investing institutions, banks and corporations to hedge against the risks posed by fluctuations in currency exchange rates. The fair forward rate is determined by the spot rate and the interest rates in the two currencies. A foreign exchange or FX swap is the combination of a foreign exchange deal and an outright forward deal with a later value date in the opposite direction. Normally one currency amount is held constant. FX swaps are used by banks to manage their cash flows in different currencies and by fund managers who wish to hedge the risks associated with investing in assets denominated in foreign currencies.

3

Forward Rate Agreements

INTRODUCTION

A forward rate agreement (FRA) is a bilateral contract fixing the rate of interest that will apply to a notional principal sum of money for an agreed future time period. In fact the notional principal never changes hands. It is simply used to calculate the compensation or settlement amount that is paid by one party to the other. One side is said to be the *buyer* and the other the *seller*.

- *Buyer.* The buyer of the FRA is compensated in cash by the seller if the reference or benchmark interest rate for the contract period turns out to be above that agreed in the contract.
- *Seller.* The seller of the FRA contract is compensated by the buyer if the benchmark interest rate turns out to be below the contractual rate.

The natural buyers of FRAs are corporate borrowers who wish to hedge against rising interest rates. Money market investors who wish to protect against declining interest rates are natural sellers of FRAs. An FRA is a derivative instrument because its value is derived from spot or cash market interest rates, that is, the interest rates on deposits and loans starting now rather than in the future.

FRAs are very similar to the short interest rate futures contracts traded on the exchanges (Chapter 5) except that FRAs are over-the-counter (OTC) transactions. As we have seen, an OTC derivative contract is a legal and binding agreement made directly between two parties. As such it cannot be freely traded and carries a counterparty risk – the risk that the other party to the deal might fail to fulfil its obligations. On the other hand, the terms of the contract are flexible and can easily be customized. FRAs are now dealt by banks in a wide range of currencies and contract periods.

FRA APPLICATION: CORPORATE BORROWER

To illustrate the applications of the instrument, we will consider the case of a corporate borrower that has an outstanding loan of £100 million. The interest rate on the loan is re-fixed twice a year at six-month sterling LIBOR plus a margin of 50 basis points (0.50%) p.a.

LIBOR – the London Interbank Offered Rate – is the key benchmark interest rate that is set every London business day by the British Bankers' Association (BBA). It is the rate at which top banks in the London market lend funds to each other. Because commercial banks fund themselves at or around LIBOR, they lend money to customers at LIBOR plus a margin, which earns a profit and provides some protection against the risk of default. LIBOR is quoted for a variety of major currencies and a range of maturity periods. Six-month sterling LIBOR is the London interbank rate for lending British pounds for a period of six months starting on the day the rate is fixed by the BBA.

Table 3.1   Forward rate agreement terms

Notional principal:	£100 million
Deal type:	Client buys FRA
Contract rate:	5% p.a.
Start date:	Now
Settlement date:	In six months
Maturity date:	In 12 months
Contract period:	A six-month period starting in six months
Reference rate:	Six-month BBA sterling LIBOR

In the case of our corporate, we will assume that the borrowing rate for the next six-month period has just been fixed. However, the finance director is concerned that interest rates for the subsequent time period might turn out to be appreciably higher; increased borrowing costs would have a detrimental effect on the company's profits, and potentially on the performance of the share price. To protect against such an eventuality the financial director decides to buy an FRA from a dealer. The terms of the contract are set out in Table 3.1.

The company will be compensated in cash by the FRA dealer if six-month sterling LIBOR for the contract period turns out to be above the contractual rate of 5% p.a. If LIBOR is fixed below 5% p.a. the company will have to make a settlement payment to the dealer. The payment will be based on a notional principal of £100 million. Both parties, the company and the dealer, sign the FRA contract, which is a legal and binding commitment. Typically deals are based on outline legal terms drawn up by the British Bankers' Association.

The settlement date in this case is six months after the contract starts. At that point the actual BBA six-month sterling LIBOR rate for the period covered by the FRA will be known to both parties. It will be announced on market information systems such as Reuters or Bloomberg. If we suppose that the LIBOR rate gets set at 6% p.a., the dealer who sold the FRA will have to compensate the company (the buyer) since LIBOR is above the contractual rate of 5% p.a. The payment due at the FRA maturity date is calculated as follows (note that the interest rates are expressed per annum but the FRA covers a six-month time period):

$$\text{Compensation payment} = £100 \text{ million} \times (6\% - 5\%) \times 6/12$$
$$= £0.5 \text{ million}$$

The company can then use this money to partially offset the interest payment it has to make on its borrowings. It has a £100 million bank loan on which it pays a rate of interest of LIBOR plus 0.5% p.a. If LIBOR for the period is fixed at 6% p.a. then its loan rate for the period will be set at 6.5% p.a. Including the compensation payment received on the FRA, its payments for the period are as follows:

Interest paid on loan = £100 million × 6.5% × 6/12 = £3.25 million
Less: Compensation received on FRA = £0.5 million
Net cost of borrowing = £2.75 million
Effective borrowing rate = £2.75 million / £100 million
= 2.75% per six months = 5.5% p.a.

Results of the FRA hedge

By entering into the FRA the corporate has in fact locked into an interest rate of 5.5% p.a. for the period of time covered by the agreement. This is demonstrated in cash flow terms in

Table 3.2   Effects of an FRA hedge

LIBOR fix (% p.a.)	Loan rate (% p.a.)	Interest (£m)	FRA payment (£m)	Net cash flow (£m)	Effective rate (% p.a.)
4.0	4.5	−2.25	−0.50	−2.75	5.5
4.5	5.0	−2.50	−0.25	−2.75	5.5
5.0	5.5	−2.75	0.00	−2.75	5.5
5.5	6.0	−3.00	0.25	−2.75	5.5
6.0	6.5	−3.25	0.50	−2.75	5.5
6.5	7.0	−3.50	0.75	−2.75	5.5
7.0	7.5	−3.75	1.00	−2.75	5.5

Table 3.2. The first column shows a range of possible rates at which LIBOR might be fixed for the contract period. The second and third columns calculate the company's borrowing rate and the interest cash flow on its loan in each circumstance. This is then combined with the FRA compensation payment to establish the net cash flow for the period and the effective interest rate paid by the company.

The results in Table 3.2 can be illustrated by a few examples.

- *LIBOR = 4% p.a.* The company's borrowing rate on its loan is 4.5% p.a. for the period. The interest is £2.25 million for six months. LIBOR is *below* the FRA contract rate of 5% p.a. Therefore the company has to pay the FRA dealer half of 1% of £100 million (for a six-month period) which comes to £0.5 million. As its net borrowing cost is now £2.75 million, effectively it is paying an annualized rate of 5.5% p.a. for the period.
- *LIBOR = 7% p.a.* The borrowing cost on the loan is 7.5% p.a. The interest payment is therefore £3.75 million. However a compensation payment of £1 million is due from the FRA dealer. The net borrowing cost is now £2.75 million and the effective interest rate for the period is 5.5% p.a.

The graph in Figure 3.1 shows the results from Table 3.2. The horizontal axis indicates a range of possible LIBOR rates for the future time period covered by the FRA deal. The dotted line shows the company's effective rate of borrowing for the period if it bought the FRA. The solid line shows what the borrowing rate would be if it had *not* purchased the FRA, i.e. if the company had left the interest rate exposure unhedged.

If it buys the FRA the company is locked into a funding rate for the period of 5.5% p.a. It is protected against increases in interest rates for that period. By the same token, however, it cannot benefit from a fall in interest rates. The company may be prepared to take this risk in return for certainty. If it fixes its borrowing cost for the period it may be easier to plan its business operations, as one source of uncertainty has been eliminated. Hedging against interest risk may also help to reduce the volatility of its earnings, and potentially boost the share price.

FRA payment dates and settlement

The various dates relating to the FRA contract discussed in the previous sections are illustrated in Figure 3.2. The notional is 100 million sterling. The start date is today. (By comparison FRAs in dollars and euros normally start two business days after the deal is agreed.) The

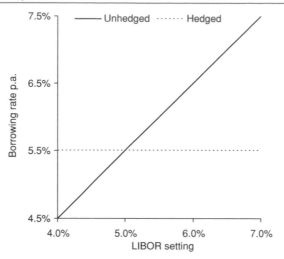

Figure 3.1   Graph of FRA hedge vs unhedged position

Figure 3.2   Key dates on the FRA deal

contract period is a period of time starting in six months and ending 12 months from today. A dealer would refer to this time period as 6v12 or 6x12.

In practice, the settlement amount on a FRA is normally paid up front on the settlement day rather than at maturity, and by convention is discounted back at the LIBOR rate. If the LIBOR rate for the contract period in our example was fixed at 6% p.a., then the compensation amount would be calculated as follows:

$$\text{Amount at maturity} = £100 \text{ million} \times (6\% - 5\%) \times 6/12$$
$$= £0.5 \text{ million}$$
$$\text{Amount if paid on settlement day} = \frac{£0.5 \text{ million}}{1 + (0.06 \times 6/12)} = £485\,437$$

The main reason why the payment is usually made on the settlement date rather at maturity is because this helps to reduce credit risk. Both parties know what is owed and any delay in payment increases the risk of default. If the compensation payment is made on the settlement date then nothing at all actually happens on the maturity date of the FRA. However it has to be stipulated in order to calculate the length of the contract period.

The FRA as two payment legs

Another way to look at the FRA deal in our case study is as a transaction with two different payment legs, as illustrated in Figure 3.3. Seen in this way, the FRA is a deal

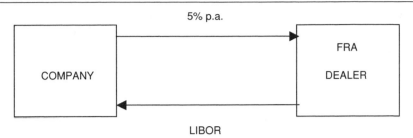

Figure 3.3   The FRA as two separate payment legs

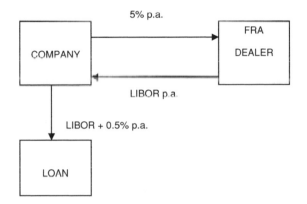

Figure 3.4   Loan plus FRA

in which:

- the company pays the dealer a rate of 5% p.a. applied to £100 million for the six-month contract period;
- the dealer, in return, pays the company the actual LIBOR rate for that period applied to £100 million;
- the amounts from each leg are netted out and one side makes a cash compensation payment to the other (discounted back to the settlement date).

For example, suppose that six-month sterling LIBOR for the contract period is fixed at 6% p.a. The settlement or compensation amount would be calculated as follows:

- The company owes £100 million $\times$ 5% $\times$ 6/12 = £2.5 million
- The dealer owes £100 million $\times$ 6% $\times$ 6/12 = £3 million
- Netted out, the dealer owes the company £0.5 million
- If payment is made on the settlement date the dealer pays the discounted value £485 437.

Figure 3.4 shows the FRA agreement the company has entered into along with the underlying loan it was seeking to hedge. It has achieved a net cost of borrowing for the contract period equal to:

$$\text{LIBOR} + 0.5\% - \text{LIBOR} + 5\% \text{ p.a.} = 5.5\% \text{ p.a.}$$

An FRA is a type of mini-interest rate swap (see Chapter 6). The main differences are that in an interest rate swap there is a series of payments on future dates, not just one; and the payments are normally made in arrears. The diagrams conventionally used to explain the structure and applications of interest rate swap deals look very much like that shown in Figure 3.4.

DEALING IN FRAs

The dealer in the case study explored in the previous sections of this chapter has sold an FRA covering a period of time starting in six months and ending 12 months after the start date. The forward interest rate agreed is 5% p.a. If this is the only deal on the dealer's trading book then there is an exposure to rising interest rates. If interest rates are set above 5% p.a., the dealer will have to make a cash settlement payment to the buyer of the FRA.

The dealer may have a view that interest rates will fall, and may be quite content to assume this risk. If the actual LIBOR rate at settlement is set below 5% p.a. the dealer will be paid compensation by the buyer. But if the dealer does not have a properly considered view on the future direction of interest rates, then it would be better to hedge or cover the risk. One way to do this is to use the exchange-traded equivalent of an FRA, an interest rate futures (see Chapter 5). Another approach would be to match the sale of an FRA with an offsetting purchase, the effect of which is illustrated in Figure 3.5.

As before, the dealer has sold a 6v12 month FRA to the company that is concerned about rising interest rates. This time it has also purchased an FRA covering the same future time period and with the same notional principal. The client for the second deal is a money manager who is worried about falling interest rates, which would adversely affect the returns made by the fund. The rate agreed on this second FRA deal is 4.95% p.a. The money manager will receive compensation on this FRA contract if the LIBOR rate for the contract period is set below 4.95% p.a. Otherwise the FRA dealer will be compensated.

The rate of 4.95% p.a. is the dealer's bid rate, the rate at which he or she buys FRAs for the future time period 6x12. The rate of 5% p.a. is the dealer's offer or ask rate. The difference – five basis points – is the dealer's spread. The spread exists partly to enable the dealer to make

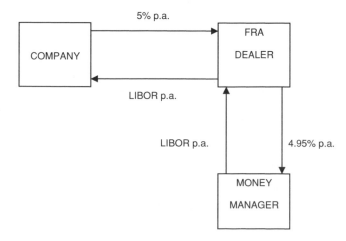

Figure 3.5   Dealer sells and buys offsetting FRAs

a profit on the FRA book, but, it also helps to provide some protection against volatile short-term interest rates. A dealer will be prepared to sell or to buy an FRA without having an exactly offsetting deal already in place, but this exposes the dealer to interest rate fluctuations until such time as an offsetting deal is agreed or some other kind of hedge can be put in place.

FORWARD INTEREST RATES

An outstanding issue concerns the way in which the parties to an FRA can determine the forward interest rate. One answer to this question is to look at arbitrage relationships. The existence of FRAs allows market participants to lock into rates for borrowing and for re-investing money on future dates. For example, a trader could carry out the following transactions today:

- Borrow pounds for one year at a fixed interest rate.
- Deposit those funds for six months at a fixed interest rate.
- Lock into a rate for re-investing the proceeds due from the deposit in six months' time for a further six months by selling a 6v12 month sterling FRA.

If the returns from investing and re-investing the pounds exceed the cost of borrowing the money in the first instance, then the trader has constructed a 'free lunch' trade – an arbitrage transaction. In an efficient financial market such a situation should not exist, or should not persist for very long. The assumption that no arbitrage is possible can be used to calculate the fair or theoretical forward interest rate at which a 6v12-month FRA should be sold on the market, based on the market rates for borrowing and lending pounds for 12 months and six months respectively.

This is true, although in practice the contract rates on FRAs are normally established through the prices at which the relevant short-term interest rate futures contracts are traded on the exchange (discussed in detail in Chapter 5). Because interest rate futures contracts in major currencies such as sterling, dollars and euros are freely and actively traded by many market participants, they are often taken as establishing the market's consensus expectations on future interest rates in those currencies. As such they are used to price a variety of over-the-counter products such as FRAs and interest rate swaps, instruments whose values depend on expected interest rates for future time periods.

CHAPTER SUMMARY

A forward rate agreement (FRA) is a contract agreed between two parties fixing the rate of interest that will be applied to a notional sum of money for a future time period. The notional is not exchanged; there is instead a cash compensation payment based on the difference between the rate agreed in the contract and the actual market interest rate for the period, as established by a benchmark such as LIBOR. The buyer of the FRA is compensated if LIBOR is found to be above the contractual rate. Otherwise the buyer compensates the seller.

FRAs are often purchased by companies concerned about rising interest rates and sold by money managers who are worried about falling re-investment rates. Dealers quote buy and sell prices for a range of currencies and contract periods. The fair or theoretical contractual rate on an FRA can be established from spot market interest rates. In practice, the rates for contracts in a major currency are normally based on the rates implied in short-term interest rate futures, which are the exchange-traded equivalents of FRAs.

4
Commodity and Bond Futures

INTRODUCTION

A futures contract is an agreement made through an organized exchange to buy or to sell a fixed amount of a commodity or a financial asset on a future date (or within a range of dates) at an agreed price. Unlike forward deals, which are negotiated directly between two parties, futures are standardized. Delivery is guaranteed by the clearing house associated with the exchange. A trader who contacts a broker and buys futures is said to have a *long position*. One who sells futures has a *short position*. The value of a trader's position is adjusted on a daily basis.

Futures are either traded by open outcry in trading pits in the form of an auction, or on electronic screen-based trading systems, although the latter is undoubtedly the way ahead. The Chicago exchanges currently (2003) operate both methods in tandem. In a pit-based market brokers transact buy and sell orders on behalf of clients including banks, corporations and private individuals; deals are also made by 'locals' who have purchased seats on the exchange in order to trade on their own account. As soon as a trade is agreed the details are entered into the exchange's price reporting system. Data from the exchanges are published throughout the world on websites and on electronic news services such as Reuters or Bloomberg. Nowadays, deals made in trading pits may be recorded on hand-held electronic devices rather than on the old cardboard tickets.

Both LIFFE and Eurex, the combined Swiss–German exchange, are wholly electronic markets. Trading on LIFFE is now effected through a computer system called LIFFE Connect; the physical trading floor finally closed for business in 2000. The main functions of an exchange are: to facilitate trading; to monitor conduct and ensure that the rules are adhered to; and to publish the prices at which trades are agreed. The exchange does not buy or sell contracts. Some exchanges, such as the CBOT, are (at the time of writing) established as not-for-profit organizations; others, such as CME, are publicly traded companies whose shares are listed on a stock exchange (in the case of CME it is the New York Stock Exchange).

Unlike over-the-counter (OTC) contracts, futures are standardized products, which encourages active and liquid trading. On the other hand, the clearing house guarantee virtually eliminates credit or default risk. To set up a long or a short position a trader has to have a margin account with a broker and must deposit *initial margin* into the account. This is a performance bond (collateral) held against the possibility that a trader may not meet the contractual obligations. The clearing house stipulates the minimum initial margin a broker has to collect. The amount varies according to the type of contract and is based on a calculation of the maximum likely movement in the value of the futures contract during the course of a day.

At the end of each day a trader's margin account is adjusted in line with the closing price of the futures contract – a process called *marking-to-market*. If a trader has a long position – that is, has bought more contracts than he or she has sold – and the price has fallen, then the loss will be subtracted from the margin account. On some exchanges this means that the trader will automatically have to make a top-up payment called *variation margin* in order to restore to its original level the amount held in the margin account. Other exchanges employ a system of so-called *maintenance margins* such that the value of a contract has to move by a certain amount before a variation margin call is triggered. Only the larger banks and financial institutions are clearing members of an exchange and have direct accounts with the clearing house. A trader who uses a smaller broker will deposit initial margin with that broker which, in turn, makes all payments to the clearing house via a clearing member.

In summary, the effect of the margining system is to provide a very high measure of protection against default. Firstly, traders have to deposit initial margin with the clearing house via their broker before they can take out a position. Secondly, all open positions are marked-to-market on a daily basis. If at the end of a trading day the futures price has fallen from yesterday's close then the accounts of the longs are debited with their losses and the accounts of the shorts are credited with their profits. If the futures price has increased then the situation is the reverse. If a trader receives a variation margin call and does not send the required funds in time, the position will normally be closed out by his or her broker.

There are three main types of end-users of futures, although the same organization or individual may take different roles in different circumstances.

- *Hedgers.* These are using futures to protect or hedge against adverse movements in commodity prices, equity indices, interest rates, bond prices, etc. Examples include farmers who are seeking protection against a fall in the market price of their crop; fund managers and banks hedging against falls in equity or bond prices; commercial banks covering exposures to changes in short-term interest rates.
- *Speculators.* These buy and sell futures contracts to profit from changes in commodity prices, interest rates, etc. They are prepared to accept risks that hedgers do not wish to assume, and they provide liquidity to the market – that is, they help to ensure that there is an active market in futures contracts with up-to-date prices, and that at any given time buyers and sellers are both in operation.
- *Arbitrageurs.* These look to exploit price anomalies by (for example) simultaneously trading in futures and the underlying assets. If a futures contract is trading 'rich', i.e. at an expensive level, an arbitrageur will short the overvalued futures and at the same time buy (go long) the underlying asset in the spot market. Overall the arbitrageur is hedged against general movements in the value of the asset since profits and losses on the short futures will offset those on the long position in the asset. However, he or she will profit as and when the futures price falls towards its correct market value.

COMMODITY FUTURES

Some readers may have seen the film *Trading Places*, released by Paramount Pictures in 1983, starring Dan Ackroyd and Eddie Murphy. One of the key scenes depicts frenzied trading in Frozen Concentrated Orange Juice (FCOJ) futures. The contracts are traded on the New York Cotton Exchange (founded 1870) and now (since 1998) part of the New York Board of Trade®.

The FCOJ-1 futures contract was first traded in 1966. Each contract was based on the delivery of 15 000 pounds of orange solids, not limited to any country of origin. The quality of the FCOJ that can be delivered is also specified, as are the licensed warehouses around the USA where delivery can take place. Starting with the May 2005 expiry the exchange will list instead two new contracts: FCOJ-A, in which juice must originate from Florida or Brazil; and

Table 4.1 FCOJ-A futures on the NYBOT®

Unit of trading:	15 000 pounds of FCOJ
Price quotation:	Prices are quoted in cents and hundredths of a cent per pound of FCOJ
Trading months:	January, March, May, July, September and November

Table 4.2 FCOJ-1 futures prices

Month	Last (cents)	Open (cents)	Volume (contracts)	Open interest (contracts)
September 2003	78.65	80.45	554	17 101
November 2003	80.55	82.25	257	4 576
January 2004	82.55	84.00	12	1 814
March 2004	84.55	82.85	20	1 064

Source: NYBOT®

FCOJ-B which is not limited by origin. The specification of the FCOJ-A contract is shown in Table 4.1. All contracts are guaranteed by the New York Clearing Corporation.

As is common with futures, very few contracts ever reach the point of delivery. Contracts are bought and sold many times, and before the delivery month is reached traders start to close out their positions. Those who are long contracts sell out and those who are short buy back. Over all the exchanges it is estimated that fewer than 4% of futures contracts ever reach delivery, in some cases fewer than 1%. This is fortunate because there are not enough physical commodities in the world to deliver against all the futures contracts that are traded.

The dominant suppliers in the orange market operate in Florida and Brazil, and much of the produce is processed into concentrate. (The structure of the FCOJ-A contract reflects this fact.) These two areas have different growing seasons so that the market operates throughout the year, without violent cycles in prices. The primary factors affecting the price of FCOJ futures contracts are the market forces of supply and demand that change the price of orange juice in the spot market.

Futures prices and the basis

Table 4.2 shows data for FCOJ-1 futures on a trading day in August 2003. The prices are quoted in cents per pound weight of FCOJ. On that day the September contracts opened at 80.45 cents. In the table 'volume' shows the number of contracts traded that day. 'Open interest' shows the total number of long or short contracts still open, not yet closed out. Notice that the open interest is at its highest with the nearby delivery month September 2003. This is typical of futures contracts generally. As a contract approaches the delivery date, traders start to close out their positions, and open interest for that delivery month tends to decline. Traders who wish to maintain their exposure will 'roll' their position by opening a new position in the next delivery month.

We saw in Chapter 2 that the theoretical forward price of an asset can be determined by what it would cost to buy the asset in the spot market, and then adding on what it would cost to 'carry' or hold the asset to deliver to a buyer on a future date. The carry costs might include funding, storage, insurance, etc. Although futures contracts operate in a slightly different way to forwards, it is conventional to extend this so-called 'cash-and-carry' method to the calculation of certain theoretical or fair futures prices. We also saw in Chapter 2 that the method works well with financial assets and some commodities but not with others. In the oil market, for example, the spot price is often higher than the futures prices although the simple cash-and-carry method suggests that the situation should be the reverse. When this happens the market is said to be in *backwardation*. When the futures prices are higher than the spot price, the market is said to be in *contango*.

It is an important aspect generally of trading futures that *the basis* – the relationship between the spot price of the underlying and the price of a futures contract – is not constant. This means, day-to-day, that a futures does not exactly track movements in the price of the underlying. Changes in the basis are determined not only by changes in 'carry' costs, such as interest rates and storage costs, but also by speculative trading activity. In some markets the futures price of an asset can be more volatile than the cash price.

As a futures contract approaches its delivery date, however, its price must converge on the spot price of the underlying because, on the actual delivery date, the futures contract becomes just another spot market transaction. On the delivery day the basis – the difference between the spot price and the futures price – must be zero. This fact allows hedgers to use contracts such as FCOJ futures to manage the risks associated with volatile commodity prices. A food-processing company that is concerned about increases in the price of orange juice can buy FCOJ futures. If the price of the commodity does rise, it can sell the futures back into the exchange shortly before the due delivery date, and realize a profit in cash that will offset the increased cost of buying orange juice in the spot market.

One of the potential pitfalls of hedging with futures was highlighted by the case of the German conglomerate Metallgesellschaft AG. The firm's energy group entered into forward contracts committing to deliver huge quantities of petroleum at fixed prices on delivery dates ranging up to 10 years ahead. It hedged the risk by buying and rolling over short-dated gasoline and heating oil futures. Unfortunately, the oil price fell and the firm was hit with very substantial margin calls on its long futures positions. Some people argued that over the long run this was balanced out by gains on the forward contracts, but senior management became seriously concerned about the cash flow implications. As a result, the company closed out the futures and cancelled the forward deals in agreement with its customers. Metallgesellschaft announced in December 1993 that its energy group was responsible for losses of about $1.5 billion.

BOND FUTURES

The 30-year US Treasury Bond Futures contract has been traded on the Chicago Board of Trade (CBOT) since 1975. Quite soon after its introduction it became the most actively traded contract in the USA, and in 1982 the exchange introduced options on Treasury bond futures. Since then the CBOT has launched a series of other bond futures contracts, including contracts on shorter-maturity US Treasury securities. Table 4.3 sets out the contract specification for the very popular 10-year US Treasury note futures. For those unfamiliar with such things, the only real difficulty here is the fact that the quotations are made in fractions of a dollar rather than in decimal format.

In simple terms, a seller of one futures contract (a 'short') is making a commitment to deliver $100 000 par value of the US Treasury notes stipulated in the contract at a fixed price. A buyer (a 'long') is committing to take delivery at a fixed price. The delivery months available are

Table 4.3   10-Year US Treasury note futures

Unit of trading:	$100 000 face or par value US Treasury note
Deliverable bonds:	US Treasury notes with between 6.5 and10 years to maturity
Tick size:	1/64 of a point
Tick value:	$15.625 per contract
Price quotation:	Points and one-half of 1/32 of a point
Contract months:	March, June, September and December
Last trading day:	Seventh business day before the last business day of the delivery month
Last delivery day:	Last business day of the delivery month

Source: CBOT Reprinted by permission of the Board of Trade of the City of Chicago, Inc. Copyright 2004. ALL RIGHTS RESERVED

March, June, September and December. Delivery can take place on any business day in the delivery month, at the choice of the short. The prices for future delivery are quoted per $100 par or face value in dollars and thirty-seconds of a dollar, to the nearest half of a thirty-second. For example, suppose that a contract is trading at 110-15.5. This is translated into decimal format as follows:

$$110\text{-}15.5 = \$110\,15.5/32 = \$110.484375 \text{ per } \$100 \text{ par}$$
$$= \$110\,484.375 \text{ on the actual contract size of } \$100\,000$$

The *tick size* (one sixty-fourth of a point) is the minimum move allowed in the price quotation. In decimal format it is $0.015625 per $100, which amounts to $15.625 on the full contract value of $100 000. So the value of one tick is $15.625. In practice what happens is that (1) long and short positions are marked-to-market at the end of each trading day based on the closing price of the contract on the exchange, and (2) profits and losses from that day's trading are added to or subtracted from a trader's margin account. For example, suppose a trader buys a contract one day at 110-15.5 and at the end of the day the contract closes exactly one tick above that value at 110-16. The trader has made a profit of $15.625 and this will be added to his or her margin account:

$$\text{Profit} = \$100\,000 \times 1/64\% = \$15.625$$

One important point to stress is that the contract is written on a *notional* or imaginary US Treasury note. This is actually very helpful, since if it was based on a real bond the contract could not be traded after that security had expired. It is not, of course, possible to deliver imaginary assets, so the CBOT publishes a list of real US Treasuries that can be delivered against a contract, plus a list of so-called *conversion factors* designed to adjust for the fact that the different securities trade at different prices in the market. (On LIFFE these are called *price factors*.) In practice, few traders actually go through the delivery process, although it does happen. Before the delivery month is reached most longs and shorts begin to close out their positions by respectively selling and buying back contracts.

The conversion factors on the US Treasury note futures are derived from pricing all the deliverable bonds at a yield or annualized rate of return of exactly 6%. In the absence of conversion factors all the 'shorts' would tend to deliver cheap, low coupon Treasuries. The factor adjusts the payment received by the short when he or she delivers securities to the long. The invoiced amount for a low and for a high coupon bond are adjusted downwards and upwards respectively. The actual method of calculating the invoice is explained in more detail later in this chapter.

Table 4.4 Euro bund futures (FGBL) specification

Unit of trading:	€100 000 par notional 6% coupon German government bond
Deliverable bonds:	German Federal bonds with 8.5 to 10.5 years to maturity
Tick size:	0.01
Tick value:	€10
Price quotation:	Per €100 par value, to two decimal places
Delivery months:	March, June, September and December
Last trading day:	Two exchange days before delivery day
Delivery day:	The tenth calendar day of the delivery month

Source: Eurex

Table 4.5 Deliverable bonds and conversion factors for December 2003 bund futures

Bond's maturity date	Bond's coupon rate (%)	Conversion factor
4 July 2012	5.00	0.934155
4 January 2013	4.50	0.897301
4 July 2013	3.75	0.839498
4 January 2014	4.25	0.870183

Source: Eurex

Gilt and Euro bund futures

A wide variety of bond futures contracts is now available around the world. For example, LIFFE offers a gilt (UK government bond) futures that is similar to the US Treasury contract traded on the CBOT. Each contract is a commitment to deliver or take delivery of £100 000 notional gilts with a 6% coupon at a fixed price. The good news is that the quotation is made in decimal format per £100 par or nominal value. The minimum move in the futures price is £0.01 per £100. This means that if a trader buys a futures at a price of (say) £110.00 and the price on the exchange rises by one tick to £110.01, then the trader has made a profit on the contract of £10.

$$\text{Tick size} = £0.01 \text{ per } £100 \text{ par value}$$
$$\text{Tick value} = £100\,000 \times 0.01\% = £10$$

The exchange publishes a list of British government bonds that are deliverable against the contract. The seller of futures has the choice of which bond and which business day in the delivery month to make delivery. The invoiced amount is adjusted by the price (conversion) factor of the bond that is actually delivered. Trading is effected through the exchange's electronic system LIFFE Connect.

As a final example, Table 4.4 shows the specification of the bund (German government bond) futures contract traded on Eurex, the German–Swiss electronic exchange. This has proved to be an extremely popular contract since its inception, and approximately 25.3 million contracts were traded in June 2003, beating all previous records. The contract is based on €100 000 par value German government bonds; the delivery months and tick size are the same as for the LIFFE gilts futures.

Table 4.5 lists the German government bonds that were deliverable against the December 2003 bund futures contracts, with their respective conversion factors. In this contract delivery can only take place on the tenth day of the delivery month.

To show how the system operates, let us assume that a trader is short one December bund futures contract and the last trading date has now been reached. The exchange calculates the final settlement or closing price of the futures (at 12:30 p.m. CET) based on the average prices of the last ten trades. The trader (the short) decides which bonds in the list he or she wishes to deliver against the contract. An invoice goes to a party who is long December bund futures and who must now take delivery. The invoiced amount is based on the final settlement price of the futures multiplied by the conversion factor of the bond that is delivered. To this is added any coupon income on the bond that is delivered that has accrued since the last coupon was paid, up to the delivery day.

The conversion factors in Table 4.5 are all below 1 because the coupon rates on these bonds are less than the 6% coupon rate on the notional bond on which the contract is written. The lower the coupon of a deliverable bond, the lower will be its conversion factor, and the lower the amount that can be invoiced if that bond is delivered against a short futures position. A deliverable bond with a coupon rate of 6% (the rate on the notional bond specified in the contract) would have a conversion factor of 1. Bonds with coupon rates greater than 6% would have factors greater than 1.

THE CHEAPEST-TO-DELIVER

When a bond futures contract with a particular delivery month first starts to trade, a list of deliverable bonds and their conversion factors is issued by the exchange. The conversion factors are fixed and do not change when the contract starts to trade. For people who are hedging a long position in bonds by shorting bond futures this is important, since they need to know the factors in order to calculate the number of contracts to sell. Unfortunately, the system is not perfect and the conversion factors do not fully adjust for the actual market values of the bonds that are deliverable against a bond futures contract. The factors are based on pricing all the deliverable bonds at exactly the same annualized rate of return, but, in reality, bonds with different maturities tend to have different yields or returns in the market.

This means, in practice, that at any one time there tends to be a so-called cheapest-to-deliver (CTD) bond. Literally, this is the bond that would make the most amount of money (or lose the least) if it were purchased on credit and delivered against a short position in the futures. The result is that most shorts will tend to deliver the CTD and longs will expect to receive that bond, so that the futures contract tends to behave rather as if it were based on the CTD and to track changes in the market value of that bond.

As if this were not enough, there is another problem. For technical reasons the bond that is the CTD can actually change over the life of a bond futures contract. It is affected by the level of interest rates in the market. This is a notoriously complex subject but, put simply, in a low-interest rate environment (when market rates are below the coupon rate on the notional bond specified in the contract) the CTD tends to be a higher coupon bond with a shorter maturity. In a high-interest rate environment it tends to be a lower coupon bond with a longer maturity.

The practical difficulty is clear enough, however. Hedgers who sell bond futures to protect against losses on a long position in a bond or a portfolio of bonds usually calculate the number of contracts they have to short on the assumption that the futures will track changes in the current CTD. That is a reasonable assumption. However, if another bond becomes the CTD then the futures will change partners and its price behaviour will be quite different from what it was previously. Consequently, the hedge will no longer be as accurate as predicted, and profits and losses on the bonds that are owned, and on the short futures, may not match particularly well.

CHAPTER SUMMARY

A futures contract is a commitment made through an organized exchange to deliver or take delivery of a specified amount of a commodity or financial asset on a fixed date in the future. In some cases there is a range of possible delivery dates. Unlike forwards, futures are guaranteed by the clearing house, but are standardized. The earliest contracts traded were on commodities such as wheat, but there is now a wide range of financial futures. The fair value of a financial futures contract can be established through a cash-and-carry calculation – the cost of buying the underlying in the cash or spot market plus the net cost of carrying it to deliver on a future date. Futures contracts do not always trade at their fair or theoretical value, and this may give rise to arbitrage opportunities. The relationship between the cash price of the underlying and the price of a futures contract on the underlying is called the basis. The basis is not constant and is affected by factors such as changes in interest rates as well as by speculative activity on the exchange.

A bond futures is a commitment to deliver or take delivery of a notional bond on a future date or between a range of dates. The exchange publishes a list of the bonds that are deliverable against a given contract, at the choice of the short, with their conversion or price factors. These factors are designed to adjust the invoiced amount according to the value of the bonds that are actually delivered. However at any one time there tends to be a bond that is the cheapest-to-deliver (CTD) against a short position and the futures tend to track changes in the CTD bond. This can cause problems for hedgers using bond futures to manage their risk on a bond or a portfolio of bonds, since the CTD can change and the hedge may not work efficiently. The bond that is the CTD is affected by changes in short- and long-term market interest rates. This can provide opportunities for speculators and arbitrage traders.

5
Interest Rate and Equity Futures

INTRODUCTION

In 1981, Chicago Mercantile Exchange (CME) introduced the Eurodollar futures contract. It is widely used by banks and other financial institutions to hedge against changes in funding and investment rates. It is also used by traders who wish to anticipate and profit from increases or reductions in short-term US dollar interest rates. In Europe, the futures contract on short-term deposits in euros (the new single currency) traded on LIFFE has also proved to be extremely popular. In 2003 a total of 137 692 241 contracts were traded, up by 30% from 2002.

The Eurodollar futures broke new ground because it was designed to be settled in cash rather than through the physical delivery of a commodity or financial asset. This technique has now been adopted for a wide range of contracts on exchanges around the world. It is used in equity index futures, so that it is now possible to profit from or hedge against changes in the level of major stock market indices without ever actually buying or selling the underlying shares. This helps to reduce transaction costs and allows traders to take a position in equities at a fraction of what it would cost to buy and sell the underlying shares.

INTEREST RATE FUTURES

The contract specification for the three-month Eurodollar interest rate futures traded on CME is set out in Table 5.1. Eurodollars are simply time deposits in US dollars held in commercial banks outside the USA. The bulk of the market is based in London. The 'Euro' prefix is historical in origin and has nothing to do with the single common European currency.

A Eurodollar deposit is a term deposit with a bank for a specific period of time such as one week, three months or six months. The great majority of deals are for maturities of one year or less. The interest rate is fixed for that period and the principal amount deposited is repaid with interest at maturity. The key reference rate for Eurodollar loans and deposits is US dollar LIBOR, which is fixed every London business day by the British Bankers' Association (BBA) based on rates submitted by a panel of contributor banks. The BBA fixes rates for a range of maturities ranging from overnight to one year. (Chapter 3 has given additional information on LIBOR rates.)

The CME Eurodollar futures contract is based on a notional $1 million three-month Eurodollar deposit starting on a specific date in the future – the third Wednesday of the contract month. In fact the notional amount never actually changes hands. The value of a contract changes on a day-by-day basis according to the *expected* interest rate for the future time period it covers. For example, the value of a September contract depends on the expected interest rate on a $1 million Eurodollar deposit starting on the third Wednesday in September and running for three months (90 days) from that date. A trader who is long or short the futures will make or lose money as that expectation changes, and as the market value of the contract fluctuates.

Table 5.1 CME Eurodollar futures contract specification

Unit of trading:	Eurodollar term deposit with a principal value of US $1 million and a three-month maturity
Contract months:	March, June, September and December plus four nearest months
Last trading:	11:00 a.m. London time two business days before the third Wednesday of the contract month
Quotation:	100.00 minus the rate of interest
Tick size:	0.01 (representing in interest rate terms one basis point or 0.01% per annum)
Tick value:	$25
Final settlement:	Based on the three-month Eurodollar LIBOR rate established at 11:00 a.m. on the last trading day

Source: CME

The last trading day of a contract is a little different. It ceases trading at 11:00 a.m. London time two business days before the third Wednesday of the contract month, because the *actual* three-month LIBOR rate for the period covered by the contract is fixed by the BBA at that point. This establishes the final settlement value of the contract. Any contracts that are still outstanding on the last trading day are automatically closed out at that value.

Trading interest rate futures

Unlike a forward rate agreement, the price of a Eurodollar futures is not quoted in interest rate terms. As Table 5.1 shows, it is quoted as 100.00 minus the rate of interest per annum for the future time period covered by the contract. For example, if a September futures is trading at 96.02, this implies that the expected interest rate for the three-month future time period starting on the third Wednesday of September is 3.98% per annum. The pricing convention was adopted to make life easier for brokers and locals on the trading pit. Traders are very familiar with the fact that the values of Treasury bills and bonds move inversely with market interest rates. If interest rates fall (rise) a trader who is long (short) Treasury bills will make a profit.

Because of the way they are quoted, exactly the same thing happens with interest rate futures. For example, suppose that the September futures is being dealt on the exchange at 96.02, implying a rate of 3.98% p.a. for the three-month period starting in September. A trader who is firmly of the view that the actual LIBOR rate for this period will be fixed below this level, buys September futures. The view turns out to be correct and on the last trading day of the contract the LIBOR rate for the period is set by the BBA at 3.80% p.a. The contract will close on its last day at a value of 100.00 − 3.80 = 96.20, above the price paid by the trader, who has made a profit. On the other hand, if LIBOR is fixed above 3.98% p.a. then the contract will close below the purchase price and the trader will suffer a loss.

One whole tick on the contract is 0.01, which represents in interest rate terms one basis point or 0.01% p.a. For example, if the price of the September futures on the exchange changes from 96.02 to 96.03, this is a one tick movement. The expected interest rate has changed from 3.98% p.a. to 3.97% p.a. The contract is based on a $1 million three-month deposit. Therefore each whole tick movement in the price of a Eurodollar futures represents a profit or loss of $25 on the total contract size.

$$\text{Tick value} = \$1 \text{ million} \times 0.01\% \times 3/12 = \$25$$

If a contract is bought at 96.02 and is later closed out at 96.20, then the total profit on the position (excluding brokerage) is calculated as follows:

Change in contract value = 96.20 − 96.02 = 18 ticks
Profit = 18 ticks × $25 = $450

In interest rate terms, buying a September futures at 96.02 is equivalent to taking the view that the actual LIBOR rate for the three-month period starting in September will be lower than 3.98% p.a. If the LIBOR rate for the period is actually fixed at 3.80% p.a. the profit on the trade can also be established as follows:

Notional principal = $1 million
Contract period = 3 months
Profit = $1 million × (3.98% − 3.80%) × 3/12 = $450

In practice, many traders tend to close out their positions before the last trading day of a contract. However, the basic principle of trading remains the same. If a trader buys a contract at a certain price and the expectation develops that the actual interest rate for the period covered by the contract will be lower than the rate implied in this price, then the price of the futures will increase on the exchange. The trader can sell the contract back into the market and realize a profit in cash.

Hedging with interest rate futures

Like forward rate agreements (see Chapter 3), Eurodollar futures can be used to lock into a rate for borrowing or re-investing cash on future dates. To illustrate this fact, we will take a typical application. Suppose that it is mid-June and in three months' time an investor will have to re-invest $1 million for a further period of three months. The cash will come from existing investments that are due to mature at that point. If the investor does not hedge this exposure, and if interest rates decline, then he or she will suffer from falling re-investment returns. To manage this risk the investor buys one September Eurodollar futures contract at a price of 96.02.

Table 5.2 demonstrates the results of the hedge. For simplicity the difference between market lending and borrowing rates and the full complications of the daily margin system on the futures are ignored in this example. Column (1) shows a range of possible levels the three-month interest rate could take in September, when the investment has to be rolled over. Column (2) calculates the interest received at that rate, based on $1 million principal for a

Table 5.2   Hedge with short interest rate futures

(1) Actual interest rate (% p.a.)	(2) Deposit interest ($)	(3) Futures close price	(4) Tick change	(5) Futures profit/ loss ($)	(6) Interest + profit/ loss ($)	(7) Effective rate (% p.a.)
3.80	9 500	96.20	18	450	9 950	3.98
3.90	9 750	96.10	8	200	9 950	3.98
4.00	10 000	96.00	−2	−50	9 950	3.98
4.10	10 250	95.90	−12	−300	9 950	3.98
4.20	10 500	95.80	−22	−550	9 950	3.98

three-month time period. Columns (3) and (4) calculate the price at which the futures would close and the change in price from a starting level of 96.02. Column (5) calculates the overall profit or loss on the futures hedge (the sum of all the daily variation margin payments and receipts over the life of the contracts).

For example, if the LIBOR rate is fixed at 3.80% p.a. then the September futures will cease trading at 96.20. This is 18 ticks above the purchase price, which results in a profit of $450 (each whole tick is worth $25). Columns (6) and (7) add the interest received from re-investing the dollars to the profit or loss on the futures contract, and calculate the effective rate of interest achieved on the basis of $1 million principal over a three-month investment period. As a result of the futures hedge the investor is locked into a re-investment rate of 3.98% p.a. for the three-month period starting in September.

Interest rate futures prices

The fact that Eurodollar futures *can* be used to lock into rates for re-investing dollars on future dates means that the market price of a future contract has to be closely related to spot or cash market dollar interest rates. (The spot market is the market for borrowing and lending funds starting now rather than in the future.) If this were not the case then arbitrage opportunities would arise.

For example, suppose, as previously, that it is mid-June but that this time the September futures could be bought on the exchange at a price of 95.00 rather than 96.02. This means that if a trader buys a contract he or she can lock into a rate of 5% p.a. for re-investing dollars in three months' time for a further three-month time period. Imagine then that the trader looks at dollar interest rates on the spot market and discovers that they are as follows:

- The rate for borrowing dollars for six months starting mid-June is 3% p.a.
- The rate for depositing dollars for three months starting mid-June is 2% p.a.

An arbitrage is then available. The trader arranges to borrow dollars for six months at 3% p.a. He or she puts the funds on deposit for three months at 2% p.a. The proceeds from this deposit will be paid out in September, and will have to be re-invested for a further three months so that cash is available in six months' time to repay the principal plus interest on the loan. The trader locks into a rate of 5% p.a. for re-investing that money by buying (also in mid-June) September Eurodollar futures contracts at 95.00. This combination of deals generates an arbitrage profit.

- Over the first three months the deposit rate is 2% p.a. but the borrowing rate is 3% p.a.
- However, over the second three months the guaranteed re-investment rate is 5% p.a. and the borrowing rate is 3% p.a.

The gains for the second three months more than offset the losses for the first three-month period and a 'free lunch' is achieved. In order for this arbitrage to disappear, the futures price would have to trade at somewhere around 96.00, so that the rate for re-investing money for three months in three months' time is approximately 4% p.a. In that case the gains and losses from borrowing and investing funds offset each other.

In fact the re-investment rate that can be achieved by buying the futures should be slightly less than 4% p.a., because of the ability to re-invest not only the original amount of dollars borrowed but also the interest received for the first three months. The rate that would cause the arbitrage to disappear is 3.98% p.a., so that the September futures should (in theory) trade at about 96.02. In practice, factors such as transaction costs do come into the equation, particularly with longer-dated interest rate futures.

EQUITY INDEX FUTURES

An equity index futures contract is an agreement:

- made between two parties;
- on an organized futures exchange;
- to exchange cash compensation payments;
- based on the movements in the level of an equity index.

One of the most liquid equity index futures contracts, which was first introduced in 1982, is the S&P 500® stock index futures traded on CME. In common with other contracts on CME, deals are currently made either electronically or on the floor of the exchange by brokers acting on behalf of clients and by 'locals' dealing on their own account. The underlying index is calculated by Standard & Poor's. The index level at any one time represents the value of a typical portfolio of 500 leading US shares. The weight of a share in the portfolio is in proportion to the market capitalization of the company (share price times the number of shares outstanding).

On the S&P 500 futures there is no physical delivery of the underlying portfolio of shares that comprise the index. This contrasts with commodity and bond futures (see Chapter 4) where there is a delivery process. It would simply be too cumbersome for a futures trader who is short contracts to deliver all 500 shares in the correct proportions. Instead, all trading profits and losses are settled in cash. In order to achieve this, each full index point is assigned an arbitrary monetary value of $250. (The exchange now also offers a very successful E-mini™ S&P 500 futures contract designed for electronic training and with a value of $50 per index point. In March 2003 trading volume exceeded one million contracts a day for the first time.)

In common with most derivatives, the futures price is quoted in the same units as the underlying – in this case the underlying is the S&P 500 index, so the futures is quoted in index points. The underlying index is usually referred to as the *cash market* since its level reflects the cash values of the 500 shares that comprise the index. The futures price on the exchange is driven up and down by changes in the cash index level, and ultimately by changes in the values of the constituent shares. However the relationship between the cash market and the futures is not completely stable. In other words, if the cash market moves by a certain number of index points it does not follow that the futures price will change by exactly the same number of points.

As we have seen before, the relationship between the cash and the futures price is known in the market as *the basis*. One reason why the basis is not constant emanates from changes to the cost of carry (the interest rate less dividends on the shares in the index). Another factor is simply supply and demand. If it looks as if there may be a slide in the market then traders rush to sell the index futures, often pushing the price down more quickly than that of the underlying cash index. If the market then rallies, traders start to buy back index futures to close out their short positions, propelling the futures price sharply upwards.

To illustrate the cash settlement process, suppose that it is now August and the September S&P 500 futures contract is trading on the exchange at 1000 index points. A day trader buys

10 S&P 500 September index futures contracts at a price level of 1000 points. The trader believes that the underlying S&P 500 index – the cash index – is set to rally strongly before the end of the day. If this happens then the futures price will rise in sympathy. The trader contracts a broker to have the order transacted, and posts the required initial margin. As we have seen previously, initial margin is simply a performance deposit and will be returned later, assuming that the trader fulfils his or her contractual obligations.

In this case we will imagine that the trader is correct in the forecast, and the September S&P 500 futures rises later that same day to a price of 1050 points, propelled upwards by a strong rally in the underlying cash market. The trader can then easily close out the long futures position by selling 10 September futures in the exchange. The profit from buying and then selling the contracts (ignoring brokerage and funding costs) is calculated as follows. The profit is realized in cash rather than through the delivery of shares.

$$\text{Profit} = 10 \text{ contracts} \times \$250 \times (1050 - 1000 \text{ points}) = \$125\,000$$

Equity index futures are not always about speculation. A portfolio manager who is concerned about losses arising from falls in the stock market can short contracts on the S&P 500 or on some other index which the portfolio tends to track. If the market falls then losses on the portfolio will be offset by variation margin payments received from the futures. There is, of course, a drawback to this type of hedge. If the market rises, then gains on the portfolio of shares would be offset by losses on the short futures position. When considering a hedge of this kind, the skill is in timing – knowing when to sell futures to manage or reduce the risk on a portfolio of shares, and knowing when to leave well alone.

THE MARGINING SYSTEM

The role of a futures exchange and the associated clearing house is to facilitate trading, to settle deals, to broadcast prices and generally to ensure an orderly market. In addition, the clearing house acts as a central counterparty and guarantees the performance of all contracts. Opening an equity index futures position (whether buying or selling) involves depositing initial margin (collateral) with a broker, who handles payments made to and received from the clearing house. At the end of a day, if a position has not been closed out it will be marked-to-market so that profits and losses are added to or deducted from the margin account.

To illustrate the margining process on a day-by-day basis, we will consider a short trading campaign based this time on FT-SE 100 index futures contracts. These are traded on LIFFE and deals are matched electronically through the LIFFE Connect system. The contract specification is shown in Table 5.3.

Trading campaign: Day 1   The September FT-SE futures is currently trading at 5000 index points. A trader decides to buy 10 contracts, and contacts a broker. The broker asks for initial margin, which is a performance deposit. The clearing house sets minimum initial margin

Table 5.3   FT-SE 100 index futures

Underlying:	FT-SE 100 index
Quotation:	FT-SE index points
Point value:	£10 per full index point
Delivery months:	March, June, September and December

Source: LIFFE Administration Management

requirements which the broker must collect from traders, based on the volatility of the market. However, a broker may ask for more. In this case we suppose that the broker asks for £3000 initial margin per contract or £30 000 on the whole trade.

The trader lodges the money with the broker, who in turn pays margin over to the clearing house. The broker transacts the order electronically and buys 10 September FT-SE futures at a price of 5000 index points. The other side of the trade is taken by a seller of the September futures. As soon as the deal is transacted, however, the clearing house interposes itself, acting as a central counterparty. It becomes the seller to the buyer, and the buyer to the seller.

The trader could close out the long futures position later the same day, simply by selling 10 September futures. Instead, the trader decides to run the position overnight. We will suppose that the futures closes at the end of the day at 4970 index points, 30 points below the price at which the position was originally opened, driven down by a fall in the cash index. The trader will receive a variation margin call via his or her broker, to make good the difference between the purchase price and the closing price (also known as the settlement price) of the September futures.

$$\text{Variation margin} = -30 \text{ points} \times 10 \text{ contracts} \times £10 = -£3000$$

The effect of the margin system is that trading profits and losses are realized on a daily basis. If the trader does not make the margin call the broker will simply sell the 10 contracts, closing out the original position, and return the initial margin that was lodged minus the £3000 trading loss and any other costs. Assuming the trader does meet the margin call, the cash is paid over to the clearing house via the broker. In this example the futures price has fallen, so the clearing house collects margin payments from the longs. The gains are credited to the accounts of the shorts – the market participants who are short FT-SE index futures contracts.

Trading campaign: Day 2   On the next trading day we suppose that the September futures closes at 5020, which is used as the settlement price to calculate variation margin payments for that day. The trader is long 10 contracts and the settlement price is 50 points higher than yesterday's value of 4970. This time the trader *receives* variation margin.

$$\text{Variation margin} = 50 \text{ points} \times £10 \times 10 \text{ contracts} = £5000$$

The futures price has risen, driven upwards by the cash FT-SE index, ultimately by the prices of the constituent shares. This time it is the shorts who have to make variation margin payments.

Trading campaign: Day 3   Finally, on Day 3 the trader decides to close the long position by putting in an order to sell 10 September futures either 'at best' (at the best available market price) or on a 'limit order' basis (at a price that is not less than a stipulated level). Suppose that the broker transacts the sell order at 5030. The trader is entitled to a final variation margin payment because the contracts were sold 10 points above the last settlement price.

$$\text{Variation margin} = 10 \text{ points} \times £10 \times 10 \text{ contracts} = £1000$$

Result of trading campaign   The position is now closed, so the trader can take back the £30 000 initial margin. The net profit on the whole trading campaign is the sum of the variation margin payments.

$$\text{Net profit} = £5000 + £1000 - £3000 = £3000$$

Alternatively, it is the price at which the futures were sold less the price at which they were bought, times the index point value, times the number of contracts traded.

$$\text{Net profit} = (5030 - 5000) \times £10 \times 10 \text{ contracts} = £3000$$

Note that this profit was achieved on an outlay of only £30 000 initial margin. At an index level of 5000 each futures contract (at £10 per point) provides a market exposure equivalent to buying shares in the index to the value of £50 000. This means that the trader in the example would have had to invest £500 000 in shares to acquire the same exposure achieved by buying 10 futures. The initial investment would have been much higher and the return on investment much lower.

The variation margin procedure is repeated every day until a FT-SE futures position is closed out. The futures contracts expire on the third Friday of the expiry month and trading ceases at 10:30 a.m. London time on that date. At the expiry of a contract, all remaining open positions are closed at the Exchange Delivery Settlement Price (EDSP), which is based on an average of the cash FT-SE 100 index between 10:10 and 10:30 a.m. on that day.

If a futures position is kept open until the last day there is a final variation margin payment based on the EDSP, and the contracts then simply expire – there is no physical delivery of shares. The procedure by which all open contracts are closed out against the level of the underlying index on the last trading day ensures that the price of a futures contract converges on the cash index level over time. During the life of a contract its price can trade some way away from the cash market, but on the last day the price of the futures must be the same as the level of the underlying index. The EDSP is based on the *average* level of the FT-SE 100 index over a 20-minute period, to help to reduce the scope for market manipulation.

SINGLE STOCK FUTURES

In January 2001 LIFFE introduced futures contracts on individual shares. Contracts are available on leading international shares quoted in US dollars, in euros and in pounds sterling. Other exchanges such as CME now offer similar products. The contract specification for the UK stock futures on LIFFE is shown in Table 5.4.

The contracts described in Table 5.4 are cash settled, so there is no physical delivery of shares. As an example of how this operates, we will take the case of an investor who wishes to take a long position in BT shares. The current share price is 500 pence or £5. The investor buys 20 BT stock futures contracts at a level of 510 pence per share, which establishes a long position in 20 000 BT shares. If the investor actually purchased the underlying shares the total purchase cost would be £5 × 20 000 = £100 000. However, one advantage of trading futures is that only a fraction of this value has to be deposited in the form of initial margin. Suppose that

Table 5.4   UK single stock futures

Currency:	Pounds sterling
Quotation:	Pence per share
Contract size:	Normally 1000 shares
Delivery months:	March, June, September, December and other months
Delivery:	Cash settled
Last trading day:	Third Wednesday in delivery month

Source: LIFFE Administration Management

the initial margin requirement on the 20 contracts is £10 000. This is only 10% of the value of the underlying shares, a quite typical figure.

Cash settlement means that although the investor bought into the futures at a price level of 510 pence per share, he or she never takes delivery of the shares and never pays the 510 pence per share purchase price. Instead, the investor earns a profit in cash if the futures price rises above 510 pence and makes a loss if it falls below that level. Suppose that later in the same trading day the price of the BT futures has increased by 10 pence per share, driven upwards by a 10 pence rise in the value of the underlying BT shares on the stock market. The investor can close out the original long position by selling 20 BT futures contracts. The profit (less brokerage and funding costs) is calculated as follows:

$$\text{Profit} = £0.1 \text{ per share} \times 1000 \text{ shares} \times 20 \text{ contracts} = £2000$$

Even more impressive is the return on capital achieved by the investor on the £10 000 originally lodged by way of initial margin.

$$\text{Return} = (£2000/£10\,000) \times 100 = 20\%$$

If the trader had bought 20 000 of the underlying BT shares at £5 each, the investment required would have been £100 000. If the share price increased by 10 pence the profit would also have been £2000 but the return on investment only 2%. The return on the futures trade is 10 times higher because the initial margin required is only 10% of what it would have cost to purchase the underlying shares.

In the UK, equity futures have (at the time of writing) a tax advantage. An investor who buys underlying shares has to pay stamp duty to the government. There is no stamp duty on cash-settled futures trades. One further advantage is that it is just as easy to take a short position on a share, or on the stock market as a whole, as a long position – it simply involves contracting a broker and selling single stock or equity index futures.

Some investors seem to dislike the daily variation margin procedure with futures, perhaps because of the inconvenience and the need to monitor the payments. Perhaps the reasons are also psychological. An investor who owns shares that perform badly can always imagine that the price will recover, and do nothing to solve the problem. The loss is only on paper. However, if a futures position performs badly the losses are felt every day because of the margin system. Although this may be an inconvenience, it actually imposes very good trading discipline. It concentrates the mind wonderfully and encourages cutting loss-making positions.

CHAPTER SUMMARY

A short-term interest rate futures contract is based on the rate of interest on a notional deposit starting at a specific point in the future. The contract price is quoted as 100 minus the expected interest rate. A seller profits if the actual rate is set above the rate built into the contract price at the time the contract was sold. A buyer profits if the rate is set below the rate built into the contract price when it was purchased. In major currencies the prices of short-term interest rate futures are used to establish the contractual rates on forward rate agreements. Because interest rate futures can be used to fix the rate of interest for borrowing and depositing money on future dates, their prices have to be closely related to cash market interest rates, otherwise profitable arbitrage opportunities can arise.

An equity index futures contract is an agreement made through an organized exchange to make and receive cash compensation payments based on the value of an equity index such as the S&P 500 or the FT-SE 100. No physical shares are exchanged. Index futures can be used to speculate on anticipated rises or falls in the market as a whole. The initial margin required is normally a fraction of what it would cost to buy the actual underlying shares. In some markets there are also tax advantages. Fund managers can hedge against losses on share portfolios by shorting equity index futures. In recent years exchanges such as LIFFE and CME have introduced futures on single shares.

6
Interest Rate Swaps

INTRODUCTION

A swap is a contract between two parties agreeing to exchange payments on regular future dates for a defined period of time, where the two payment legs are calculated on a different basis. The most common type of interest rate swap (IRS) is a fixed/floating deal in which the payment made by one party is based on a fixed rate of interest, and the return payment is based on a variable or floating rate. The floating rate is reset periodically according to a benchmark such as the London Interbank Offered Rate (LIBOR). A variant on this type of structure is the *cross-currency swap* in which the payments are made in two different currencies, based on floating or fixed interest rates.

In an *equity swap* one payment leg is based on the change in the value of a share, or a basket of shares, or an equity index such as the S&P 500 or the FT-SE 100 (see Chapter 7). In a *commodity swap* one leg is based on the value of a physical commodity such as oil. Swaps of all kinds are used by corporations, by investing institutions and by banks to manage their exposures to interest rates, currencies, share values, commodity prices and loan default rates. They can also be used to take speculative trading positions.

STERLING INTEREST RATE SWAP

The most common type of interest rate swap is the fixed/floating swap, often referred to as a 'plain vanilla' deal. The characteristics of a vanilla IRS contract are as follows:

- The notional principal is fixed at the outset and never varies.
- The notional is never exchanged; it is used to calculate the payments.
- One party agrees to pay a fixed rate of interest applied to the notional principal on regular future dates.
- The other party agrees to make a return payment on regular future dates based on a variable rate of interest applied to the same notional principal.
- When a floating payment is made, the rate is reset to establish the next floating payment in the sequence, based on a benchmark reference rate such as LIBOR.

To illustrate the basic deal, let us suppose that two parties A and B contract a vanilla interest rate swap between themselves. The terms of the transaction are set out in Table 6.1 and the payment structure is illustrated in Figure 6.1.

The first payment due on the swap is made in arrears, one year after the start date. Notice that the LIBOR rate that establishes the first floating leg payment is actually set at the outset, when the terms of the deal are agreed by both parties. Therefore both sides know exactly what the first payment on the swap will be on the first payment date. In this example LIBOR is set at the outset at 3.75% p.a. while the notional for both legs is £100 million. The cash flows on

Table 6.1   Sterling interest rate swap

Notional principal:	£100 million
Fixed payer:	A pays fixed at 5% p.a.
Floating rate payer:	B pays 12-month sterling LIBOR p.a.
Payments (both legs):	Annually in arrears
Start date:	Today
Maturity:	10 years
First LIBOR fix:	3.75% p.a.

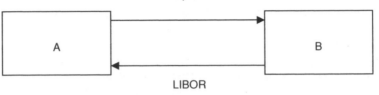

Figure 6.1   Interest rate swap payment legs

the first payment date are calculated as follows:

- A owes 5% of £100 million, a payment of £5 million.
- B owes 3.75% of £100 million, a payment of £3.75 million.
- Since the payments are due on exactly the same date they can be netted out, so that A pays over the difference to B, which amounts to £1.25 million.

That, of course, is not the end of the story, because there are nine further payments due on the swap, the second of which will be made two years after the start date. The LIBOR rate that establishes the second floating payment will be set at the 12-month sterling LIBOR rate on the day the first swap payment is made. The floating rate for the third payment will be set when the second payment is made. And so on. Note in Figure 6.1 that the position of A is akin to being long a floating-rate bond and short a fixed-rate bond, at least in terms of exposure to changes in interest rates. Its counterparty B has the reverse profile.

Hedging with interest rate swaps

It might seem odd in the last example that A would be prepared to enter a deal in which it knows for certain that it will have to make a payment of £1.25 million in one year. Why should it agree to such a deal? The kind of payment structure illustrated in this case – in which the fixed rate payer makes net payments towards the beginning of the life of a swap – is typical of the situation in which the market is anticipating future increases in interest rates. Assuming that interest rates do rise at a later stage, the fixed rate payer A will expect to receive net payments in the later years of the swap transaction. The fixed rate on the swap is essentially an average of the first LIBOR rate stipulated in the contract and the forward or expected LIBOR rates for subsequent years. (Forward interest rates are covered in Chapters 3 and 5.)

To see why A might enter the swap transaction, suppose that A is a company that has borrowed £100 million from a bank and 10 years remain until the maturity of the loan. The interest payment on the loan is made annually in arrears, with the next payment due in exactly

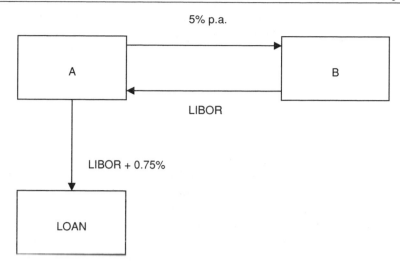

Figure 6.2   Loan plus interest rate swap

one year's time. The rate of interest is reset every year according to the 12-month sterling LIBOR rate plus a margin charged by the lending bank of 75 basis points (0.75%) p.a.

Since the rate of interest on the loan is reset annually, A is exposed to rising interest rates, which would increase its borrowing costs and could potentially have an impact on its profitability. So A approaches B, a bank which deals in swaps, and agrees the contract shown in Table 6.1 and illustrated in Figure 6.1. The combination of the interest payments on the underlying loan and the swap is illustrated in Figure 6.2.

Imagine that for one year during the life of the loan and the swap the sterling LIBOR rate is set at 6% p.a. Then for that year company A would have to pay 6.75% or £6.75 million on its loan. It pays 5% or £5 million on the fixed leg of the swap, and it receives 6% or £6 million on the floating leg. Its net borrowing cost for that year is therefore £5.75 million, equivalent to an interest rate of 5.75% p.a. on £100 million. To see how this applies in different circumstances, Table 6.2 takes a range of different possible LIBOR rates and calculates the company's loan and swap payments at each rate. The final column nets out all the payments.

Table 6.2   Net payments with loan plus swap

LIBOR (% p.a.)	Loan rate (% p.a.)	Loan interest (£m)	Swap fixed payment (£m)	Swap floating receipt (£m)	Net payment (£m)
4.00	4.75	−4.75	−5.00	4.00	−5.75
5.00	5.75	−5.75	−5.00	5.00	−5.75
6.00	6.75	−6.75	−5.00	6.00	−5.75
7.00	7.75	−7.75	−5.00	7.00	−5.75

The table shows that, whatever the LIBOR rate turns out to be for a given year, the company's net payment is always the same. By entering into the swap it has effectively moved from a floating rate liability linked to LIBOR to a rate fixed at 5.75% per annum. To put it another way, if LIBOR rates rise steadily in the future then the company will receive a stream of cash payments from the swap which will compensate for the increasing cost of borrowing on its loan. The net effect for A of entering into the swap can also be assessed by looking back to the values in Figure 6.2. The LIBOR element on the loan is cancelled out by the LIBOR receipt on the swap. What remains is the 5% fixed payment on the swap plus the margin of 0.75% on the loan.

DOLLAR INTEREST RATE SWAP

The example considered in the last section is a very simple swap, and in fact it is a little unusual in that the payments on both legs are made annually. In this section we will look at a more detailed example, this time based on a swap denominated in US dollars.

Table 6.3 sets out the terms of the deal. The parties concerned are a bank and its client ABC Corporation. The bank receives a fixed and pays a floating rate. The notional principal is $100 million. As is common with US dollar swaps, the swap starts on the spot date, two business days after the trade date when the deal is priced and the terms are agreed. Payments are made every six months in arrears, starting spot. The day-count method for calculating interest is the actual/360 method, which derives from the US money market and is also used in US dollar LIBOR interest calculations.

The first swap payment is a floating payment which the bank will make to its counterparty six months after spot, on 4 February 2004. The LIBOR rate has been set for this period at 1.13875% p.a. There are 184 calendar days in this time period, so the bank's payment is calculated as follows. Notice how the actual/360 convention works. The per-annum interest rate is de-annualized by multiplying by 184 calendar days and dividing by a fixed 360-day year.

$$\text{Floating payment made} = -\$100 \text{ million} \times 1.13875\% \times 184/360$$
$$= -\$0.582 \text{ million}$$

At this point the LIBOR rate is reset in order to establish the next floating rate payment in the sequence, which is due in a further six months' time on 4 August 2004. This is a period of 182 days. Let us suppose that LIBOR is reset for the period at 2% p.a. Then the bank's payment on 4 August 2004 would be calculated as follows:

$$\text{Floating payment made} = -\$100 \text{ million} \times 2\% \times 182/360$$
$$= -\$1.0111 \text{ million}$$

Also, on 4 August 2004 the bank is due to receive a fixed payment from its swap counterparty; these are made annually. The fixed rate is 4.75% p.a. and there are 366 days from 4 August

Table 6.3 US dollar interest rate swap

Notional principal:	$100 million
Counterparty:	ABC Corporation
Bank receives fixed at:	4.75% p.a. paid annually
Bank pays floating at:	Six-month USD LIBOR, paid every six months and reset every six months
Day-count for both legs:	Actual/360
Trade date:	31 July 2003
Start date:	4 August 2003
Maturity date:	4 August 2013
First LIBOR setting:	1.13875% p.a.

2003 to 4 August 2004. The payment due to the bank is calculated as follows:

$$\text{Fixed payment received} = \$100 \text{ million} \times 4.75\% \times 366/360$$
$$= \$4.8292 \text{ million}$$

Since the swap has 10 years to maturity there will be a total of 10 fixed rate and 20 floating rate payments, the last on 4 August 2013. The swap will then terminate. As is standard in these deals, the notional principal is never exchanged.

SUMMARY OF IRS APPLICATIONS

Interest rate swaps (IRS) can be used to take directional views on interest rates. For example, a speculator who believes that rates will rise more sharply than anticipated by the rest of the market could agree to pay fixed and receive floating on a swap. If rates do increase as predicted, then the fixed rate payments will be exceeded by the floating rate receipts. However, most interest rate swaps are entered into by companies seeking to improve their cost of funding or to hedge their interest rate risks; or by investing institutions that wish to move from a fixed to a floating rate of return, or vice versa. The following outline case studies illustrate some basic applications of interest rate swaps:

- *Problem 1:* A well-known company with a top credit rating will pay LIBOR plus a margin if it borrows money from a bank. It would like cheaper floating rate debt.

  Solution: The company issues a fixed-rate bond on which it pays a relatively low coupon, given its top credit rating and name recognition. It enters a swap receiving a fixed rate of interest which it uses to service the coupon payments on the bond, paying a floating rate in return. Depending on swap rates, top name borrowers can often achieve sub-LIBOR funding through this method.

- *Problem 2:* A money market investor has made a deposit that is due to mature but is concerned that interest rates are falling and the returns on re-investing the cash will be poor.

  Solution: The investor enters into an IRS paying the dealer a floating rate of interest and receiving fixed. This has the effect of locking the investor into a fixed rate of return on his or her underlying investments for the lifetime of the swap.

- *Problem 3:* An investor owns a fixed coupon bond but believes that interest rates are likely to rise and hence the value of the bond will fall. The investor could sell the bond but feels that the problem is short term and wishes to retain the bond in his or her portfolio.

  Solution: The investor arranges an IRS paying a fixed rate and receiving a floating rate. If interest rates rise sharply the investor will receive a stream of positive cash flows from the IRS, offsetting the fall in the value of the bond.

- *Problem 4:* A money market investor will earn a sub-LIBOR return by depositing funds with a bank. LIBOR is the bank's lending rate; it will pay out less on incoming deposits. The investor would like a higher return.

  Solution: The investor buys a fixed coupon bond from a dealer and enters into a swap paying fixed and receiving LIBOR. (This combination is called an *asset swap*.) If the fixed rate paid on the swap is less than the return earned on the bond, then the package produces a net return that is higher than LIBOR.

- *Problem 5:* A mortgage-lending bank funds itself on a floating-rate basis but wishes to create fixed-rate loans. If it does so it runs the risk that interest rates will rise and it will pay more in funding than it receives in interest on the mortgage loans.

  Solution: The bank enters into a swap paying a fixed rate and receiving a variable rate of interest, which it can use to service its borrowing requirements.

- *Problem 6:* A company has borrowed funds by issuing a bond that pays a fixed coupon, but believes that market interest rates are set to fall sharply and it will lose out on the resulting cheaper borrowing costs.

  Solution: The company enters into an IRS receiving fixed and paying floating. If short-term interest rates fall sharply, the company will receive net payments from the swap transaction.

Since swaps are OTC contracts negotiated directly between two parties, the terms can be extremely flexible. The payment dates and the notional principal amounts can match the requirements of users. In addition, there is a wide variety of non-standard structures available that adjust some of the features of vanilla interest rate swaps. On some deals the notional principal changes over the life of the swap. In a so-called *amortizing* swap the notional steadily reduces over the term of the contract. This is useful for a company that wishes to use a swap to manage the interest rate risk on a loan it has raised or a bond it has issued on which principal amounts are repaid during its life in addition to interest payments.

SWAP RATES AND CREDIT RISK

Table 6.4 shows a sample of recent swap rates on dollar-, sterling- and euro-denominated swaps extracted from a market rates page of the *Financial Times*. Rates can be obtained from dealers on request for maturities out to 30 years and even longer.

To take just one example from the table, dealers were paying a fixed rate of 4.73% p.a. on 10-year sterling-denominated swaps and asking in return sterling LIBOR. This is their bid rate. For the same maturity and currency, dealers were paying sterling LIBOR asking in return a fixed rate of 4.78% p.a. This is their ask or offer rate. The dealer's spread is 0.05% or 5 basis points.

It is noticeable in Table 6.4 that the fixed swap rates increase with time to maturity. This is because the market was anticipating increases in LIBOR rates over the ensuing 10 years. Therefore a receiver of fixed on a swap has to earn a rate that is likely to compensate for the steadily rising floating leg payments he or she will have to make over the life of the transaction. As discussed previously, the fixed rate on an interest rate swap is an average of the first LIBOR rate set under the terms of the contract and the forward LIBOR rates for the subsequent payment periods. If LIBOR rates are expected to keep rising then the fixed rate – the average of the

Table 6.4   Swap rates 18 August 2003. All rates % per annum

Maturity	Euro €		Sterling £		US $	
	Bid	Offer	Bid	Offer	Bid	Offer
1 year	2.32	2.35	3.81	3.84	1.36	1.39
5 years	3.60	3.63	4.54	4.58	3.78	3.81
10 years	4.27	4.30	4.73	4.78	4.93	4.96

Source: ICAP plc quoted in the *Financial Times*

LIBORs – will be greater on five-year than on one-year swaps, and greater still on 10-year deals.

On the day that the figures quoted in Table 6.4 were published, 10-year gilts were providing returns (yields) of around 4.62% p.a. The fixed rate on 10-year sterling swaps (on the bid side) was 4.73% p.a., which is an extra 11 basis points. The difference arises because gilts are free of default risk, whereas it is possible that the counterparty on an interest rate swap might default on its obligations. The additional 11 basis points – the *spread* over the return on 10-year gilts – compensates for that additional risk. Since most IRS deals are agreed between banks and other financial institutions, the level of default risk anticipated in this spread is around the average for the banking sector.

We saw above that, in terms of exposure to interest rate changes, an IRS is akin to being long a variable-rate bond and short a fixed-rate bond or vice versa. However, it is important to appreciate that the credit or default risk is not exactly the same. An investor who buys a bond will suffer serious losses if the par or principal amount is not repaid. On an interest rate swap the principal amount is never actually exchanged. Credit risk arises when one side is expecting a stream of positive cash flows, based on the difference between a fixed and a floating rate of interest, and the counterparty defaults on making its due payments.

Default risk on swaps was treated with some complacency until the late 1980s when a major disaster hit the market. The London authority of Hammersmith & Fulham defaulted on almost £3 billion notional in swap transactions. When UK interest rates rose sharply the contracts became loss-making for the local authority. Unfortunately for the banks who were the counterparties, the UK courts declared the transactions *ultra vires*, that is, the local authority had no power to enter into the deals. The swaps were cancelled and some banks lost heavily as a result.

Interest rate swaps in US dollars are now so liquid and the market so vast that the fixed rates on swaps are sometimes used as benchmarks when a company is issuing a bond and has to decide the rate of interest it will have to pay to attract investors.

CROSS-CURRENCY SWAPS

In a cross-currency interest rate swap, cash flows in one currency are exchanged on regular dates for cash flows in another currency. The principal amounts are normally exchanged at the spot foreign exchange rate at the start of the swap and then re-exchanged at the same rate on the final payment date. The interest payments can be calculated on a fixed-rate or a floating-rate basis.

In the following example, one party, Americo, is a US company with a top credit rating. The other party, Britco, is a less highly-rated UK company. Both sides wish to borrow money on a fixed-rate basis. Americo wishes to borrow £100 million and to pay interest in sterling to finance its UK operations. Britco wishes to borrow $150 million and to pay interest in dollars, to fund activities in the USA. The spot foreign exchange rate is £/$1.5, that is, 1 pound sterling buys 1.5 US dollars. The 10-year borrowing rates for each company in dollars and in sterling are set out in Table 6.5. Interest in all cases is payable once a year, in arrears.

Americo can borrow more cheaply than Britco in either currency, reflecting its higher credit rating. It has an absolute advantage in the rates it will pay on both dollar and sterling loans. However, it has a significant relative or comparative advantage in dollars due to its greater 'name recognition' in its home market in the USA. It pays 1.5% p.a. less than Britco on dollar loans but only 0.75% p.a. less on sterling loans. In order to exploit this opportunity, Americo arranges dollar borrowings of $150 million at 5% p.a. for 10 years. Britco arranges sterling

Table 6.5   Fixed borrowing rates for US and UK companies

Borrower	$ fixed rate (% p.a.)	£ fixed rate (% p.a.)
Americo	5.00	6.00
Britco	6.50	6.75

borrowings of £100 million at 6.75% p.a. for 10 years. The two firms then approach a swap dealer who agrees the following transactions.

1. *Swap with Americo*

   • The dealer takes £150 million principal from Americo and gives the firm the £100 million it needs for its business operations. The principals will be re-exchanged at the same FX rate in 10 years' time on the final swap payment date.
   • The dealer agrees to pay Americo 5% p.a. on $150 million every year for the next 10 years and will receive in return 5.75% p.a. annually on £100 million.

2. *Swap with Britco*

   • The swap dealer takes the £100 million from Britco raised through its funding and gives the firm $150 million. The principals will be re-exchanged at the same FX rate on the final swap payment date.
   • The dealer agrees to pay Britco 6.75% p.a. annually on £100 million for the next 10 years. In return Britco will pay 6.35% p.a. on $150 million.

Gains from cross-currency swap

Figure 6.3 shows the flows of principal payments at the start of the various transactions. Americo raises dollars on its loan but pays these over in the swap transaction to obtain the pounds it requires. Britco sells the sterling it raises on its borrowing via the swap and receives

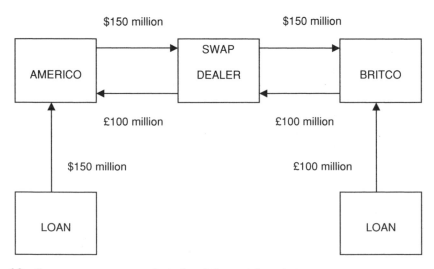

Figure 6.3   Cross-currency swaps principal cash flows at the outset

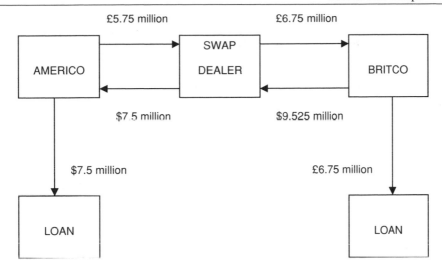

Figure 6.4   Cross-currency swaps annual interest payments in pounds and dollars

the dollars it needs for its business operations. Next, Figure 6.4 shows the annual interest payments on the swap deals and on the underlying loans. The positions of the two companies are as follows:

- Americo pays 5% p.a. on its $150 million loan, which is $7.5 million. However on the swap it receives 5% p.a. on $150 million which is also $7.5 million. So the dollar amounts cancel out. On the swap it pays in return 5.75% p.a. on £100 million which is £5.75 million.
- Britco pays 6.75% p.a. on its £100 million loan, which is £6.75 million. However on the swap it receives 6.75% p.a. on £100 million, which is also £6.75 million. So the sterling amounts simply cancel out. On the return leg of the swap it pays 6.35% p.a. on $150 million which is $9.525 million.

Finally, Figure 6.5 shows the principal payments in 10 years' time. Through the swaps, Americo receives the $150 million and Britco the £100 million they both need to repay the principal amounts on their loans. The net borrowing cost for Americo is 5.75% p.a. on £100 million. This is a saving of 0.25% p.a. compared to its funding cost if it had borrowed sterling directly rather than going through the swap (see Table 6.5). The net borrowing cost for Britco is 6.35% p.a. on $150 million. This is a saving of 0.15% p.a. compared to its funding cost if it had borrowed dollars directly (see again Table 6.5). So both parties are satisfied with the arrangements. The position of the swap dealer is as follows:

- The dealer receives and pays over the principal amounts to the two other parties, so the net effect is zero.
- Each year the dealer receives 6.35% and pays 5% on $150 million. This results in a positive cash flow of $2.025 million per annum.
- Each year the dealer pays 6.75% and pays 5.75% on £100 million. This is a negative cash flow of £1 million per annum.

The dealer can enter into a series of forward FX deals arranging to sell some of the dollar receipts each year to cover the negative cash flows in sterling. At the current spot rate of

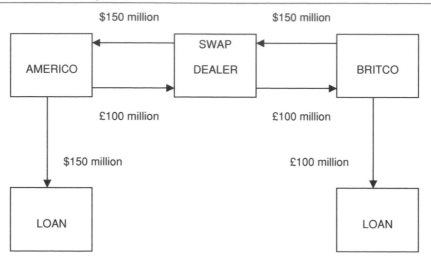

Figure 6.5   Cross-currency swaps principal cash flows at maturity

£1 = $1.5 it would only cost $1.5 million to buy £1 million, leaving surplus dollars each year as a profit. As a result of using the swap market the US and British firms have lowered their borrowing costs and the swap dealer has also booked a profit.

How does everyone seems to 'win' in this case? The answer lies with comparative advantage in funding costs. If you look back to Table 6.5 you will see that Americo has a substantial advantage over Britco in borrowing in its home currency (the US dollar) where its name is well known. Britco is a lower-rated company but it is much better recognized in the UK than in the USA, and the gap between the borrowing rates in sterling is much less than in dollars. So it makes good sense for Americo to borrow dollars, for Britco to borrow pounds, and then (via the dealer) for both parties to swap into the currencies they really need.

CHAPTER SUMMARY

A swap is an agreement made between two parties to exchange payments on regular dates in the future. In a 'plain vanilla' interest rate swap (IRS) one payment leg is based on a fixed rate of interest and the other on a variable rate which is reset periodically according to a benchmark such as LIBOR. Interest rate swaps have many applications. They are used by companies to lower their cost of funding or switch between fixed and floating borrowing. They are used by investors who wish to move from a fixed to a variable return or vice versa. The fixed rate on a standard or 'vanilla' IRS is an average of the first LIBOR rate agreed at the outset and the forward LIBORs expected over the life of the contract. It is normally higher than the rate on a Treasury bond with the same maturity because in a swap transaction there is default risk.

A cross-currency swap is a deal in which the payment legs are in two different currencies. Normally the notionals are exchanged at the outset and at maturity at the same FX rate. If a company wishes to borrow in a foreign currency it may find it beneficial to arrange a loan in its home currency in the first instance and then use a cross-currency swap to acquire the foreign currency and make interest payments in that currency.

7

Equity and Credit Default Swaps

EQUITY SWAPS

An equity swap is the over-the-counter alternative to equity index and single stock futures. It is an agreement between two parties:

- to exchange payments at regular intervals;
- over an agreed period of time;
- where at least one of the payment legs depends on the value of a share, a basket of shares or a stockmarket index.

In a *total return* deal a payment is also made which reflects the dividends on the share or basket or index. A typical equity swap application occurs when a company owns a block of shares in another firm (this is sometimes known as a corporate cross-holding) which it would like to 'monetize', i.e. to sell for cash. However, the company wishes to retain the economic exposure to changes in the value of the shares for some time period. The company sells the shares and enters into an equity swap in which it receives the return on the shares paid in cash on a periodic basis.

MONETIZING CORPORATE CROSS-HOLDINGS

To illustrate the idea, suppose that a company owns a block of 100 million shares in another firm. The shares are worth €1 each, with a total value of €100 million. It sells the shares to a bank and at the same time enters into a one-year equity swap. The notional principal is set at the outset at €100 million, although this will be reset later depending on what happens to the value of the shares. In the swap the bank pays the company the total return on the block of shares (capital gains or losses plus dividends) on a quarterly basis. In return, the company pays Euribor on a quarterly basis. Euribor is a key reference rate for short-term lending in euros, calculated by the Brussels-based European Banking Federation (FBE). The quarterly payments are illustrated in Figure 7.1.

There will be four payments on the swap, the first being due three months after the start date. The Euribor rate for that first payment is fixed at the start of the contract. Let us suppose that it is set at 4% p.a. or 1% for the quarter, so that the company will owe the bank €1 million on the interest rate leg of the swap. Suppose also that on that first payment date the shares are worth €102 million. The bank then owes the company €2 million for the increase in the value of the shares from the starting level of €100 million. We will assume that there are no dividends that quarter. Then all the payments are as follows:

- The company owes an interest payment of €1 million.
- The bank owes €2 million for the increase in the value of the shares.
- The payments are netted out and the bank pays the company €1 million.

Figure 7.1   Equity swap payment legs

The notional principal amount and the Euribor rate are now reset to help to calculate the cash flows due on the next quarterly payment date (six months after the start date of the swap). The notional principal value is reset to €102 million, the current value of the shares. For simplicity we will assume that the Euribor rate is unchanged at 4% p.a. and that no dividends are paid in the next quarter. Suppose that on the second payment date the shares are worth €99 million. The payments due on the swap for that quarter are calculated as follows:

- The company owes 1% of €102 million in interest which is €1.02 million.
- The company also owes €3 million for the *fall* in the value of the shares from a level of €102 million.
- The company pays the bank a total of €4.02 million.

If the shares increase in value during a quarter, the bank pays the company for the increase, but if the shares fall in value the company pays the bank. This replicates the economic exposure the company would have if it actually retained the shares. It is also possible to fix the notional on an equity swap throughout the life of the contract. A floating or resetting notional swap replicates an exposure to a fixed number of shares. A fixed notional equity swap replicates an exposure to a fixed *value* of shares, such that if the share price rose or fell the investor would sell or buy shares to maintain a constant allocation.

OTHER APPLICATIONS OF EQUITY SWAPS

Equity swaps are extremely versatile tools and have many applications for companies, banks and institutional investors. Because they are over-the-counter deals negotiated directly between the two parties, they can be tailored or customized to suit the needs of clients. A dealer will normally agree to pay the return on almost any basket of shares, provided some means can be found to hedge or at least to mitigate the risks on the transaction.

This can be useful, for example, for an investor who wishes to gain exposure to a basket of foreign shares but faces certain restrictions on ownership. A swap dealer will agree to pay the return on the shares (positive and negative) every month or every three months for a fixed period of time. In return, the investor will pay a floating or fixed rate of interest applied to the notional principal. The deal can be structured such that all the payments are made in a familiar currency such as the US dollar or the euro.

In this kind of case, it is possible that if the investor actually purchased the underlying shares then, as a foreigner, he or she would have to pay tax on the dividend income. If this is the case, the investor can enter into an equity swap transaction with a dealer who is not subject to the tax or can reclaim it. The dealer borrows money to buy the shares, and in the swap transaction the

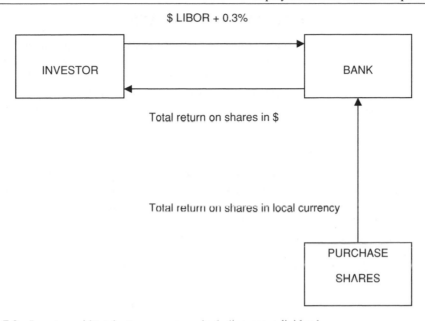

$ LIBOR + 0.3%

INVESTOR

BANK

Total return on shares in $

Total return on shares in local currency

PURCHASE

SHARES

Figure 7.2   Investor paid total return on a swap including gross dividends

dealer pays the total return on the shares to the investor, including *gross* dividends. In return the investor pays a funding rate which the dealer uses in part to service the loan and in part to make a profit on the transaction. The series of transactions involved in this type of deal is illustrated in Figure 7.2. In this swap the bank pays the total return on the shares to the investor in US dollars. The investor pays US dollar LIBOR plus 30 basis points.

The bank borrows money to buy the shares and uses the dollar LIBOR payment from the swap to help to pay the interest on the loan; assuming that it can borrow at LIBOR it will make 30 basis points per annum on the deal. It will need this, not just to make a profit, but also because its hedge is unlikely to be perfect and it will have to manage the risks. For example, although the bank has agreed to pay over the return on a specific basket of shares it may decide to hedge by buying a subset of shares in the basket in order to save on transaction costs. It will also have to manage the currency translation since it is making payments on the swap in US dollars whereas the returns on the underlying shares will be achieved in local currency.

By entering into an equity swap, it is just as easy for a client to take a 'short' position in a share or a basket of shares as it is to take a long position. The client agrees to pay over to the swap dealer any changes (positive and negative) in the value of a share. If the share price falls the client will receive payments from the swap dealer; if it rises the client will have to make payments to the dealer. Economically, this is the equivalent of a short position.

Of course it is also possible to take long and short positions in shares by trading equity index and single stock futures (see Chapter 5). One drawback of futures is that there is a daily margin system in operation, which may be inconvenient. With an equity swap there are a set number of payments, made weekly, monthly or quarterly. Swaps can also be customized to meet the needs of clients. On the other hand, futures are guaranteed by the clearing house, whereas swaps are over-the-counter transactions and, as such, carry counterparty default risk.

EQUITY INDEX SWAPS

In a standard equity index swap contract one party agrees to make periodic payments based on the change (positive or negative) in the value of an equity index such as the S&P 500, the DAX, the Nikkei 225, the CAC 40 or the FT-SE 100. In return it receives a fixed or a floating rate of interest applied to the notional principal. The swap can be structured such that the notional principal remains constant over the life of the deal, or varies according to the changing level of the index.

The term sheet for a typical equity index swap transaction is set out in Table 7.1. The deal is also illustrated in Figure 7.3 (the Δ sign simply means 'change'). The swap dealer has agreed to pay the total return on the FT-SE on a quarterly basis, including a payment representing the dividend yield on the index. In return the dealer receives three-month sterling LIBOR plus 25 basis points applied to the notional principal. The notional is fixed at £100 million, the LIBOR rate and dividend yield for the first payment have been set at 3.75% p.a. and 3% p.a. respectively, and the starting index level is fixed at 5000 points. This is based on the level of the cash FT-SE 100 index when the deal is agreed.

The first payment on the swap is due three months after the start date. We will assume that the FT-SE 100 index is trading at 5100 at that point, which is a rise of 2% from the starting level of 5000. The payments due on the swap are then calculated as follows:

- The dealer pays 2% of £100 million for the rise in the index, i.e. £2 million.
- The dividend yield was set at 3% p.a., which is 0.75% for the quarter. Applied to the notional of £100 million, this means that the dealer pays £0.75 million.
- The LIBOR rate was fixed at 3.75% p.a. Including the spread, the client owes 1% of £100 million for the quarter, i.e. £1 million.
- Payments are netted out and the dealer pays £1.75 million to the client.

Table 7.1   Equity index swap on the FT-SE 100

Client receives:	Change in the value of the FT-SE 100 index plus the dividend yield on the index
Dealer receives:	Three-month sterling LIBOR + 0.25%
Payments for both legs:	Quarterly
Start date:	Today
Maturity:	In one year
Notional principal:	£100 million fixed
First LIBOR setting:	3.75% p.a.
First dividend yield setting:	3% p.a.
Start FT-SE level:	5000

Three-month £ LIBOR + 0.25% p.a.

CLIENT

SWAP DEALER

Δ FT-SE 100 + dividend yield

Figure 7.3   Equity swap payment legs

The key variables are reset to help to establish the second payment on the swap, which is due after a further three months. The variables are as follows:

- the FT-SE 100 index level, which in this case will be reset at 5100
- the interest rate, which is re-fixed according to three-month sterling BBA LIBOR
- the dividend yield on the FT-SE 100 index.

Since the swap has a maturity of one year with quarterly payments, this means that there will be a total of four payments, all calculated in the manner illustrated above. At maturity the final payment takes place and the swap expires. The swap enables the client to achieve a diversified exposure to the UK stock market, without having to physically buy the shares, which could incur significant spreads and other transaction costs. The client pays LIBOR plus a set spread. In fact the interest rate could easily be fixed by adding an interest rate swap to the package.

Hedging equity swaps

In the above example, the dealer pays the total return on the FT-SE 100 index to the client. If the index rises the dealer pays the client for that increase, but if the market falls the client pays the dealer. In effect, the dealer has a short position in the FT-SE 100 index. The dealer can hedge the risk if he or she buys FT-SE 100 index futures (see Chapter 5). This establishes a long position in the market so that profits and losses on the futures contracts will offset those on the swap. The dealer would, however, have to buy futures contracts that match the payment dates on the swap, and there is the risk that the contracts might be expensive, i.e. trading above their fair or theoretical value.

As an alternative, the dealer could borrow money and buy a basket of shares designed to track the FT-SE 100 index, and use the LIBOR-related receipts on the swap to service the interest payments on the loan. The hedge is illustrated in Figure 7.4. The dealer simply pays

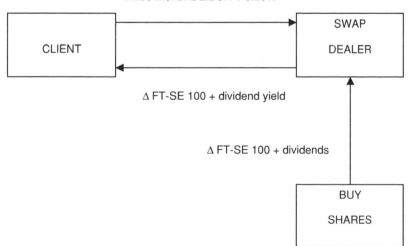

Figure 7.4   Equity swap hedged in the cash market

Payment contingent on credit event

Figure 7.5   Credit default swap

away the returns on the shares to the client in the equity swap transaction. Assuming the loan can be funded at exactly LIBOR, then the dealer has covered the equity exposure and has made 25 basis points on the set of transactions. The dealer also has to consider counterparty or default risk on the swap; in practice, the client may be asked for collateral when the deal is agreed to cover this risk.

CREDIT DEFAULT SWAPS

Generally, a credit derivative is a contract whose payout depends on the creditworthiness of some organization such as a multinational corporation. Specifically, a credit default swap (CDS) is a form of insurance against default on a loan or a bond. There are two parties to a deal:

* The buyer of protection.
* The seller of protection.

The asset that is to be protected is known as the *referenced asset*. It can be a loan or a bond or a set of such obligations. The borrower or issuer of the bond is called the *referenced credit* or *entity*. In the standard type of deal the buyer of protection pays a periodic premium to the seller of so many basis points per annum applied to the par value of the referenced asset (this can also be made in a single up-front payment). If, during the life of the swap, any one of a number of specified credit events occurs then the seller of protection has to take delivery of the referenced asset and pay a set amount of money to the buyer of protection (normally the par value of the asset). The swap can also be set up such that if a credit event occurs the buyer of protection retains the asset but is paid cash in compensation. The basic deal is illustrated in Figure 7.5.

A range of credit events affecting the referenced credit can be stipulated that will trigger the contingent payment by the seller of protection. This can include items such as bankruptcy, insolvency, failure to meet a payment obligation when due, a credit ratings downgrade below a certain threshold. The payout on a *basket CDS* is based on a basket of assets with different issuers. In a first-to-default deal the credit event that triggers payment depends on the first of the referenced assets in the basket that defaults. Buyers of protection in credit default swaps include commercial banks who wish to reduce their exposure to credit risk on their loan books, and investing institutions seeking to hedge against the risk of default on a bond or a portfolio of bonds. Sellers of protection include banks and insurance companies who earn premium in return for insuring against default.

Most deals are structured such that if a credit event occurs the buyer of protection sells the referenced asset to the seller of protection at a set price. However, some assets cannot be

Table 7.2   Users of credit derivatives 2003

Types of institution	Protection buyer (%)	Protection seller (%)
Banks	52	39
Securities houses	21	12
Hedge funds	12	21
Corporates	4	16
Monoline/re-insurers	3	5
Insurance companies	3	3
Mutual funds	2	2
Pension funds	1	2
Governments/agencies	2	0

Source: British Bankers' Association, Lehman Brothers. Quoted in *Financial News*

transferred for legal reasons, in which case the buyer of protection is given the right to substitute a similar asset that can be transferred. If the deal is structured such that the protection buyer actually retains the asset but is compensated in cash for the fall in its value, then some means has to be found to establish the value of the asset after a credit event occurs. This is often estimated through a series of dealer polls, since it is not likely that the asset would be actively traded in such circumstances.

To give some idea of the size of the market, the International Swaps and Derivatives Association (ISDA) estimated that the notional principal amount outstanding on credit derivatives generally at mid-year 2003 was $2.69 trillion, compared to $2.79 trillion on equity derivatives. (These values are adjusted for double-counting.) ISDA provides important services for the market, including standard documentation for credit default swaps. Table 7.2 shows the users of credit derivatives in 2003 and the proportions that bought and sold protection.

Credit default swap premium

The periodic premium paid on a credit default swap is related to, but not normally exactly the same as, the *credit spread* on the referenced asset. The credit spread is the additional return that investors can currently earn on that asset above the return available on assets that are free of default risk – in effect, Treasury bonds.

For example, suppose that a five-year corporate bond pays a return of 5% p.a. and the return on five-year Treasuries is only 4% p.a. Then the bond's credit spread is 1% p.a. or 100 basis points. The size of the spread depends to a large extent on the rating of the bond, which measures the probability of default. It also depends on other factors such as the expected *recovery rate* if it defaults – the percentage of the par value the investors can hope to recover from the issuer. The seller of protection in a credit default swap assumes the credit risk on the referenced asset and should therefore be paid a premium that reflects the level of default risk on that asset – i.e. one that is related in some way to its credit spread.

Suppose that an insurance company has invested in risk-free Treasury bonds. The returns are safe but not very exciting. It decides to enter into a credit default swap in which it receives a premium in return for providing default protection against a referenced asset. The position of the insurance company is illustrated in Figure 7.6.

By entering into the swap the insurance company has moved from a risk-free investment to a situation that involves credit or default risk. To an extent this replicates the sort of position

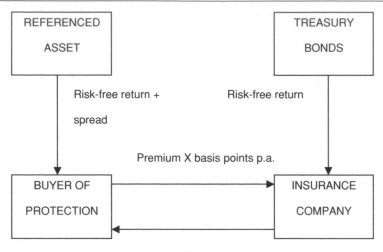

Figure 7.6   Treasury bonds plus credit default swap

it would be in if it sold the Treasuries and bought the referenced asset itself. The premium received from the buyer of protection in the swap should therefore be related to the additional return over the risk-free rate (the credit spread) available on the referenced asset. In practice, credit default swap premiums are not usually exactly the same as the spread over Treasuries on the referenced asset for a variety of reasons. The spread is affected by the liquidity of the asset as well as its default risk. As another complicating factor, the two parties in a credit default swap also acquire a credit exposure to each other.

There are a number of ways in which the premiums on credit default swaps are established. One is by modelling the probability of default on the referenced asset, based on the credit spread and/or the historical behaviour of assets of that credit quality. The ratings agencies publish historical default rates and recovery rates on different classes of assets with different credit ratings. They also publish so-called *transition matrices* which provide historical data on the occurrence of ratings downgrades on assets with different credit qualities.

When calculating the CDS premium it is necessary to take into account the expected recovery rate on the referenced asset – that is, the percentage of its par value that can be recovered in the event of default. This will depend on factors such as the seniority of the asset and whether it is secured on collateral such as property.

CHAPTER SUMMARY

An equity swap is an agreement between two parties to exchange cash flows on regular future dates where at least one of the payment legs depends on the value of a share or a portfolio of shares. The notional principal on a deal can be fixed or floating. Traders and investors can replicate long and short positions in shares by receiving or paying the change in the value of the underlying in an equity swap. In a total return deal, dividends are also paid. In an equity index swap one of the payment legs is based on a stockmarket index such as the S&P 500 or the FT-SE 100. A deal can be hedged by trading index futures or by buying or shorting the underlying shares.

In a credit default swap the buyer of protection pays a premium to the seller of protection. In return he or she receives a contingent payment depending on whether one of a number of credit events occurs during the life of the agreement. Credit events can include default or ratings downgrades or financial restructurings. The premium on a credit default swap depends on the probability that a credit event will occur and also on any money that can be recovered on the asset or assets being protected. Buyers of protection include fund managers and commercial banks seeking to reduce the level of credit risk on portfolios of bonds or loans. Sellers of protection include dealers in banks, and insurance companies who are trying to enhance the returns on their investments by earning premium.

8
Fundamentals of Options

INTRODUCTION

In Chapter 1 we saw that options on commodities such as rice, oil and grain have been in existence for many years. Options on financial assets are more recent although activity has expanded rapidly since the introduction of listed contracts on exchanges such as the Chicago Board Options Exchange (CBOE), LIFFE and Eurex. The buyer of a European-style option contract has the right but not the obligation:

- to buy (call option) or sell (put option) an agreed amount of a specified asset, called the underlying;
- at a specified price, called the exercise or strike price;
- on a future date, called the expiry or expiration date.

European options can only be exercised at expiry, whereas American-style contracts can be exercised on any business day up to and including expiry. These labels are purely historical. The majority of exchange-traded options around the world are American-style, modelled on the contracts first traded on exchanges in the USA. Over-the-counter (OTC) options are often European, because the buyers do not wish to pay extra premium for the ability to exercise before expiry. An American call on a dividend-paying share will be more expensive than a European call, since there are occasions when it is beneficial to exercise the contract early and receive the forthcoming dividend on the share. A *Bermudan* option is a half-way house. It can be exercised on a set number of days before expiry, such as one day per week.

Unlike a forward, an option contract has built-in flexibility because the holder is not obliged to exercise or take up the option. For this privilege the buyer of an option has to pay an initial premium to the seller (also known as the writer) of the contract. As we will see in Chapter 13, the premium is determined by calculating the expected payout, and a key input to establishing this value is the volatility of the price of the underlying asset. The more volatile the underlying asset, all other things being equal, the greater the expected payout from an option on that asset, and the greater the premium charged by the writer.

Consider the example of a one-year European call on a share struck at $100. The holder of the option has the right but not the obligation to purchase the share for $100 after one year. If the price of the share is highly volatile this increases the chance that it will be substantially above the strike at expiry. The greater the value of the underlying at expiry, the greater the profit achieved by the owner of the call. Of course, a high level of volatility also increases the chance that the share price at expiry will be *below* the $100 strike of the call. However the holder of the option is not obliged to exercise the contract. The loss is limited to the initial premium paid.

Exchange-traded options are largely standardized but their performance is guaranteed by the clearing house associated with the options exchange. OTC options are agreed directly between two counterparties, one of which is normally a specialist dealer at a bank or securities firm. As

Table 8.1   Bought call option contract

Type of option:	Long call
Underlying share:	XYZ
Spot share price:	$100
Number of shares in the contract:	100
Exercise price:	$100 per share
Exercise style:	American
Expiry:	1 year
Premium:	$10 per share

a result, the terms of OTC contracts can be tailored to meet the needs of clients. For example, the strike price or the time to expiry can be adjusted; or the contract can be based on a basket or portfolio of shares rather than a single asset. The contract can also be designed such that profits and losses are settled in cash rather than through the physical delivery of the underlying asset. This is an advantage for clients who do not wish to go through the inconvenience and expense of an actual delivery process.

CALL OPTION: INTRINSIC AND TIME VALUE

A call option is the right but not the obligation to buy a commodity or a financial asset at a fixed strike or exercise price. Table 8.1 gives details of an equity call option contract purchased by a trader. The option is American-style, so it can be exercised on any business day up to and including expiry, in one year's time. The underlying share is trading at $100 in the cash or spot market and the exercise price of the call is also $100. The premium charged by the writer of the contract is $10 per share or $1000 on 100 shares.

The holder of the call has the right to purchase each share for $100. The *intrinsic value* of an option is defined as any money that can be realized through immediately exercising the contract. In this case the share is trading at $100 in the cash market and the strike is also $100, so the holder cannot release any value by immediate exercise. The option has zero intrinsic value. Since the strike price is exactly the same as the spot price, the call is said to be *at-the-money*.

Imagine, however, that some time after the option is purchased the spot price of the share jumps to $120. The option is now *in-the-money* since the owner has the right to buy a share for $100 that is worth $120. The option contract now has $20 intrinsic value per share. Note that this is not the *net profit* the holder would achieve by actually exercising the call. To establish this value the initial $10 premium has to be deducted from the intrinsic value. Table 8.2 calculates the option's intrinsic value if the spot price of the share moves to a range

Table 8.2   Intrinsic value of $100 strike call for a range of spot prices

New share price	Intrinsic value now	Option is now ...
$80	$0	Out-of-the-money
$90	$0	Out-of-the-money
$100	$0	At-the-money
$110	$10	In-the-money
$120	$20	In-the-money

of different possible levels. Notice that intrinsic value is never negative because the owner of an option is never obliged to exercise an out-of-the-money contract.

More formally, the intrinsic value of an American-style call option can be defined as the spot price of the underlying asset minus the strike, or zero, whichever is the greater of the two. This definition is commonly also applied to European options, although the profit from exercise can only be realized at expiry.

Any money paid for an option in addition to its intrinsic value is called *time value*. In the contract shown in Table 8.1, the buyer pays $10 per share in premium, even though the option has no intrinsic value at all. The $10 consists of time value, and the buyer is obliged to pay this money because there is some chance or probability that the share price *might* rise above the strike before expiry. This possibility provides profit opportunities for the buyer of the contract and serious risks for the writer. If the contract is exercised the writer is obliged to deliver a share at a fixed price of $100, whatever its value in the market happens to be at that point in time. The buyer of the call has to pay for that chance or opportunity and the writer has to be compensated for that very considerable risk. The two components – intrinsic and time value – together make up the total premium paid for an option.

$$\text{Option premium} = \text{Intrinsic value} + \text{Time value}$$

The expression *time value* derives from the fact that normally, all other things being equal, a longer-dated option has more time value than a shorter-dated contract. The probability of a share price doubling in the course of a year is much greater than over the course of a day. This increases the potential payout to the buyer of a call on the share. It also increases the potential losses to the writer, who has to charge a higher premium in compensation. Talk of 'time value' can be a little misleading, however, since time to expiry is not the only factor that determines how much a buyer has to pay for an option over and above its intrinsic value. It is also determined by factors such as the volatility of the underlying, and the general level of interest rates in the market. We will return to this issue in Chapter 13.

Long call expiry payoff

If an option is at- or out-of-the-money at expiry it has zero intrinsic value. The contract will simply not be exercised and will be worthless. On the other hand, if the option is in-the-money it will have positive intrinsic value. This is calculated as the difference between the share price and the strike price. At expiry an option has zero time value, since the outcome of the contract is no longer in question.

To illustrate these effects, we return to the bought or 'long' call option contract discussed in the previous sections. The strike is $100 and premium paid is $10 per share. Table 8.3 shows the intrinsic value for a range of different possible share prices at expiry. The break-even point occurs when the underlying is trading at $110. The owner of the call can realize $10 intrinsic value by exercising the contract, by purchasing a share for $100 that is worth $110. This exactly offsets the initial premium, and the net profit and loss per share is zero. (This ignores any transaction and funding costs.)

The results from Table 8.3 are presented graphically in Figure 8.1, which shows the net profit and loss on the option contract for a range of possible share prices between $50 and $150. The maximum loss to the buyer of the call is $10 per share. The maximum profit is unlimited since the share price (in theory) could rise to any level.

Table 8.3 $100 strike call: intrinsic value and net P&L at expiry per share

Share price at expiry	Call intrinsic value	Net profit and loss
50	0	−10
60	0	−10
70	0	−10
80	0	−10
90	0	−10
100	0	−10
110	10	0
120	20	10
130	30	20
140	40	30
150	50	40

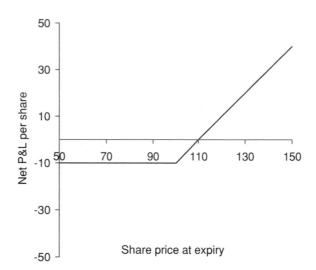

Figure 8.1 Profit and loss per share on long $100 strike call at expiry

Short call expiry payoff

In the jargon of the market, the buyer of an option contract has *limited downside* (potential losses) but *unlimited upside* (potential profit). Like an insurance policy, the most money that can ever be lost is the initial premium that was paid. Also, if the option is exchange-traded it can easily be sold back before expiry, recouping at least some of that initial outlay.

However the position of the seller or writer of a call option is very different. Figure 8.2 illustrates the payoff profile at expiry for the writer of the call option explored in the previous sections. The maximum profit is the initial premium collected. If the share price is trading above the strike at expiry then the option will be exercised at a profit to the holder and a loss to the writer. For example, suppose the share price is $150. Then the writer will have to deliver a share at a fixed price of $100 which costs $150 to buy in the spot market, so losing $50 on exercise. From this is deducted the initial premium received of $10, leaving a $40 loss per share on the deal (ignoring funding and transaction costs).

Table 8.4   Bought put option contract

Type of option:	Long put
Underlying share:	XYZ
Spot share price:	$100
Number of shares:	100
Exercise price per share:	$100
Exercise style:	American
Expiry:	1 year
Premium:	$10 per share

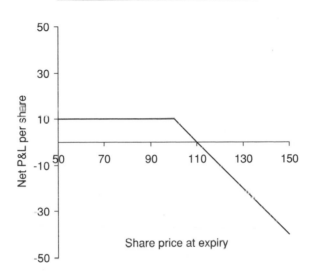

Figure 8.2   Profit and loss per share on short $100 strike call at expiry

The graph in Figure 8.2 shows the profit and loss profile of a 'naked' or unhedged short call. The position has *limited upside* gains (limited to the initial premium collected) and potentially *unlimited downside* losses. In practice, professional traders do not routinely sell options contracts unhedged. That would be much too risky. As we will see in Chapter 15, a short or sold call option can be hedged by buying a quantity of the underlying. If the share price increases, the dealer will lose money on the call but gain on the hedge. This methodology is known in the market as *delta hedging*. When a dealer has sold an option and has traded the appropriate quantity of the underlying to match the risk, then the overall position is said to be *delta neutral*.

PUT OPTION: INTRINSIC AND TIME VALUE

A put option is the right but not the obligation to sell the underlying at the strike or exercise price. Table 8.4 sets out the terms of a purchased or long put option contract. The strike is $100 per share, the time to expiry is one year and the premium is $10 per share. Buying a put option is a 'bear' position on the underlying. The holder profits from a fall in the share price, although the maximum loss is restricted to the initial premium paid. Since the strike and the spot price in this example are both $100 the option is at-the-money and has zero intrinsic value. It is not possible to realize any value by immediately exercising the contract.

Table 8.5 Intrinsic value of $100 strike put for a range of share prices

New share price	Intrinsic value now	Option is now
$80	$20	In-the-money
$90	$10	In-the-money
$100	$0	At-the-money
$110	$0	Out-of-the-money
$120	$0	Out-of-the-money

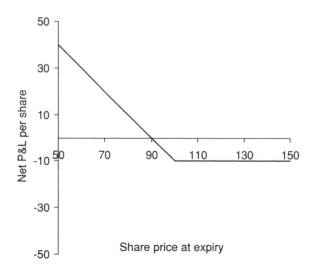

Figure 8.3 Profit and loss per share on long $100 strike put at expiry

The intrinsic value of a put option is the strike less the spot price of the underlying asset, or zero, whichever is the greater of the two. In this example the option is at-the-money and its intrinsic value is zero. Therefore the premium consists entirely of time value. It is paid on the possibility that the share price *might* fall below the strike, in which case the option would move into-the-money and would acquire positive intrinsic value.

Suppose that some time after the contract was purchased the share price had fallen to $80. The owner of the put could purchase the share in the cash market for $80, then exercise the option, thereby selling the share for $100 and earning $20 (less the premium paid at the outset). The contract would now be in-the-money with $20 intrinsic value. On the other hand, if the share price increased to (say) $120, the option would be out-of-the-money and the intrinsic value zero. It would not make sense to exercise the contract and sell for only $100. Table 8.5 calculates the intrinsic value of the put option if the share price moved to a number of different levels.

Long put expiry payoff

Table 8.6 and Figure 8.3 illustrate the profit and loss profile of the put option discussed in the previous section at expiry and from the perspective of the buyer of the contract. The values are shown per share; the strike price is $100; the initial premium paid is $10; and the maximum loss is the premium. If the underlying is trading below the strike price, the option will have

Table 8.6 $100 strike put option intrinsic value and net
profit/loss at expiry

Share price at expiry	Intrinsic value	Net profit and loss
50	50	40
60	40	30
70	30	20
80	20	10
90	10	0
100	0	−10
110	0	−10
120	0	−10
130	0	−10
140	0	−10
150	0	−10

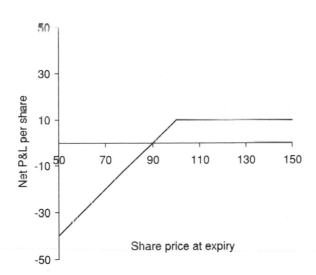

Figure 8.4   Profit and loss per share on short $100 strike put at expiry

positive intrinsic value and will be exercised. The intrinsic value measures the gain that can be released by exercising the contract; the net profit and loss figure subtracts from this the initial premium paid.

Short put expiry payoff

The buyer of a put option has limited downside (potential loss), restricted to the initial premium paid. The maximum upside or profit potential is not in fact unlimited, since share prices do not fall below zero, but normally it is still very substantial. The major risk is taken by the writer of the contract. If it is exercised the writer is obliged to take delivery of the underlying and pay a predetermined price – the strike – whatever the actual value of the share happens to be in the cash market.

Figure 8.4 illustrates the position of the writer of the put option contract at expiry explored in the previous section. The strike is $100 per share and the premium received is $10 per share.

As long as the share is trading at or above the strike the contract will not be exercised. The profit is the initial premium received. However, if the underlying is trading below the strike then the contract will be exercised. The writer will be obliged to pay $100 for an asset that is worth less than that in the cash market. The break-even point for the writer is reached when the share is trading at $90, in which case the loss on exercise matches the initial premium received.

The position illustrated in Figure 8.4 is that of an unhedged or 'naked' sold put option. As we remarked above, professional traders normally try to hedge or cover the bulk of the risks they acquire when selling contracts. The risk, when selling a put, is that the share price may fall sharply, and one method of hedging this is to establish a short position in the underlying – that is, to borrow shares and sell them into the cash market, with a promise to return them later to the original owner. If the shares fall in price the option writer can then buy them back cheaply and return them to the original owner. The profit achieved by doing this will help to offset losses on the put option. This is an example of a delta hedge and of establishing a position that is *delta neutral* – one that is not exposed to small changes in the value of the underlying (see Chapter 15 for further details).

CHAPTER SUMMARY

A call option conveys the right but not the obligation to buy the underlying asset at a fixed strike or exercise price. A put conveys the right to sell the underlying at a fixed strike or exercise price. An American-style contract can be exercised at or before expiry but a European-style option can only be exercised at expiry. The buyer of an option has flexibility – he or she is not obliged to exercise the contract – and for this privilege pays an initial premium to the seller or writer of the contract. The maximum loss is therefore the initial premium paid, but the potential gains can be unlimited. The writer of an option has a quite different risk/return profile. The maximum profit is restricted to the initial premium earned while the maximum loss can be unlimited.

There are two components of an option premium: intrinsic and time value. The intrinsic value of a call is the spot price of the underlying minus the strike, or zero, whichever is the greater of the two. The intrinsic value of a put is the maximum of zero and the strike minus the spot price of the underlying. Intrinsic value is never negative because an option contract that is out-of-the-money will not be exercised. Anything paid for an option in addition to its intrinsic value is time value. Even if a contract has zero intrinsic value there is still a chance that it *might* move into the money prior to expiry. This provides profit potential for the holder of the option and is reflected in its time value. All other things being equal, a longer-dated option on the same underlying normally has greater profit potential than a shorter-dated option. Time value is also linked to other factors such as the volatility of the underlying asset, interest rates and dividends.

9

Hedging with Options

INTRODUCTION

Institutional investors such as pension funds and insurance companies are exposed to changes in the values of shares, bonds and other financial assets. Company profits can be eroded by movements in borrowing rates, currency exchange rates and the market prices of physical commodities such as oil. Food producers find it very difficult to manage their businesses if crop prices are highly volatile.

All of these risks, and more, can be hedged by the use of forwards, futures or swaps. An investor concerned about potential losses on a portfolio of US shares can short S&P 500 index futures. If the shares fall in value the investor will earn compensation in the form of variation margin receipts on the futures contracts. A business due to receive foreign currency can enter into an outright forward FX deal with a bank to sell the currency at a fixed rate of exchange. A company concerned about rising interest rates can use an interest rate swap to fix its borrowing costs. A farmer can hedge against volatility in the market price of a crop by shorting exchange-traded futures contracts.

Hedging exposures of this kind with forwards, futures and swaps has many advantages. But all the strategies discussed above share one common characteristic. The exposure to the market variable is hedged out, but at the expense of being unable to benefit fully from favourable movements in that variable.

An equity investor who sells index futures is protected against losses arising from falls in the stock market. But if the market rallies, gains on the portfolio will be offset by losses on the short futures position. A company that agrees to sell foreign currency on a future date at a predetermined rate cannot gain if the movement in the spot rate is favourable. The forward contract must be honoured at the stipulated rate of exchange. A company that switches from a floating to a fixed liability by entering into an interest rate swap is protected against rising borrowing costs but cannot take advantage of falling market interest rates.

Hedging with options is quite a different proposition. Options can protect against adverse movements in a market variable while still permitting some level of benefit if the movement in the variable is favourable. In the jargon of the market, options can be used to provide 'downside protection' while still retaining some degree of 'upside potential'. The drawback of course is that purchasing options costs money, the premium due to the writer. In this chapter we explore a number of hedging strategies involving equity options, which also serve to illustrate the close relationship between European-style options and forward contracts. Chapters 11 and 12 consider hedging strategies using currency and interest rate options.

FORWARD HEDGE REVISITED

The case investigated throughout this chapter is that of an investor owning a share trading at a price of exactly 100 in the cash market. This could be pounds or dollars or euros. Since the

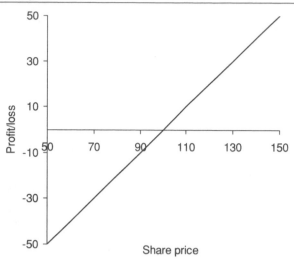

Figure 9.1   Profit/loss profile for a long position in a share trading at 100

investor has a long position in the share, he or she will incur losses if the price falls and will gain if it rises. The diagonal line in Figure 9.1 illustrates the relationship between the spot price of the share and the investor's profits and losses. If the share price falls to 50 the investor loses 50. If it rises to 150 the profit is 50. And so on.

Suppose that the investor is concerned about short-term factors in the market that could cause the share price to fall. An obvious solution of course is to sell and switch into another asset, perhaps into cash, until the problems are resolved. There are many practical reasons why this may not be a particularly attractive solution. The share might be a long-term investment and the bearish indicators only hold for the next two or three months. If it is sold now it may have to be repurchased later, incurring heavy transaction costs. The investor may be trying to generate returns that exceed but do not deviate too far from a benchmark index. If the share is a 'blue chip' and a major component of the index, it may be very difficult to sell outright without diverging too far from the benchmark. The investor could sell a proportion of the holding, but if the deal is large enough this could actually contribute towards depressing the market value of the share.

An alternative strategy is to short a forward contract on the stock, or a futures, if one exists. Suppose the investor wishes to hedge against a fall in the share price over the next three months. The interest rate is 4% p.a. and the share pays a dividend yield of 2% p.a. The net carry on the stock is therefore $4\% - 2\% = 2\%$ p.a. or 0.5% for the quarter year. The theoretical forward price of the stock in three months is given by the cash-and-carry calculation we discussed in Chapter 2.

$$\text{Three-month forward price} = 100 + (100 \times 0.5\%) = 100.50$$

The investor enters a contract with a dealer agreeing to 'sell' the stock forward in three months' time at a price of 100.5. The intention is not actually to deliver the share, so the contract is set up such that it will be settled in cash. If in three months' time the share is trading below 100.5 the investor will be paid the difference in cash by the dealer. If it is trading at a price above 100.5 then the investor will have to pay the dealer the difference between that price and 100.5.

Figure 9.2 shows the investor's profits and losses on the share for a range of possible share prices at the expiry of the forward contract in three months' time. It also shows the payout on the

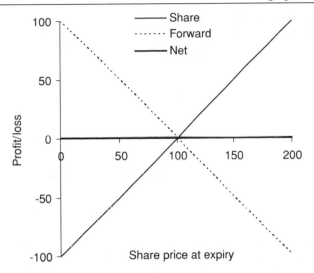

Figure 9.2   Net payoff from hedging a share with a short forward contract

short forward contract. This appears as a diagonal line sloping to the left and cutting through the horizontal axis at the forward price of 100.5. If the share price at the expiry of the forward is zero the profit on the short forward is 100.5; if it is 200 the loss on the short forward is 99.5; and so on.

Figure 9.2. also shows the combination payoff profile for the long position in the share plus the short forward deal. It appears in the graph as a horizontal line 0.5 above the *x* axis, labelled 'net'. To see why this is the case, we can take some possible levels at which the share might be trading at the expiry of the forward contract in three months' time and calculate the net profit and loss.

- *Share price* = 90. The investor has lost 10 on the share but has made 100.5 − 90 = 10.5 on the short forward. The net figure is plus 0.5.
- *Share price* = 110. The profit on the share is 10 and the loss on the short forward is 100.5 − 110 = −9.5. The net figure is once again plus 0.5.

In fact the net profit and loss is the same for all possible share prices in three months' time. At first glance this may appear to be an excellent deal, since the investor always seems to 'make' 0.5 out of the hedged position whatever happens to the share price. However this is something of an illusion. It does not take account of the fact that by continuing to hold the share for three months rather than selling it and depositing the proceeds, the investor is actually losing the interest that could be earned. This opportunity loss cancels out what appears to be a 'gain' on the hedged position.

Overall, however, the benefit of the hedge is that the investor is insured against falls in the stock price over a three-month period. The downside is that he or she cannot benefit from an increase in the price. The gains would be paid to the counterparty on the forward contract.

PROTECTIVE PUT

As an alternative, the investor can consider buying a put option on the share. The choice of strike depends on the level of protection the investor requires, balanced against how much premium he or she is prepared to pay. Suppose the investor contacts a dealer and is offered a

Table 9.1   Profit/loss on share, on put option, and on the combination

Share price at expiry	Share P&L	Put net P&L	Combined P&L
70	−30	21.54	−8.46
80	−20	11.54	−8.46
90	−10	1.54	−8.46
100	0	−3.46	−3.46
110	10	−3.46	6.54
120	20	−3.46	16.54
130	30	−3.46	26.54
140	40	−3.46	36.54

three-month out-of-the-money European put on the stock with a strike of 95. The dealer asks for a premium of 3.46.

In this deal, the option contract will be settled in cash. This means that if the spot price of the share is below the strike at expiry, then the dealer will pay the difference to the investor – in other words, the dealer will pay the intrinsic value of the option, depending on how much it is in-the-money. Unlike the forward contract, however, if the share price is *higher* than the strike the investor will have no obligation to make further payment (the put will have zero intrinsic value). The other side of the coin is that, unlike the forward contract, the investor has to pay a premium to buy the put option.

The first column in Table 9.1 shows a range of possible spot prices for the share at the expiry of the put option in three months. The second column calculates the profit or loss on the share, given that it was initially worth 100. The third column in the table is the net payout on the 95 strike put option, its intrinsic value at expiry less the initial premium paid. The fourth column is the total profit and loss on the combined hedged position, that is, long the stock and long the 95 strike put option.

A few examples from Table 9.1 will help to explain how the values are calculated.

- *Share Price = 70.* The loss on the share is 30. The cash payment due to the investor on the put (its intrinsic value) is $95 − 70 = 25$. The net payout on the put less the premium is $25 − 3.46 = 21.54$. The total loss on the combined position is therefore 8.46.
- *Share Price = 140.* The gain on the share is 40. The intrinsic value of the put is zero and the loss on the option is just the premium of 3.46. The total profit on the combined position is therefore 36.54.

The break-even point on the combined position at the expiry of the option is reached when the share is trading at 103.46. At that point the gains on the share will recoup the option premium. Because it is reached when the share increases in price, this is called the *upside break-even* point. The maximum loss on the combined position is 8.46. This is reached when the share price is 95. At 95 the put has zero intrinsic value so the losses are 5 on the share plus 3.46 premium. Below 95, cash payments are received on the put that compensate the investor for any further falls in the share price.

PAYOFF PROFILE OF PROTECTIVE PUT

Figure 9.3 illustrates the expiry payoff profile of the long 95 strike put option considered in the previous section for a range of possible share prices at expiry. It also shows the profile

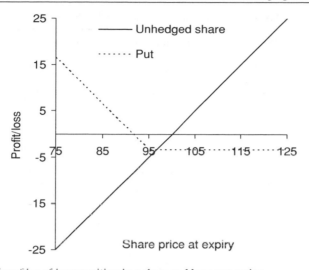

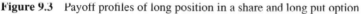

Figure 9.3 Payoff profiles of long position in a share and long put option

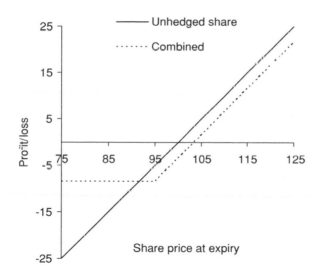

Figure 9.4 Combined payoff profile long share plus long put option

of the long position in the share – this represents the profit or loss on the share if it remains unhedged. The graph shows that when the share price falls below the strike, the payment due on the put option begins to balance out the loss on the share.

The dotted line in Figure 9.4 shows the profit and loss on the *combined position* – long the stock, long the 95 strike put. For comparison purposes, the solid line in the graph shows the profile of an unhedged position in the share. The maximum loss on the combined position is 8.46, and is reached when the share price is at 95. Buying an out-of-the-money put means that the share price has to fall (in this case by 5) before the protection afforded by the option comes into effect. Below 95, the loss on the hedged position stays at 8.46 because any further losses on the share are offset by gains on the put option. As we saw before, the upside break-even

Table 9.2   Maximum loss and upside break-even levels for different strikes

Strike	Premium	Maximum loss	Upside break-even point
90	1.89	−11.89	101.89
95	3.46	−8.46	103.46
100	5.68	−5.68	105.68

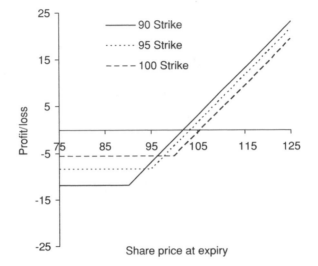

Figure 9.5   Maximum loss and upside break-even levels for different strike puts

point on the combined strategy is 103.46. Note also that the combined payoff profile resembles that of a long call struck at 95.

Changing the put strike

Suppose that the investor decides to explore a number of different strikes for the protective put. The option dealer offers two alternatives, both three-month European puts.

Strike	Premium payable
90	−1.89
100	−5.68

Table 9.2 and Figure 9.5 show the investor's maximum loss on the combined hedged position for both of these options and for the 95 strike contract. By choosing higher strike options, the investor can reduce the maximum loss, but at the expense of pushing the upside break-even point further and further away from the spot price of the share.

EQUITY COLLAR

The advantage of the out-of-the-money put is clearly that it provides a fair level of downside protection at reasonable cost. If the share price rises it does not have to increase by too much for the investor to recover the premium – the upside break-even point is not shifted too far to the right. It is fairly obvious why the investor would not want to spend too much money paying premium, but why does the upside break-even point matter so much?

The answer depends on the goals and objectives of the investor. If he or she is an equity fund manager, the performance of the portfolio will probably be evaluated against a benchmark index. This could be the FT-SE All-Share, or the S&P 500, or a global benchmark such as the Morgan Stanley Capital International (MSCI) world index. Assuming that the investor is an 'active' manager then he or she will be given the task of outperforming the index. Generally, there will also be constraints on the extent to which the performance of the portfolio can deviate from the index.

There is, then, a problem with buying a put option: if the share price rises rather than falls, the premium paid acts like a dead-weight on the performance of the fund, since the share will have to rise by the extent of the premium before the fund starts to gain. Meantime, other investors who have not bought put options are registering profits. The risk is that the fund will underperform in a rising market and do less well compared to rival funds managed by competitors.

One solution is to buy a deeply out-of-the-money put, which will be very cheap. However, the level of protection afforded may be so low as to be almost worthless. Another possibility is to buy a put and at the same time sell an out-of-the-money call on the underlying. This is often agreed as a package or combination with an option dealer. The investor receives premium on the short call which helps to offset the cost of the long put. If he or she believes that the share price is unlikely to rise above the strike of the call, then it will probably never be exercised. In any case, the risk arising from selling the call is strictly limited because the investor actually owns the underlying stock.

Suppose that the investor now approaches an option dealer and agrees the following package of European options on the underlying share. The net premium payable is 0.85.

Contract	Expiry	Strike	Premium
Long put	3 months	95	−3.46
Short call	3 months	110	+2.61

As before, the options will be settled in cash without a physical delivery process. If, at expiry, the share price is below 95 the dealer will pay the intrinsic value of the put to the investor. If the share price is above 110, the investor will pay the intrinsic value of the call to the dealer. The combination of a bought put option and a sold call with a long position in the underlying share creates an *equity collar*.

Figure 9.6 shows the payoff profile of the collar at expiry. The maximum loss is 5.85. This is reached when the share price falls to 95. It comprises a loss of 5 on the share and net premium paid of 0.85. Below 95 any further losses on the share are compensated for by cash payments from the dealer who sold the put option as part of the package. The maximum profit is 9.15. This is reached when the share price is 110. It comprises a profit of 10 on the share less 0.85 net premium. Above 110 any further gains on the share are paid over to the dealer on the short call.

The upside break-even point – when the payoff from the collar is zero – is reached when the share price is at 100.85. This compares with a break-even point of 103.46 if the 95 strike put is purchased on its own. The advantage of the collar for the investor is that it reduces the potential for underperformance if the share price rises, as long as it does not rise by too much. The problem is that if it moves above the strike of the short call, the returns are capped. The investor will then underperform against competitors who own the share and who have not entered into the collar strategy. However if the investor believes it is unlikely that the share

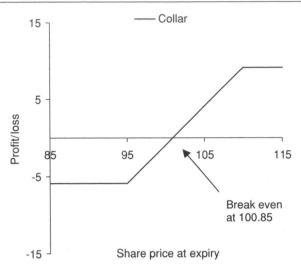

Figure 9.6   Equity collar with put strike 95 and call strike 110

price will increase sharply over the next three months, the strategy is perfectly reasonable. It provides a good level of downside protection at low premium cost.

Zero-cost equity collar

A zero-cost equity collar is one that is constructed with zero net premium. However, it is important to understand that this does *not* mean that there are no potential losses. If the share price rises sharply the profits are capped – there is a risk of losing out from a market rally. To illustrate how the strategy works let us assume that the investor agrees the following package of options with a dealer:

Contract	Expiry	Strike	Premium
Long put	3 months	95	−3.46
Short call	3 months	107	+3.46

The strike on the call this time is lower than before (107 rather than 110) such that the premiums cancel out. The expiry payoff profile for the zero-cost collar is shown in Figure 9.7. The maximum loss is 5, reached when the share price has fallen from 100 to 95. After that the investor will receive compensation on the 95 strike put option to offset any further losses on the share. The maximum gain is 7, reached when the share price has risen from 100 to 107. After that profits are capped.

The advantage of the zero-cost collar is that it provides a good level of protection with no net premium to pay. There is the risk of underperformance if the share price rises, but the investor may consider this a remote possibility and the risk worth taking.

COLLARS AND FORWARDS

The exploration of hedging strategies in this chapter started with a forward hedge. To complete the circle, it is interesting to see what happens if the zero-cost collar is arranged with the strikes

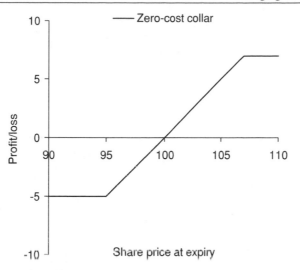

Figure 9.7   Zero-cost equity collar

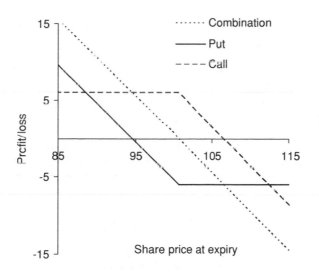

Figure 9.8   Short forward composed of long put and short call

of the long put and the short call set at the fair forward price of the share, which in this case is 100.5. The details of the option package this time are as follows.

Contract	Expiry	Strike	Premium
Long European put	3 months	100.5	−5.94
Short European call	3 months	100.5	+5.94

The premiums completely cancel out. In fact the two options combined simply replicate a short forward position in the share at a price of 100.5. This is illustrated in Figure 9.8, which shows the long put and the short call and the combination payoff profile – a short forward, just like the position illustrated earlier in this Chapter in Figure 9.2.

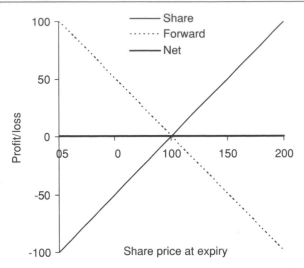

Figure 9.9   Long share, long put, short call, strikes set at the forward price

Finally, Figure 9.9 shows the total of all the positions – long the share at 100, short a forward through the two options, and the ultimate result. This is a horizontal line with a profit of 0.5 for all possible levels of the share price at expiry. This is exactly the same result that is achieved by holding the share and selling a three-month forward contract at 100.5 – and as illustrated in Figure 9.2 earlier in the chapter.

This last example demonstrates a very important principle for European options, known as *put–call parity*. (The rules do not hold for American options.)

- *Short forward.* The combination of a long put and a short call on the same underlying with the same time to expiry both struck at the forward price produces a short forward position.
- *Long forward.* The combination of a long call and a short put on the same underlying with the same time to expiry both struck at the forward price produces a long forward position.

Put–call parity is very useful in practice, since it is possible to create forwards out of options where it is difficult to find counterparties to forward deals. It also means that the premiums on European options and forward prices must be in alignment, otherwise arbitrage opportunities arise. For instance, if a trader could buy a forward and sell a forward at a higher price through a combination of options this would create an arbitrage profit.

PROTECTIVE PUT WITH BARRIER OPTION

The key issue for the investor in the case study considered in the previous sections is how to hedge the risk at reasonable cost. An at-the-money put would be relatively expensive and if the share price rose the investor would underperform the rest of the market. An out-of-the-money option would be cheaper but it does not offer much protection. The investor could create a collar strategy, but at the expense of capping potential gains on the share. A short forward has no premium, but the investor would not benefit if the share price increased. The risk of underperformance in a rising market may simply be unacceptable.

All these alternatives have their advantages and disadvantages, but they are by no means the only choices available. The creation of new generations of so-called exotic options dramatically

Table 9.3   Barrier options

Barrier option type	Characteristic
Up-and-out:	Ceases to exist if the price of the underlying rises to hit the barrier level. A knock-out option
Up-and-in:	Comes into existence if the price of the underlying rises to hit the barrier level. A knock-in option
Down-and-out:	Ceases to exist if the price of the underlying falls to hit the barrier level. A knock-out option
Down-and-In:	Comes into existence if the price of the underlying falls to hit the barrier level. A knock-in option

increases the range of possibilities. One such product is the *barrier option* (Table 9.3). A barrier is a contract whose payoff depends on whether or not the price of the underlying reaches a certain threshold level (the barrier) during a specified period of time over the life of the option. A *knock-in* call or put only comes into existence if the underlying price hits the barrier. A *knock-out* call or put ceases to exist if the underlying price reaches the barrier. Some contracts have both knock-out and knock-in features. Sometimes the buyer is paid a rebate on the initial premium paid if a contract is knocked out.

The investor in the case study may wish to consider buying an up-and-out put with a barrier level set above strike. This is a regular put option with a fixed strike, but with the difference that, if during a defined time period the share price rises and hits the barrier level, then the contract will cease to exist. Let us suppose that the investor contacts a dealer and is offered a contract with the following terms (the spot price of the underlying is 100):

Contract	Expiry	Strike	Barrier	Premium
Long up+out put	3 months	95	105	−2.92 (no rebate)

The contract is set up such that if the share price reaches the 105 barrier (also known as the out-strike) at any point during the three months, then the option ceases to exist. The premium is lower than that on a standard or vanilla put option. The dealer can afford to sell the up-and-out put at a reduced premium because the expected payout is lower and the risk to the dealer is that much less. There is a set of circumstances (if the share price hits 105) when the option will go out of existence.

The advantage to the investor is clear. The option is cheaper, and if the share price rises the potential underperformance against the market is reduced. If the investor believes that the share price is unlikely to hit the barrier then he or she may feel comfortable about incorporating the up-and-out barrier feature into the contract. The real risk is that if the share price rallies during the life of the option and hits the barrier, the contract will cease to exist. The investor would lose any protection against a subsequent fall in the share price and would also have lost the premium.

The behaviour of barrier options is interesting. Figure 9.10 shows how the value of the up-and-out put discussed above (solid line) would change in response to an immediate change in the spot price, still with three months remaining to expiry and all other factors remaining constant. For reference it also shows (dotted line) the value of a standard or vanilla put also struck at 95 for different spot prices. As the share price rises towards the barrier at 105, the value of the up-and-out put falls sharply towards zero, as it becomes increasingly probable that the option will be knocked out. The vanilla put also loses value but it will continue to exist and the loss is much more gradual.

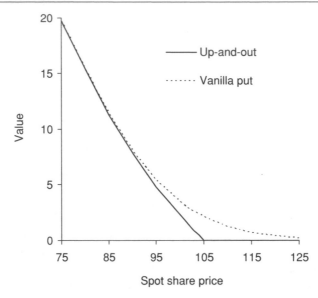

Figure 9.10   Values of barrier and vanilla put options

COVERED CALL WRITING (BUY–WRITE)

One final possibility for the investor to consider is a covered call strategy. This consists of selling an out-of-the-money call on the share. It is sometimes known as a *buy–write* strategy, since it involves buying or owning a share and writing a call against it. This is not actually a hedge but it does generate premium income that can offset at least a portion of any losses on the share. Suppose, as previously, that the investor owns a share trading at 100. The investor sells a three-month call on the stock struck at 110 with the following details:

Contract	Expiry	Strike	Premium
Short call	3 months	110	+2.61

The expiry profit and loss profile on the covered call strategy – long the share and short the 110 call – is illustrated in Figure 9.11. The solid line shows the profit and loss profile of the share on its own. The premium generated by the call means that the share price can fall to 100 − 2.61 = 97.39 before the strategy starts to record a loss. Without the call, losses start as soon as the share price falls below 100.

The maximum profit at expiry is 12.61, reached when the share price is at 110. It consists of a gain of 10 on the stock plus the premium on the call. Above 110 any gains on the share have to be paid over to the buyer of the call, so the profit is capped at that level. If the investor thinks it is unlikely that the share price will reach 110 in the next three months, then the covered call strategy makes good sense.

Covered call writing is often used as a means of generating additional income in a flat market, when share prices are relatively static. The strategy is fairly low risk, since owning the underlying covers potential losses on the short call. The greatest risk is that of underperformance – if the share price rises sharply the profits on the covered call strategy are capped. One way to manage this risk is to keep track of the price, and if it looks like rallying the call can be repurchased.

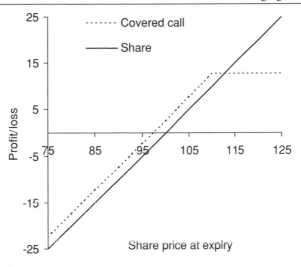

Figure 9.11   Covered call strategy expiry payoff profile

CHAPTER SUMMARY

An investor who owns a share can short a forward or futures contract to hedge against potential losses. The problem is that potential gains are also eliminated or severely curtailed. As an alternative the investor can buy a protective put as a type of insurance. If the share price falls, the payoff from the put will compensate for the loss in the value of the share. If the share price rises, the put need not be exercised. Unfortunately buying an option involves paying premium which can reduce investment performance. One alternative is an equity collar strategy, which can be set up with zero premium. This consists of buying a put and selling an out-of-the money call while retaining the long position in the underlying. A collar produces a maximum loss but a capped profit. Another possibility is to save on premium by buying a put option with a barrier feature such that it is knocked out if the share price rises.

Put–call parity is a fundamental result for European-style options. It shows that a forward position can be created from a pair of options with the same expiry date, both struck at the forward price of the underlying. A covered call or buy–write strategy consists of holding a stock and selling an out-of-the-money call on the asset. This generates premium income which can boost investment performance in a flat market. The risk is that the share price rises sharply and gains above the strike of the short call are capped.

10

Exchange-Traded Equity Options

INTRODUCTION

Call and put options on the shares of individual companies can be bought over-the-counter (OTC) from dealers, or traded on major exchanges such as Eurex, LIFFE and the Chicago Board Options Exchange (CBOE). Exchange-traded contracts that are actively traded can be bought and sold in reasonable quantity without greatly affecting the market price. The performance of contracts is guaranteed by the clearing house associated with the exchange which eliminates any possibility of default.

In recent years some exchanges have introduced so-called FLEX option contracts which allow investors to tailor certain terms of a contract. However, most exchange-traded options are standardized. There are a set number of strikes and expiry dates available, and it is not generally possible to trade options on the shares of smaller companies. By contrast, in the OTC market dealers will sell and buy options on a wide range of shares, as long as they can find a way to manage the risks associated with such deals. Also, dealers offer a huge variety of non-standard contracts known collectively as exotic options.

On some exchanges and with some contracts the buyer of an option is not required to pay the full premium at the outset. Instead, the purchaser deposits initial margin that is a proportion of the premium due on the contract. In the case of the individual stock options traded on LIFFE, the full premium is payable upfront. However, the writers of options are subject to margin procedures. They must deposit initial margin at the outset, and will be required to make additional variation margin payments via their brokers to the clearing house if the position moves into loss. The initial margin depends on the degree of risk involved, calculated according to factors such as the price and volatility of the underlying and the time to expiry of the contract. In practice, in order to cover margin calls, brokers often ask for more than the minimum initial margin figure stipulated by the clearing house.

The derivatives exchanges also offer listed option contracts on major equity indices such as the S&P 500, the FT-SE 100 and the DAX. Contracts are of two main kinds. Some are options on equity index futures, and exercise results in a long or short futures position. Other contracts are settled in cash against the spot price of the underlying index. If a call is exercised the payout is based on the spot index level less the strike. If a put is exercised the payout is based on the strike less the spot index level. Options on indices and other baskets of shares can also be purchased directly from dealers in the OTC market.

Some dealing houses issue securities called *covered warrants* which are longer-dated options on shares other than those of the issuer. Warrants are usually listed and trade on a stock market such as the London Stock Exchange. The term 'covered' means that the issuer is writing an option and hedges or covers the risks involved, often by trading in the underlying shares. Warrants are purchased by both institutional and retail investors (historically the retail market has been more active in Germany than in the UK). Warrants can be calls or puts and written on an individual share or a basket of shares. They are sometimes settled in cash, and sometimes through the physical delivery of shares.

UK STOCK OPTIONS ON LIFFE

Table 10.1 shows some recent prices for stock options on Royal Bank of Scotland Group plc (RBOS) traded on LIFFE. These are the offer or sale prices for contracts posted by dealers placed on the exchange's electronic dealing system, LIFFE Connect. At the time the quotations were taken the options had just over two weeks remaining until expiry and the underlying RBOS share price was 1781 pence or £17.81.

The stock option contracts on LIFFE are American-style and can be exercised on any business day up to and including expiry. Table 10.1 only shows a small sample of the strikes available in RBOS options at the time. Most market participants tend to deal in options that are around the at-the-money level. As the share price fluctuates in the cash market, the exchange creates additional strikes so that there are sufficient contracts available that are likely to appeal to buyers and sellers. The quotations are in pence per share, but each contract is based on a lot size of 1000 RBOS shares.

These contracts are physically settled. If the holder of one long (bought) RBOS call contract exercises the option then he or she will receive 1000 shares. In return, the 'long' will have to pay the strike price times 1000. A market participant who is short the contract will be 'assigned' at random by the clearing house and required to deliver the shares in return for cash. The delivery of shares and the payment of cash is always made via the clearing house, to eliminate any possibility of default.

The open interest figures in the table show how many long and short contracts were still outstanding at the time. Some traders keep track of the open interest in call and put options as a means of gauging market sentiment. An excess of put options being traded may indicate that investors and speculators are bearish about the share, and are actively buying put options from dealers in anticipation of a sharp decline in the price of the underlying. An excess of calls may indicate the reverse. To explore the values in a little more detail, we will take a number of examples from the data in the table.

- *1600 strike calls.* The buyer of a contract has the right but not the obligation to buy 1000 shares at a cost of £16 per share. The option is being offered at a premium of £1.865 per share or £1865 on a contract. The option is in-the-money (it is the right to buy a share for £16 that is worth £17.81). The intrinsic value per share is £1.81. Therefore the time value is £1.865 − £1.81 = £0.055 per share. This is quite low, partly because there are only a few weeks to expiry, and partly because there is not much uncertainty about what is going to happen to the option – it is very likely to expire in-the-money.
- *1800 strike calls.* These are out-of-the money. The intrinsic value is zero and the time value is £0.275 per share. There is a reasonable chance that the share price will trade above £18

Table 10.1   Call and put option premiums and open interest on RBOS share options

Strike	Call premium (pence)	Calls open interest	Put premium (pence)	Put open interest
1600	186.5	37	3.5	102
1700	92	255	14.5	171
1800	27.5	224	58.5	62
1900	4	62	134	0
2000	2	0	—	0

Source: LIFFE Administration Management

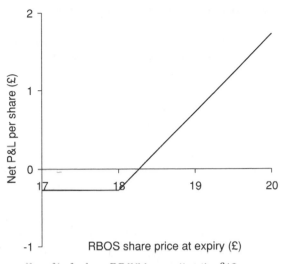

Figure 10.1 Expiry payoff profile for long RBOS long call strike £18

at or before expiry, and the purchaser of the contract has to pay for that possibility. On the same day 1800 strike calls on RBOS with an extra month to expiry were being offered at £0.50 a share. The chances of the share price moving above the strike is that much greater with a longer expiration date.

- *2000 strike calls.* These are struck well out-of-the money, since they convey the right to buy shares for £20 each. The intrinsic value is zero and the entire premium cost of £0.02 per share is time value. The time value is low and the option is cheap because there is only a remote chance that the share price (currently £17.81) will be trading above £20 by expiry in a few weeks' time.
- *1700 strike puts.* These contracts are slightly out of the money, since they represent the right to sell RBOS shares below the current cash price of £17.81. The intrinsic value is zero and the premium cost of £0.145 per share is all time value.

STOCK OPTIONS: CALL EXPIRY PAYOFF

Figure 10.1 illustrates the profit and loss at expiry for one of the RBOS options considered in the previous section: the 1800 strike call. The profile is shown from the perspective of a holder of the option and profits and losses are shown in pounds per share. It is assumed that a contract has been purchased at a premium cost of £0.275 per share. The option will only be exercised at expiry if the share is trading above £18. Otherwise it will expire worthless and the purchaser of the contract will have lost the initial premium paid. Ignoring funding and transaction costs, the option strategy will break even when the share is trading at £18.275 at expiry.

> Premium paid per share = £0.275
> Break-even point = Strike + Premium = £18 + £0.275 = £18.275

At £18.275 the intrinsic value is £0.275, which just recovers the initial premium, therefore the net profit and loss is zero. A buyer of the call would have to be fairly confident that the share price will trade above £18.275, otherwise the deal will make no money. In reality the share would have to trade a little higher to recover additional costs such as brokerage and the cost of borrowing money to buy the option (or the interest forgone from not putting the money used to buy the option on deposit with a bank).

The writer of the call option bears a much higher level of risk than the buyer, which is why the position will be subject to margin procedures on the exchange. In addition, there is the risk of early exercise. The single stock options on LIFFE are American-style, which means that a long (a buyer) can exercise a contract on any business day up to and including expiry. If a call is exercised early by a long the exchange will nominate or 'assign' one of the writers, who will be obliged to deliver the underlying shares and receive in return the contractual strike price.

The terms of stock options on exchanges such as LIFFE are adjusted for certain so-called 'corporate actions', such as rights issues and stock splits and some special dividends. However, they are not adjusted for regular ordinary dividend payments. When a share is declared 'ex-dividend' a purchaser after that date is not entitled to receive the forthcoming dividend payment. As a result the market price of the share will fall, and so too will the value of a call on the share. Sometimes this makes it optimal for the holder of an in-the-money American call to exercise the contract just before the ex-dividend date, in order to receive the share dividend and not suffer from the fall in the value of the option.

US-LISTED STOCK OPTIONS

Table 10.2 shows some recent historical prices for one-month options on Microsoft shares, traded on the Chicago Board Options Exchange (CBOE). The lot size is 100 shares per contract, and the option premiums are quoted in dollars per share. The contracts are American-style and are physically exercised rather than cash-settled. Again, the terms of a contract will be adjusted for certain corporate actions such as stock splits (when the share is split into smaller units) but not for regular ex-dividend dates. The information in the table is based on the latest trade prices at the time the data was captured. At that time the underlying Microsoft (MSFT) shares were trading at $26.17 on NASDAQ, the US electronic stock market.

Again, we will take some examples from the data in Table 10.2 to explain the values and illustrate the potential returns on the option contracts.

- *22.50 strike put.* Since the underlying stock is trading at $26.17, this option is quite deeply out-of-the-money, which is reflected in the low premium. The premium is all time value. It is paid for the (quite remote) chance that the stock *might* fall sharply in price at or before expiry in one month. If the contract is purchased for $0.15 then the share would have to trade at £22.50 − $0.15 = $22.35 (less funding and transaction costs) at expiry just to break even.

Table 10.2   Call and put option premiums and open interest on MSFT share options

Strike ($)	Calls premium ($)	Open interest (contracts)	Puts premium ($)	Open interest (contracts)
22.50	3.90	903	0.15	760
25.00	1.85	3250	0.60	10420
27.50	0.55	39740	1.80	12613

Source: CBOE

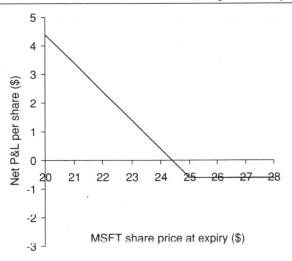

Figure 10.2 Expiry payoff of long MSFT put strike $25
Source data: CBOE

- *25.00 strike put.* This contract is closer to the at-the-money level, though it still has zero intrinsic value since the strike is below the cash price of the share. However, it is a 'better bet' than the $22.50 put and this means that the cost of the option is that much higher.

Figure 10.2 shows the profit and loss profile of the $25 strike Microsoft put, assuming a trader bought a contract at a premium of $0.6 per share and held it to expiry. The values in the graph are in dollars per share. Ignoring brokerage and funding costs, the break-even point at expiry is reached when the share is trading at $24.40. At this level the intrinsic value of the put is $0.60 per share, which simply recoups the initial premium cost of the contract. If a trader were to purchase the option then he or she would have to be quite confident that the stock would trade below that level at or before the expiration of the option in one month.

CME OPTIONS ON S&P 500® INDEX FUTURES

In addition to options on individual shares it is also possible to trade options on stock market indices on the exchanges. Table 10.3 shows the specification for one of the most actively traded contracts, the options on S&P futures available on Chicago Mercantile Exchange (CME). The underlying here is a *futures contract* on the S&P 500 index – an index of 500 leading US shares calculated by Standard and Poor's. (Chapter 5 discussed details of the equity index futures contract.)

Table 10.3   CME options on S&P 500 futures

Contract size:	One S&P 500 futures contract
Regular tick size:	0.1 index point
Tick value:	$25 per contract
Contract months:	All 12 calendar months

Source: CME

Table 10.4   Sample closing prices for CME options on September S&P 500 futures

Strike (index points)	Call premium (index points)	Open interest (contracts)	Put premium (index points)	Open interest (contracts)
965	35.90	3	21.30	5
970	32.70	284	23.10	137
975	29.70	910	25.10	646
980	26.90	591	27.30	446
985	24.30	3	29.70	25
990	21.90	479	32.30	468

Source data: CME

If the owner of a call exercises the contract then he or she will acquire a long position in an S&P 500 index futures contract with a specific expiry month. If the owner of a put exercises, he or she will acquire a short position in a futures. The contract months for the underlying futures are March, June, September and December. On the options, as on the futures, each full index point is worth $250. A one tick movement in the price of an option is 0.1 index point and is worth £250 × 0.1 = $25. Contracts are traded on floor of CME and then after hours on the exchange's electronic trading system, GLOBEX.

Table 10.4 shows a recent sample of closing prices for a range of September CME call and put options on S&P 500 futures. The premiums are quoted in index points. On the day these data were taken the underlying September futures closed at 979.6 index points. The open interest figures show the number of long and short option contracts at that strike and expiry date that were outstanding.

Some examples from Table 10.4 will serve to explain the values and the potential profits and losses from trading the option contracts.

- *990 strike call.* A buyer of one contract has the right but not the obligation to buy a September S&P 500 futures at a strike of 990 index points. The premium is 21.9 points, which in cash terms equals 21.9 × $250 per point = $5475. Since the futures is trading at 979.6, the contract is out-of-the-money and the premium represents time value.
- *990 strike put.* This option is in-the-money. It is the right to sell one September futures contract at a price of 990 points when the market price of the futures is 979.6. The intrinsic value is 990 − 979.6 = 10.4 index points. The total premium is 32.3 points, of which 21.9 is time value.

Suppose that a trader buys one 990 strike call at a premium cost of 21.9 points or $5475. Imagine further that, at the expiry of the option and of the futures in September, the underlying S&P 500 index is trading at 1050 points. The call option will be exercised and, as a result, the trader will acquire a long position in one S&P futures contract at a price of 990. Since the futures has reached its expiry point it will be closed out at the cash index level, which in this case is assumed to be 1050 index points. The cash paid out to the trader and the net profit and loss are calculated as follows:

$$\text{Cash settlement from exercise} = (1050 - 990) \times \$250 = \$15\,000$$
$$\text{Net profit} = \$15\,000 - \$5475 = \$9525$$

The break-even point on the option contract at expiry is reached when the S&P 500 index is trading at 1011.90. At that level the payment received on the option (its intrinsic value) is 21.90 index points or $5475, which recoups the initial premium paid.

Break-even point = Strike + Premium = 990 + 21.9 = 1011.90

FT-SE 100 INDEX OPTIONS

Index options traded on exchanges can also be settled directly in cash rather than through the acquisition of a position in a futures contract. Table 10.5 lists details of the FT-SE 100 index options contract traded on LIFFE through its electronic trading system LIFFE Connect. This is the European-style contract. The exchange also lists an American option on the FT-SE 100, which can be exercised on any business day up to and including expiration (it is far less actively traded). In either case, if a contract is exercised in-the-money the owner is paid cash in sterling based on the difference between the spot price of the underlying FT-SE 100 index at that point and the strike of the option. No shares ever change hands.

On the FT-SE 100 index option each full index point is worth £10 and the tick size (the minimum movement in the price quotation) is 0.5 point, so each one-tick move in the price of an option results in a profit or loss per contract of £5. The exchange creates new strikes as the underlying index level changes. The full option premium is payable on the day after an option is purchased.

To illustrate how the LIFFE contract works, suppose that the underlying FT-SE index (the cash index) is trading at 4103 index points and dealers on the LIFFE Connect system are offering August 4125 strike calls on the index at a premium of 74 points. There are about two weeks remaining to expiry. If a trader buys 10 of these contracts, the total premium cost is calculated as follows:

Premium cost = 10 contracts × 74 index points × £10 = £7400

The trader holds the contracts to expiry on the third Friday of August, at which time we will suppose that the FT-SE 100 index is trading at 4300. The trader exercises the calls and is paid a settlement amount in cash. The cash settlement amount and the trader's net profit are calculated as follows:

Cash settlement = 10 contracts × (4300 − 4125) × £10 = £17 500
Net profit = £17 500 − £7400 = £10 100
Alternatively: Net profit = 10 contracts × (4300 − 4125 − 74) × £10
= £10 100

Table 10.5   FT-SE 100 index option (European-style exercise)

Index point value:	£10 per point
Delivery months:	March, June, September and December, plus additional months so that the next four calendar months are available
Quotation:	In FT-SE 100 index points
Tick size:	0.5 point
Tick value:	£5
Last trade:	Third Friday in the expiry month
Exercise day:	Exercise on the last trading day only

Source: LIFFE Administration Management

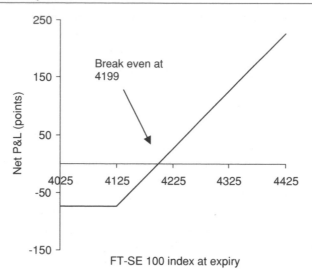

Figure 10.3   Expiry payoff profile for FT-SE 100 index call strike 4125

EXPIRY PAYOFF OF FT-SE 100 CALL

Figure 10.3 illustrates the expiry payoff profile of the 4125 strike FT-SE 100 call considered in the previous section. The profit and loss figures on the vertical axis are shown per contract and in index points. The break-even point is reached when the index is trading at 4199 at expiry. At that level the trader will be paid a settlement amount of 74 points or £7400 on 10 contracts, recovering the initial premium. The maximum loss is restricted to the premium whereas the maximum gain is (in theory) unlimited.

The option also provides the advantage of gearing or leverage, because the initial premium is a relatively small proportion of what it would cost to buy the underlying shares in the index. This has the effect of magnifying the return on capital invested. For example, suppose as before that the trader buys 10 call option contracts struck at 4125. The premium is 74 points per contract or £7400 in total. Suppose also that at expiry the FT-SE 100 index is trading at 4300 so that the net profit on the 10 contracts is £10100. The return on the initial outlay is even more impressive.

$$\text{Return on capital} = (\pounds 10\,100/\pounds 7400) \times 100 = 136\%$$

Suppose that instead of buying the calls the trader had purchased a portfolio of UK shares in exactly the correct proportions required to track changes in the FT-SE 100 index. At the time the options were offered at 74 points the cash index was trading at 4103. So by buying an index-tracking portfolio at that point the trader would be establishing a position in the index at a level of 4103 points. Assuming that the portfolio does indeed match the index, then its value will rise and fall in line with the market.

If the FT-SE increases to 4300 points this represents a rise of 197 points or 4.8%. Therefore, the returns on the tracker portfolio will also be 4.8%. This is a healthy return, but is a great deal less than the 136% achieved on the options. Of course there are some snags to the option strategy. For example, this analysis ignores the effects of dividends. The shares will pay out cash dividends that can be re-invested in the market; the options do not. Also, the options do not last for ever. If the market has not risen above the strike at expiry the cost of the premium will have been lost.

EXERCISING FT-SE 100 INDEX OPTIONS

What happens to FT-SE 100 index options on the last trading day? The answer is that they are cash settled against the underlying index on that day, then they simply expire. The level used is known as the Exchange Delivery Settlement Price (EDSP). It is an average of the cash market index taken between 10:10 and 10:30 a.m. on the last trading day. The averaging process reduces the scope for market manipulation. Many traders chose not to retain their positions up to the expiration date. Speculators who are long calls will hope that the market rises and they can sell the contracts back into the exchange at a higher premium before expiry. Equally, those who are long puts are hoping for a fall in the index to enable them to sell the contracts back at a higher premium.

The American-style FT-SE 100 index option contracts traded on LIFFE provide the additional advantage that they can be exercised early. However, if a trader wishes to realize the gains from a purchase of an exchange-traded option it is usually preferable to sell the contract back into the exchange. For example, suppose that a trader owns an American call on the FT-SE struck at 4000 and with around six weeks to expiry. The cash market level today is 4103 and the contract is trading at a premium of 155 index points (£1550) on the exchange. If the trader exercises now the settlement amount received would be £1030.

$$\text{Settlement amount from early exercise} = (4103 - 4000) \times £10$$
$$= £1030$$

It would make more sense to sell the option back into the market and receive a total premium of £1550. When an American option is exercised early all that is received is the intrinsic value – the extent to which the contract is in-the-money – and this simply kills off any remaining time value. In this example the option still has six weeks to expiry. If the trader sells the option, he or she will receive the intrinsic value, plus some additional time value.

CHAPTER SUMMARY

An equity option conveys the right but not the obligation to buy or to sell an underlying share or basket of shares at a predetermined strike price. Exercising an exchange-traded option on an individual share (a stock option) results in the delivery of the underlying share. In the over-the-counter market contracts can be set up to enable them to be settled in cash. The terms of exchange-traded stock options are not adjusted for ordinary dividends, although they are adjusted for certain exceptional events such as stock splits and rights issues. American-style contracts can be exercised before expiry, although this kills off any remaining time value and, in many cases, it is better to retain the option or sell it back into the market. Exceptions include some deeply in-the-money puts and some call options just before an ex-dividend date.

Exchange-traded options on stock market indices are either settled against the level of the cash index or result in a long or short position in a futures contract on the underlying index. Equity index options offer a diversified exposure to a large number of shares and can provide leverage opportunities – the return on investment can be much higher than that achieved by investing in the actual shares that comprise the index. On the other hand, there is no opportunity to re-invest dividends and the options have a defined life. If at expiry the contracts are not in-the-money the premium has been lost and cannot be recovered. One alternative to exchange-traded equity options is the covered warrant. This is a longer-dated option that is issued by a dealer and trades in the form of a security on a stock market. It can be a call or a put based on a single share or a basket or an index.

11

Currency Options

INTRODUCTION

A European-style currency or FX option is the right but not the obligation to exchange two currencies at a fixed rate (the strike rate) on an agreed date in the future (the expiry date). American-style contracts can be exercised before expiry. Contracts are either negotiated directly between two parties in an over-the-counter transaction, or traded through an organized futures and options exchange.

The right to sell one currency is also the right to buy the other currency involved in the contract. Suppose that an FX option contract conveys the right but not the obligation to sell €10 million and to receive in return $11.5 million. The contract is a euro put (the right to sell euros) and at the same time a dollar call (the right to buy US dollars). The strike or exercise price is €/$ 1.15, i.e. each euro buys 1.15 US dollars. Currency options are widely used by corporations, institutional investors, hedge funds, traders, commercial and investment banks, central banks and other financial institutions. They can be used to:

- limit the risk of losses resulting from adverse movements in currency exchange rates;
- hedge against the foreign exchange risk that results from holding assets such as shares or bonds that are denominated in foreign currencies;
- enhance returns on foreign currency investments;
- speculate on the movements in currency rates with limited risk.

Because they offer flexibility, currency options can be attractive hedging tools. As we saw in Chapter 2, a firm that is due to receive a fixed quantity of foreign currency on a future date can cover its exposure to movements in the spot exchange rate by entering into an outright forward FX transaction. This is an obligation to exchange two currencies on a future date at a predetermined rate. As such it has none of the flexibility of a currency option contract. An option need not be exercised if the buyer of the contract can find a better rate of exchange in the spot market. The drawback is, of course, that buying an option costs premium.

In recent years more advanced or 'exotic' currency option products have been developed. Partly this is because advanced 'financial engineering' techniques required to build such instruments and manage the risks have been discovered by specialists in the field. However, the primary force driving innovation is the need for products that banks and securities firms can use to tailor solutions to meet the problems of their clients. Business and investment have become much more global and the volume of currency transactions has exploded; as a result, currency risk-management problems have become both pervasive and more complex. In response, the solutions have become ever more sophisticated.

CURRENCY OPTIONS AND FORWARDS

In this section we consider the case of a commercial bank that wishes to hedge the currency risk on a transaction on which it is due to receive €10 million in three months' time. Its home currency is the US dollar and it would like to hedge against adverse movements in the spot €/$ rate over that time period. If it does nothing the bank will have to sell the euros in three months and will receive an unknown quantity of US dollars.

The first recourse is to consider entering into an outright forward FX contract – a legal and binding contract to sell the €10 million in three months and to receive in return a fixed amount of dollars. We saw in Chapter 2 that the fair forward exchange rate can be calculated from the spot rate and the interest rates in the two currencies. This uses the classic cash-and-carry methodology. If the actual forward rate differs from the theoretical value, then arbitrage or 'free lunch' trades can be constructed. Suppose we have the following data for the two currencies:

> Spot rate: €/$1.15
> Three-month outright forward rate: €/$1.1470

If the two currencies are exchanged in the spot market then 1 euro buys 1.15 US dollars. However, if the deal is to exchange the two currencies in three months' time, then 1 euro will buy only 1.1470 dollars. The euro is at a discount to the US dollar in the forward market compared to the spot rate, i.e. it buys fewer dollars. As we saw in Chapter 2, this is because the euro is the higher interest rate currency of the two. Imagine that the bank in this case enters into a forward contract with a dealer to sell the €10 million in three months' time and to receive $11.47 million at the forward exchange rate. The problem is that it will be obliged to go through with the deal. If the euro strengthens against the dollar and the actual rate in three months' time was (say) €/$ 1.20, then €10 million would have bought $12 million in the spot market.

As an alternative, suppose the bank agrees the following European-style currency option contract with a dealer. It is the right to sell the €10 million for dollars at a strike rate of 1.15. It is a euro put and a dollar call. The expiration is three months and the total premium payable on €10 million is $198 000.

Contract	Expiry	Strike	Premium per €1	Premium on €10 million
Long euro put and US dollar call	3 months	1.15	−$0.0198	−$198 000

It would be common practice to describe this contract as being at-the-money, since the strike is the same as the spot exchange rate. However, the option can only be exercised at expiry, and the real benchmark rate for selling euros in three months is not today's spot rate but the three-month forward rate. In relation to the forward rate of €/$ 1.1470 the contract is in fact slightly in-the-money. It conveys the right to sell €10 million and receive $11.5 million rather than only $11.47 million at the forward rate. Some dealers would say that while the contract is 'at-the-money spot' it is 'in-the-money forward' – that is, in relation to the forward exchange rate.

The clear advantage the option has over the forward is that it need never be exercised. If at expiry the exchange rate is higher than 1.15, then the contract is discarded and the bank sells its surplus euros for dollars on the spot market. If the spot is lower than 1.15 the bank exercises the contract and receives $11.5 million for its euros. Whether the option is exercised or not, however, the bank has to net out from its dollar receipts the $198 000 premium initially paid for the contract.

RESULTS FROM THE OPTION HEDGE

The first column in Table 11.1 shows a range of possible spot exchange rates in three months' time when the bank in the case study receives its €10 million. The second column calculates

Table 11.1   Effective rate achieved by FX option hedge

Spot	$ Unhedged	$ Forward hedge	$ Option hedge	Effective rate
1.00	10 000 000	11 470 000	11 302 000	1.1302
1.05	10 500 000	11 470 000	11 302 000	1.1302
1.10	11 000 000	11 470 000	11 302 000	1.1302
1.15	11 500 000	11 470 000	11 302 000	1.1302
1.20	12 000 000	11 470 000	11 802 000	1.1802
1.25	12 500 000	11 470 000	12 302 000	1.2302
1.30	13 000 000	11 470 000	12 802 000	1.2802

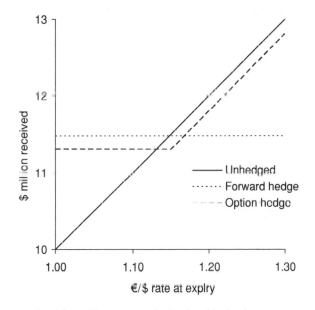

Figure 11.1   Dollars received for selling euros unhedged and hedged

the total amount of US dollars the bank would earn by selling those euros if it did not hedge the exposure. For example, if the two currencies are at parity, the dollar receipt is $10 million, while at a rate of €/$ 1.30 the amount is $13 million. The third column confirms that if the bank takes out the forward hedge at a rate of 1.1470 it will always receive $11.47 million for selling its euros.

The fourth column calculates the dollars received with the FX option hedge in place, net of the premium paid. If the spot rate is below 1.15 the bank will exercise the option, sell the euros and receive $11.5 million less the premium. If the rate is above 1.15 the option expires worthless and the euros are sold at the spot rate; however the initial premium paid has once again to be netted out from the dollar proceeds. The final column calculates the effective exchange rate achieved by the option strategy for different spot rates at expiry. For example, if the spot is at parity, the option is exercised and the effective rate achieved net of the premium is $1.15 - 0.0198 = 1.1302$. If the spot is 1.30 the option expires out-of-the-money and the effective rate achieved is $1.30 - 0.0198 = 1.2802$.

Figure 11.1 illustrates the results of the various strategies – leaving the exposure unhedged; selling the euros forward at 1.1470; and buying the euro put option (dollar call) at a strike of

1.15. The vertical axis shows the quantity of dollars the bank receives for selling its €10 million from each of these three strategies. One interesting fact here is that, with the benefit of hindsight, the option hedge is never the best solution. The reason for choosing it is that hindsight is not available at the outset. The hedge offers a little bit of both worlds; it insures against the risk of the euro weakening over the next three months, but still permits some level of benefit if the currency strengthens.

The drawback of course is the cost of the option premium, although the bank may think it is a reasonable price to pay to manage its currency exposures. If it wished to save premium it could choose an out-of-the-money option. For example, with the same data used to price the 1.15 strike put, a 1.14 strike contract would only cost around $150 000. However, it would only guarantee a minimum receipt at expiry of $11.25 million for selling the euros compared to $11.302 million from the 1.15 strike contract.

ZERO-COST COLLAR

The stumbling block with using options to manage currency risks is the cost of the premium. We saw in Chapter 9 how this affects institutional investors, since it represents potential underperformance for the fund. Equally, banks and companies contemplating buying currency options are faced with paying premium that can erode profit margins and adversely affect business performance. A company considering the takeover of a foreign business and paying in cash will normally pay the consideration in foreign currency. If it hedges the currency exposure using FX options then this adds to the overall cost of the deal, and perhaps reduces its prospects of success.

The premium cost can be reduced or even eliminated by a combination package of options, some purchased and some sold. Let us return to the story of the commercial bank, explored in previous sections, and its future receipt of €10 million. At the same time as purchasing a euro put the bank could also sell an out-of-the-money euro call. If the strike of the call is set appropriately, the premium received will completely offset the premium due on the put. This is a zero-cost collar strategy. The other side of the coin is that the gains that would result from a strengthening euro will be capped at the strike of the short call option.

To illustrate how this strategy would work, we suppose that the bank negotiates the following package of options with a dealer. As before, the spot is currently 1.15 and the fair three-month forward rate is 1.1470. The put option this time is struck out-of-the-money, which makes it a little cheaper; and the cost is offset by the premium received for selling an out-of-the-money euro call. Both options are European-style and are written on €10 million.

Contracts	Expiry	Strike	Premium per €1	Premium on €10 million
Long euro put	3 months	1.10	−$0.0034	−$34 000
Short euro call	3 months	1.20	+$0.0034	+$34 000

Figure 11.2 shows a range of possible spot rates in three months' time and the dollars received at expiry for selling the €10 million at each rate, assuming the exposure is unhedged. It also shows the dollars received if the euros are sold forward at a rate of 1.1470 and if the zero-cost collar strategy is adopted.

The zero-cost collar will work as follows. If the spot rate at expiry is in the range 1.1 to 1.2, neither option will be exercised and the bank will sell its euros for dollars at the spot rate. If the rate is below 1.1, the bank will exercise its put and sell the euros at the strike of 1.1 and receive in return $11 million. However if the rate is above 1.2 the call option will be exercised by

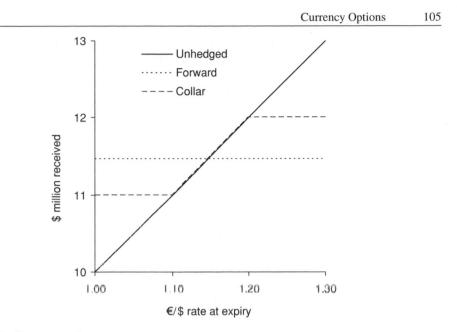

Figure 11.2   Zero-cost collar

the bank's counterparty. The bank will be required to deliver the €10 million and will receive exactly $12 million.

The collar is zero cost, in the sense that there is no initial premium to pay, but not in the sense that the bank can never lose out as a result of the deal. If the spot rate in three months is above 1.2, its gains from a strengthening euro will be capped. However the bank may be prepared to surrender such potential gains in return for a hedge that affords a reasonable level of protection against a decline in the value of the euro and with zero net premium.

REDUCING PREMIUM ON FX HEDGES

A tremendous amount of ingenuity has gone into finding ways of reducing, or at least making more palatable, the premium cost of hedging currency exposures with FX options. One method, which we explored in the previous section, is to negotiate a package of options and to set up a zero-cost collar. However the gains on the spot rate are capped at the strike of the short call.

Another route is to use barrier options (see Chapter 9). For example, the first suggestion the bank considered was the purchase of a three-month put on the euro struck at 1.15. Unfortunately the premium cost was $198 000. However, the contract could also be structured as an up-and-out put struck at 1.15 and with a barrier level set (for example) at 1.175. If at any time during the life of the contract the spot rate hits 1.175 then the option ceases to exist. The bank might reason that if the euro strengthens it will become increasingly unlikely that the put option will ever be required (it will simply sell the euros for dollars in the spot market). Therefore it may be content to have the barrier feature built into the option contract in return for a lower premium.

With the same data used to price the vanilla 1.15 strike put option, the incorporation of an 'out' barrier set at 1.175 would lower the cost of the contract to about $163 000. The premium could be reduced still further by lowering the barrier or 'out-strike' level. However, there is a risk for the bank that the spot rises, the option is knocked out, but the euro later weakens against the dollar and there is no longer any protection in place. One way to reduce this risk is to structure the contract so that it can only be knocked out if the spot hits the barrier during specific periods of time.

A further possibility that might be attractive to the bank in the case study is a *pay-later* or contingent premium option. With this type of deal there is no premium to pay unless the option is exercised. If it expires out-of-the-money, that is the end of the story. However, the contract *must* be exercised and the premium paid if it is in-the-money at expiry, even if the intrinsic value received through exercise is less than the cost of the premium. Alternatively, both parties might agree that the premium payment can be made in instalments. This can be combined with a feature that allows the buyer of the option to cancel the contract early without having to pay any further instalments. However, if the contract is held to expiry the total premium paid by instalments is greater than the premium that would have been paid on a standard or vanilla option.

COMPOUND OPTIONS

A compound option is an option on an option. The contracts that are most likely to appeal to corporations and institutions hedging currency exposures are of two types.

- A call on a call – the right to purchase a call option at a later date at a fixed cost.
- A call on a put – the right to purchase a put option at a later date at a fixed cost.

The most common application occurs when a company is participating in a tender and realizes that it may need to buy a call or a put option to hedge its currency exposures if it is successful. However, the company is not yet sure that it will win the tender and does not wish to pay the full premium for an option that may never be required.

To take a very simple example, suppose a US company is pitching for some business in the Eurozone and is asked by its potential client to quote a fixed price in euros. The cash will be paid in three months. At the current spot rate €/$ 1.15 it could afford to quote a total price of €10 million, which it believes will be competitive. At the spot rate this would translate into $11.5 million, which would cover its costs and achieve a satisfactory profit margin. However, if it quotes €10 million and the euro weakens appreciably over the next three months it would lose money on the deal; the dollar proceeds from selling the euros would fail to cover its costs.

The company could enter into a forward FX deal at a forward rate of 1.1470. The problem is that it does not know whether it is going to win the tender, and it would be obliged to go through with the forward deal whatever happened. Alternatively, it could buy a three-month put on €10 million struck at 1.15 for a total premium cost of $198 000. This, however, is a lot of money for an option that it will not need if the company fails to get the business. Suppose that the company will find out whether or not it is successful in the tender in one month. As a third possibility, it could buy a compound option. It contacts a dealer and is offered the following terms. The contract is written on €10 million. It is a call on a put – the right but not the obligation to buy a euro put option after one month at a predetermined premium cost.

Contract	First expiry	First strike	Second expiry	Second strike	Call on put premium
Long call on euro put	1 month	$0.0198 per €1	3 months	$1.15 per €1	−$0.0057 per €1

The stages in the life of the contract are as follows:

- The company agrees the terms and pays $57 000 for the compound option (i.e. $0.0057 × 10 million).
- The first decision point is one month later, when it has to decide whether or not to exercise the compound option. If it does not then nothing further happens and it has lost $57 000. If it does, then it pays the first strike of $0.0198 per €1 or $198 000 on the contract size. It now owns a standard put option on €10 million struck at €/$ 1.15 and with two months to expiry.
- If the standard put option is exercised at expiry the company sells €10 million and receives $11.5 million at the second strike rate. Otherwise the contract expires worthless.

The decision on whether or not to exercise the compound option on the first expiry date really depends on the value of the underlying put at that stage. If it is worth more than its purchase cost at the first strike – in this case $198 000 – then the compound option should be exercised. Otherwise it should not. Of course there is a drawback to this strategy. If the company wins the tender and exercises the compound option it will end up paying a total of $57 000 + $198 000 = $255 000 for the put option it requires. It could have purchased that option in the first instance for $198 000. That is the price of flexibility.

EXCHANGE-TRADED CURRENCY OPTIONS

Currency option contracts were first offered on the Philadelphia Stock Exchange (PHLX) in 1982. The exchange offers (at the time of writing) standardized contracts on six major foreign currencies: the Australian dollar, the British pound, the Canadian dollar, the euro, the Japanese yen and the Swiss franc. All deals are made against the US dollar. There is a range of expiration dates and both European- and American-style contracts are traded. If a contract is exercised the two currency amounts are exchanged at the strike rate. Currently, trading is conducted both on the trading floor and electronically. Table 11.2 shows the foreign currencies available for trading (in 2003) on standardized PHLX contracts, and the contract sizes.

The strike prices are expressed in terms of US cents per unit of foreign currency. For example, suppose that a trader buys a call option contract on euros struck at 116, i.e. $1.16 per euro. On the contract size this conveys the right to buy a total of €62 500 and to pay in return 62 500 × 1.16 = $72 500. The option premiums are also quoted in US cents per euro. If a trader buys a euro call at a premium of 1.26, then the total premium payable is 62 500 × $0.0126 = $787.50.

PHLX also offers a range of customized options on major currencies and on the Mexican peso. The expiration dates, the strikes and the way in which the premiums can be quoted

Table 11.2 Currency option contracts on PHLX

Foreign currency	Contract size
Australian dollar	50 000 Australian dollars
British pound	31 250 British pounds
Canadian dollar	50 000 Canadian dollars
Euro	62 500 euros
Japanese yen	6 250 000 yen
Swiss franc	62 500 Swiss francs

Source: PHLX

are more flexible than on standardized contracts. These options are primarily designed for institutional investors and restrictions apply on the minimum number of contracts that can be traded at any one time. Settlement on all PHLX contracts is guaranteed by the Options Clearing Corporation (OCC).

Hedging with exchange-traded options

The applications of exchange-traded options are fundamentally the same as those employing standard over-the-counter option contracts. The example we looked at earlier in this chapter was that of a commercial bank due to receive €10 million in three months and keen to hedge its exposure to a weakening euro. The spot rate €/$ is 1.15 and the three-month forward rate is 1.1470. Suppose that the bank decides to hedge the exposure with PHLX contracts by purchasing 114 strike put options on the euro. The contracts are being offered on the exchange at 1.5 US cents. The first thing to work out is how many contracts the bank has to purchase.

$$\text{Number of contracts} = €10\,000\,000/€62\,500 = 160$$

The premium is $0.015 per €1 per contract. So the total premium payable is calculated as follows:

$$\text{Total premium} = 160 \text{ contracts} \times 62\,500 \times \$0.015$$
$$= \$150\,000$$

The 160 contracts taken together give the bank the right to sell a total of €10 million and to receive in return dollars calculated according to the strike of the contracts. The strike is 114 cents or $1.14 per euro.

$$\text{Dollars received if exercised} = 160 \times 62\,500 \times \$1.14$$
$$= \$11.4 \text{ million}$$

From this must of course be deducted the cost of buying the contracts. To see how the hedge would work out in practice, suppose the €/$ spot exchange rate at the expiry of the option contracts is either 1.1 or 1.2.

- *Spot rate 1.1*. If the bank sold the euros at the spot rate it would only receive $11 million. So it exercises the puts and receives $11.4 million. Net of the initial premium paid its dollar receipts are $11.4 million – $0.15 million = $11.25 million.
- *Spot rate 1.2*. The puts are out-of-the-money so are left to expire. The bank sells the euros on the spot market and receives $12 million. Net of the initial premium its dollar receipts are $12 million – $0.15 million = $11.85 million.

Figure 11.3 illustrates the results of hedging with the 114 strike puts at expiry. The solid line shows the number of dollars the bank would receive if the currency exposure is unhedged, i.e. it sells the euros in the spot market. This is based on a range of possible spot prices in three months' time. The dotted line represents the dollars received using 114 strike contracts to hedge the currency risk. The least amount of dollars received (taking into account the premium paid) is $11.25 million. Unlike a forward hedge, however, there is no limit to the potential gains the bank can achieve from a strengthening euro. Exchange-traded options have the additional advantage that if they are no longer required they can easily be sold before expiry, recouping some premium.

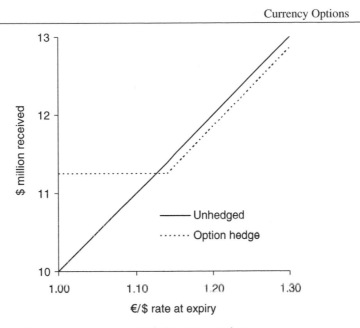

Figure 11.3   Currency hedge using exchange-traded currency options

The two lines in Figure 11.3 cross when the spot rate is 1.125. At that level the dollars received on the unhedged position is also $11.25 million. If the spot is below that level the option hedge outperforms the unhedged position and produces more dollars for the euros. Above that level the unhedged position actually produces more dollars than the hedged position. This is the effect of paying premium to buy the option contracts. The put option offers protection against a weakening euro, and a reasonable level of gain if the euro strengthens, but not the same level as on an unhedged position.

FX COVERED CALL WRITING

The final currency option strategy investigated in this chapter is not a hedge, but a means by which a corporation or financial institution can generate additional income by writing FX options without incurring too much risk. Writing 'naked' or unhedged options is extremely dangerous, but here the risk is covered through other underlying currency transactions. The case we will explore is that of a US money manager. The manager holds £10 million in sterling-denominated assets. The returns are acceptable but not spectacular, and the manager would like to enhance the performance of the fund without taking too many risks. The spot rate is £/$ 1.59. Two-month European-style sterling calls struck at $1.63 per pound are trading at 0.55 cents per pound.

The manager decides to write calls on sterling against the £10 million assets. If the calls are ever exercised the manager will have to deliver pounds in return for dollars, but can liquidate the assets to have the necessary sterling available. At a strike of 1.63 the dollars received would be $16.3 million, which is rather better than the dollars received from liquidating the portfolio at the current spot rate of 1.59. In the meantime, the calls will generate welcome premium income.

$$\text{Premium received} = 10\,000\,000 \times \$0.0055 = \$55\,000$$

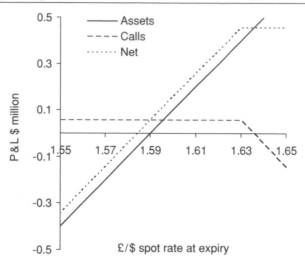

Figure 11.4   Outcome of FX covered call strategy

Figure 11.4 illustrates the profits and losses the investor would achieve as a result of movements in the exchange rate between the pound and the dollar. This is shown at the expiry of the option contracts and for a range of spot rates from 1.55 upwards. The vertical axis represents profits and losses in millions of dollars. Note that the assumption throughout is that the sterling value of the assets is unchanged at £10 million.

The solid line in the graph shows profits and losses on the underlying sterling assets resulting from changes in the exchange rate. For example, the spot rate at the outset is 1.59 and the sterling assets are worth $15.9 million. If the rate is unchanged, the profit and loss from currency movements is zero, but if the pound strengthens or weakens, the dollar value of the assets will change, resulting in gains or losses to the fund. The graph also shows the profits and losses on the calls at expiry, and the net profit and loss on the combined covered call strategy.

A few examples will help to explain the values in the graph. Suppose the spot rate at expiry is either 1.55 or 1.63 or 1.65:

- *Spot Rate = 1.55.* The sterling-denominated assets are now worth only $15.5 million where originally they were worth $15.9. This is a loss of $400 000. However, premium received from writing the calls adds back $55 000 so the net loss is only $345 000. The options expire out-of-the-money and worthless.
- *Spot Rate = 1.63.* The sterling-based assets are now worth $16.3 million. This is a currency gain of $400 000 million. To this is added the premium, so the net gain is $455 000. The options expire at-the-money and worthless.
- *Spot Rate = 1.65.* Above 1.63 the written calls will be exercised. The manager has to deliver £10 million and will receive $16.3 million. The currency gain on the assets is $400 000. To this is added the premium, so the net gain is again $455 000. In fact the gain is capped at this level.

The strategy is a known as a covered call because the money manager owns assets denominated in British pounds which can be liquidated to cover the risks on the short call options. The currency gains on the portfolio can reach $400 000 before the calls are exercised and the gains are capped. In addition, the strategy generates premium income of $55 000. If the money manager did not actually wish to liquidate the portfolio, an alternative approach is to buy the calls back if the spot price looks like rising above the strike of 1.63.

CHAPTER SUMMARY

A currency or FX option conveys the right but not the obligation to exchange two currencies at a predetermined rate. In a European-style contract the currencies can only be exchanged on the expiry date. Exchange-traded options are generally standardized, although the exchanges have introduced contracts that allow for some flexibility in the strikes and expiry dates and quotation methods. FX options can be used to hedge currency exposures. Because they need not be exercised, they can protect against adverse movements in an exchange rate while permitting some degree of benefit if the rate moves in a favourable direction. The problem is the cost of the premium. One way to reduce or eliminate the premium cost is a collar strategy. If the strikes are set appropriately there is zero net premium to pay. The snag is that gains from currency movements are capped at a certain level.

Another way to reduce premium when buying options to hedge currency exposures is to incorporate a barrier feature into the contract. A company bidding for a contract that includes currency risk may decide to buy a compound option. This conveys the right but not the obligation to buy a standard or 'vanilla' option at some future date. Institutional investors who purchase assets denominated in foreign currencies can construct a covered call strategy. This involves selling an out-of-the-money FX call on the foreign currency. If the call is exercised the investor is covered because he or she can liquidate the assets. The premium income adds to the performance of the fund. The disadvantage is that gains from favourable currency movements are capped.

12

Interest Rate Options

INTRODUCTION

In Chapters 3, 5 and 6 we explored products such as forward rate agreements (FRAs), interest rate futures and interest rate swaps. FRAs and futures can be used by banks, traders, corporations and institutional investors to manage exposures to or speculate on changes in interest rates. However the potential gains are balanced by the potential losses. The buyer of an FRA is paid compensation if the interest rate for the contract period turns out to be above the contractual rate, but otherwise has to compensate the seller. If the contractual rate is the expected rate for the period then the expected payout from the deal is zero. Interest rate futures have similar characteristics, although settlement takes place daily and because of the different quotation method it is the short who is paid out if interest rates rise.

A standard or 'vanilla' interest rate swap is the exchange of fixed for floating cash flows on regular dates. The initial floating or variable cash flow is based on a cash market interest rate (normally LIBOR). The subsequent cash flows are based on a sequence of future interest rates. As such, it can be priced using the first cash market rate and the interest rate futures that best match its payment periods. The fixed rate on a par swap is the rate that makes the present values of the expected future cash flows equal to zero. The expected payout on a par swap is zero. An interest rate option is different. The expected payout to the buyer (ignoring the premium) is positive since the contract need not be exercised in unfavourable circumstances. This flexibility has a price, the option premium. The premium restores the balance between the buyer and the writer.

The interest rate option products explored in this chapter are over-the-counter and exchange-traded options on short-term interest rates; interest rate caps, floors and collars; swaptions (options to buy or to sell interest rate swaps); and bond options. We look at how the products are quoted and at some practical applications. The payoff in all of these products depends on what happens to market interest rates in the future, so that their valuation relies on an ability to understand and model the behaviour of interest rates.

OTC INTEREST RATE OPTIONS

Interest rate options provide investors, traders and corporations with a flexible means of hedging and managing interest rate risk. In recent decades the central banks of the major economies have relaxed or abolished controls on currency exchange rates and tend to rely on short-term interest rates as the major weapon to control inflation and regulate the economy. Among other factors, this has led to increased volatility in interest rates and the need for sophisticated risk-management tools.

In Chapter 3 we explored the structure and applications of forward rate agreements (FRAs). The purchaser of an FRA is compensated in cash by the seller if the actual LIBOR rate for the future time period covered by the contract is above the fixed contractual rate. Otherwise the buyer compensates the seller. The contractual rate is a forward interest rate. In theory, it can be established from cash market interest rates, although in practice it tends to be determined by the prices at which the appropriate short-term interest rate futures contracts are trading.

A European over-the-counter (OTC) interest rate call option is essentially a call on a forward rate agreement for settlement on the option's expiry date. The strike is the FRA fixed or contractual rate. If at the expiry of the contract the LIBOR rate for the contract period is set above the strike, then the owner of the call exercises and has a long position in an FRA, which is settled in cash in the normal way. However, if the LIBOR rate is below the strike, the option simply expires and no further payment is made. The buyer has to pay premium to the writer at the outset based on the expected payout from the option contract.

As interest rate calls are used as components of interest rate caps (which we consider in the next section), they are sometimes known as *caplets*. To illustrate how they work we take a simple example of a European caplet. The notional principal is £10 million. This is used to calculate the settlement payment on the underlying FRA if the contract is exercised. Additional details of the contract are as follows:

Contract	Contract period	Expiry	Strike rate	Premium
European caplet	6v12 months	In 6 months	4% p.a.	0.16% p.a.

The contract confers the right but not the obligation to buy an FRA with a notional of £10 million at a strike rate of 4% p.a. The future time period covered by the underlying FRA begins in six months and ends six months later, i.e. a 12-month period. This time period is often expressed in the market as '6v12' or sometimes as '6x12'. The caplet expires in six months. If it is exercised at that point it will become a long position in the underlying FRA. Assuming the strike rate is the same as the forward rate for the contract period then the caplet is at-the-money. The premium is expressed in terms of a per annum rate, though the underlying FRA covers a six-month time period. The actual cost in sterling terms is calculated as follows.

$$\text{Premium cost} = £10 \text{ million} \times 0.16\% \times 6/12 = £8000$$

The buyer of the caplet – the interest rate call – pays the premium to the writer, and then nothing more is done until six months after the start date. At that point the LIBOR rate for the contract period will be announced by the British Bankers' Association (BBA). If we assume that the rate is actually set at 5% p.a., then buyer of the call will exercise and have a long position in an FRA at a contractual rate of 4% p.a. In practice this simply means that the writer has to make a compensation payment based on the difference between 5% p.a. and 4% p.a. for a six-month time period.

$$\text{Compensation payment} = £10 \text{ million} \times (5\% - 4\%) \times 6/12 = £50\,000$$

This is the compensation amount due at the end of the contract period, i.e. 12 months after the option purchase date. As we saw in Chapter 3, it is conventional to make the settlement payment after the actual LIBOR rate for the period is announced. In this example the payment, to be made at the option expiry date, would be £50 000 discounted back for six months at LIBOR. The real benefit of the caplet is that if the LIBOR rate is set at or below 4% then the buyer is not obliged to exercise the contract. The maximum loss is the initial premium of 0.16% p.a., or £8000.

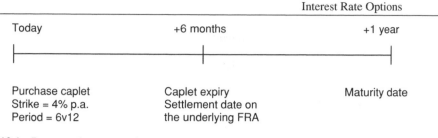

Figure 12.1 Payment dates on caplet

Hedging with interest rate calls

Imagine that the buyer of the caplet discussed in the previous section is a company that has borrowed money and pays a variable or floating rate of interest on the loan. The details of the company's loan are as shown below:

Principal: £10 million
Interest rate: Six-month sterling LIBOR + 0.75% p.a.
Interest rate reset: Every six months
Payment dates: Payable in arrears every six months

There is exactly six months to the next interest payment on the loan. At that point the rate of interest for the following six-month period will be reset at six-month sterling LIBOR plus 75 basis points (0.75%) per annum. The interest payment for the period will be made in arrears. Suppose that the company is concerned that interest rates for this period might rise, increasing its borrowing costs and affecting its profitability. It could buy a 6v12 FRA to cover the risk. If LIBOR is set above the contractual rate the company will receive a payment on the FRA. Unfortunately, if LIBOR is below that rate the company would have to make a settlement payment to the seller of the FRA.

As an alternative, the company could purchase a call on the FRA (a caplet) – the right but not the obligation to buy the FRA, with the terms as set out in the previous section. The premium is 0.16% p.a. or £8000, the notional is £10 million, the contract period for the underlying FRA is 6v12 and the strike is 4% p.a. Figure 12.1 shows the key payment dates on the caplet.

If the LIBOR rate in six months time for a six-month period is fixed at (say) 5% p.a. then the company's cost of borrowing on its underlying loan will be set at 5.75% for that period. However, it can exercise the caplet and will receive a compensation payment on the underlying FRA contract. Its net cost of borrowing is 4.91% p.a. calculated as follows:

Borrowing rate on loan = LIBOR + 0.75% p.a. = 5.75% p.a.
Plus premium paid for call = 0.16% p.a.
Less: compensation payment received on FRA = 1% p.a.
Net borrowing rate for the period = 4.91% p.a.

On the other hand, if LIBOR is set at or below the strike of the caplet, then the contract simply expires worthless and the company need make no further payment. If, for example, LIBOR is set at 3% p.a., the company's net cost of borrowing is calculated as follows:

Borrowing rate on loan = LIBOR + 0.75% = 3.75% p.a.
Plus premium paid for call = 0.16% p.a.
Net borrowing rate for period = 3.91% p.a.

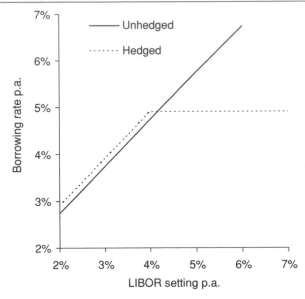

Figure 12.2   Unhedged and hedged exposure to LIBOR

The graph in Figure 12.2 compares the company's position if it does not hedge the interest rate exposure (solid line) to its situation with the caplet in place (dotted line). By buying the caplet the company establishes a maximum borrowing cost for the period of 4.91% p.a.

CAPS, FLOORS AND COLLARS

The caplet explored in the last section limits the company's borrowing rate only for the six-month future time period covered by the contract. The company may decide that it also wishes to protect itself against increases in interest rates for the subsequent payment periods on its loan. To do this it could buy a series or strip of caplets. The first, as before, would cover its interest payment on the loan for the time period 6v12 (for six months starting in six months); the second caplet would cover the time period 12v18 (for six months starting in 12 months); and so on.

If the strikes are all set at the same level this creates an *interest rate cap*. As the name suggests, it is used to cap or limit a borrower's effective funding rate for a series of future interest payment periods. If for any one of the periods the LIBOR rate is set above the strike, then the buyer of the cap is compensated in cash by the writer of the contract. The cap premium is simply the sum of the premiums of the constituent caplets. It is either paid in a lump sum at the outset, or in instalments, often on dates that match the interest payments made on the underlying loan.

A caplet is priced in relation to the forward interest rate for the period it covers. A caplet covering a period 6v12 is priced against the forward interest rate for the period 6v12. If the market is expecting increases in LIBOR rates over the years ahead and the forward rates are higher than cash market rates, this can mean that the premium cost of a cap with a strike set around current interest rate levels is prohibitively expensive. The writer of the cap would have to take into account the fact that he or she will most likely be making a number of compensation payments to the buyer over the life of the contract. In other words, the expected payout from the cap is high, and this has to be factored into the premium that is charged.

Normally in this type of case the cap strike is set above current interest rate levels. Additionally, a borrower may choose to combine the purchase of a cap with the sale of an *interest rate floor* with a strike set at a lower rate. It would normally agree this as a package deal with an option dealer. The combined strategy is called an *interest rate collar*, and operates as follows. If the LIBOR rate for a payment period is set above the cap strike, the borrower receives a compensation payment from the dealer. However, if the LIBOR rate is set below the strike of the floor the borrower has to make a compensation payment to the dealer. The effect for the borrower is to establish a maximum and a minimum funding rate. If the strikes of the cap and floor are set appropriately the premiums cancel out and there is zero net premium to pay on the deal. This structure is called a *zero-cost collar.*

We return to the case of a company that has borrowed £10 million on a variable or floating rate basis. Interest payments are made every six months in arrears and the payment for a given period will be set at the start of the period at LIBOR + 0.75%. p.a. This time the company agrees a zero-cost collar strategy with a dealer based on a notional of £10 million, in which it buys a cap struck at 7% p.a. and writes a floor struck at 5%. p.a. Payouts on the collar are made every six months to match the payments on the underlying loan. Suppose that during one of the loan payment periods the LIBOR rate for that period is set at 4%, at 6% or at 8% p.a.

- *LIBOR = 4% p.a.* The rate on the underlying loan will be set at 4.75% p.a. The floor is struck at 5% p.a. and LIBOR is 1% lower than this, therefore the company has to pay 1% p.a. compensation to the dealer. As there is no premium to pay on the collar, the company's net borrowing cost for the period is 4.75% + 1% = 5.75% p.a.
- *LIBOR = 6%.* The rate on the underlying loan will be set 6.75% p.a. There is nothing to be paid on the floor and nothing is received on the cap, so the net cost of borrowing is simply 6.75% p.a.
- *LIBOR = 8%.* The rate on the underlying loan will be set at 8.75% p.a. The company receives 1% p.a. on the cap, since the strike is 7% p.a. The net cost of borrowing is therefore 8.75% − 1% = 7.75% p.a.

Because of the hedge the company's minimum cost of borrowing is 5.75% p.a. and the maximum is 7.75% p.a. The result of the zero-cost collar hedge for a range of possible LIBOR rates is illustrated in Figure 12.3.

SWAPTIONS

As another alternative, the company might consider an interest rate swap, in which it receives a floating rate linked to LIBOR and pays in return a fixed rate of interest. The notional on the swap would be set at £10 million and the payments would be made every six months in arrears to match its underlying loan. (See Chapter 6 for further information on interest rate swaps.) Suppose that the fixed rate on the swap is set at 6% p.a. In practice, this would be calculated from the forward interest rates that cover the time periods to maturity. The effect of hedging the loan with the interest rate swap is illustrated in Figure 12.4.

As a result of entering into the swap the company can fix its borrowing costs at 6.75% p.a. The advantage of this strategy is that if interest rates rise sharply the company will not suffer as a result. It has known borrowing costs for the lifetime of the swap and it can plan its business activities accordingly. The drawback is that it cannot benefit from any decline in interest rates. Compare this with the zero-cost collar strategy, where the company can gain from declining interest rates as long as they do not fall below the strike of the floor.

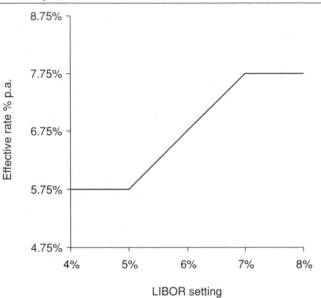

Figure 12.3 Zero-cost interest rate collar

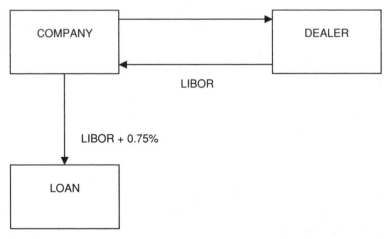

Figure 12.4 Loan plus swap

As another alternative, the company can consider a European *payer swaption*. This confers the right but not the obligation to enter into an interest rate swap at some point in the future (at the expiry of the swaption). In the actual swap it would pay a fixed rate of interest and receive LIBOR in return. The notional principal, the payment dates and the interest calculations on the underlying swap would all be specified in the contract. The swaption provides flexibility. The company has the choice over whether or not to exercise and to enter into the swap specified in the contract. In addition, if at expiry the fixed rates on interest rate swaps in the market are higher than the fixed rate agreed in the contract, a payer swaption would be in-the-money and could be closed out at a profit.

For example, suppose the company buys a swaption conferring the right in six months' time to enter into a swap paying 6.25% p.a. and receiving LIBOR. If in six months' time the fixed rate on swaps is 6.5% p.a., then the swaption has a positive value. In theory, the buyer of the swaption could exercise the contract, enter into a swap paying a fixed rate at 6.25% p.a., and at the same time make an offsetting deal in the spot market in which it receives 6.5% p.a. In practice the swaption contract can be set up such that if it expires in-the-money the company is paid the intrinsic value in cash by the writer of the contract. This, of course, would only happen if swap rates rise, in which case the company's borrowing costs would also increase.

There are two important differences between the zero-cost collar and the swaption strategies. Firstly, there is premium to pay on a swaption. Secondly, the swaption can only be exercised once. If exercised, the company acquires a position in an interest rate swap. The collar consists of a series of interest rate options covering different time periods, each of which individually may or may not be exercised depending on how the actual LIBOR rate for that period compares with the strikes of the cap and of the floor. In practical terms, the company in the case study will have to make its decision on which product to choose based on its attitude to risk, its views on the likely direction of interest rates and its willingness or otherwise to pay premium. It has a number of choices to consider (these are by no means exhaustive).

- Do nothing. In which case its borrowing costs will increase if interest rates rise.
- Buy an FRA. This will fix its effective borrowing rate for one time period only.
- Pay fixed on a swap. This will fix its effective borrowing rate for a series of future time periods. If interest rates fall it cannot benefit.
- Buy a call on an FRA (a caplet). This will cap its effective borrowing rate for one future time period only. However, it incurs premium costs.
- Enter into a zero-cost collar. This establishes a minimum and a maximum borrowing rate for a series of future time periods. There is no premium. However, the company can no longer benefit if interest rates fall below the strike of the floor.
- Buy a payer swaption, the right to enter a swap at some point in the future as the payer of fixed and the receiver of a variable rate. If rates rise this can fix its effective borrowing rate for a series of future time periods, and if rates fall the contract need not be exercised. However, it incurs premium costs.

EURODOLLAR OPTIONS

Chapter 5 has details of the Eurodollar futures contracts traded on Chicago Mercantile Exchange (CME). They are widely used by financial institutions to manage their exposures to changes in short-term interest rates. Contracts are based on a three-month $1 million notional deposit starting in the future. The quotation is made in terms of 100 minus the interest rate for that future time period. The notional principal is never exchanged. Instead, there are a series of margin payments based on the changing price of the contract in the market.

A movement of 0.01 in the futures price is equivalent to a change of one basis point (0.01%) in the interest rate for the future time period covered by the contract. It is worth $1 million $\times$ 0.01% $\times$ 3/12 = $25. Sellers or shorts gain if the interest rate increases. Buyers or longs gain if the rate falls. Interest rate futures are used to price forward rate agreements, which are their OTC relatives. CME also offers an *option* on the Eurodollar futures contract. The premiums are quoted in a similar way to the futures prices. In dollar terms a premium of 20 basis points is worth 20 $\times$ $25 = $500.

- A call option is the right to buy and a put is the right to sell a Eurodollar futures contract at a fixed price, the strike price, on or before expiry.
- If a long call is exercised it results in a long position in a futures contract, which benefits from falling interest rates.
- If a long put is exercised it results in a short position in a futures contract, which benefits from rising interest rates.
- In-the-money contracts are automatically exercised at expiry.
- The options are American-style. If an option is exercised early a trader who is short a contract is randomly assigned a futures position. If it is a call this results in a short position in the futures for the assigned trader. A put results in a long position.

To illustrate how the contracts work, suppose that a trader buys one December Eurodollar put struck at 98.62. The December futures is trading at 98.71. The agreed premium is 10 basis points. Each point is worth $25 so the dollar premium is calculated as follows:

$$\text{Premium cost} = 10 \text{ points} \times \$25 = \$250$$

The put is out-of-the money since it confers the right to sell a futures at only 98.62 when it is trading above this level on the exchange. Therefore the option has zero intrinsic value and the premium cost is purely time value. The futures price is based on the expected rate of interest for the three-month period starting in December. The expected rate is $100 - 98.71 = 1.29\%$ p.a.

The closing price of the December futures at expiry is based on the *actual* LIBOR rate set for the period covered by the contract. Suppose it is set at 2% p.a. at expiry. Then the December futures will close at $100.00 - 2.00 = 98.00$. The trader owns a put that provides the right to sell a Eurodollar futures at 98.62. The net profit is calculated as follows:

Intrinsic value in points $= 9862 - 9800 = 62$ points
Value in dollars $= 62 \times \$25 = \$1550$
Net profit (intrinsic value less premium) $= \$1550 - \$250 = \$1300$

The net profit can also be calculated as 62 points intrinsic value less 10 points premium which is 52 points $\times$ $25 = $1300. Suppose, on the other hand, that the December futures closes at expiry at (say) 99.00 based on a LIBOR rate set at 1.00% p.a. Then the put option will simply not be exercised. For the buyer of the contract, the worst that can happen is that the option expires out-of-the-money and the initial premium has been lost.

EURO AND STERLING INTEREST RATE OPTIONS

Very similar interest rate option contracts are traded in Europe. The three-month Euribor futures traded on LIFFE (through its electronic network) is based on a €1 million deposit starting in March, June, September or December plus certain other months. A Euribor option contract is the right to buy or to sell one Euribor futures. Each one-point move in the market value of a contract is worth €25 though the price is allowed to change in half-point intervals. Exercise can take place on any business day and results in a position in the futures with the expiry month associated with that option. For example, the exercise of a long December call results in a long position in the December futures. The exercise of a long March put results in a short position in the March futures.

LIFFE also offers a option on the three-month sterling interest rate futures. The main difference here is that the underlying futures is based on a notional £500 000 deposit, so each full point move in the price quotation is worth £12.50. The premium is not paid in full when an option is purchased. Instead, initial margin is posted at the outset and a series of daily variation margin payments or receipts are made, depending on the changing market value of the contract.

BOND OPTIONS

Bond options are classified as interest rate options because bond prices are critically affected by changes in market interest rates. Many bond options in the OTC market are European-style contracts. A European bond option is the right but not the obligation to buy or sell a bond on a specified date at an agreed price, the strike or exercise price. By contrast, exchange-traded contracts are options on bond futures and can be exercised on any business day up to and including expiry. Here are some of the most important applications of OTC bond options.

- *Hedging.* The owner of a bond is concerned about a short-term rise in interest rates (which would lead to a fall in the value of the bond) but would prefer not to sell out. One possibility is to short bond futures, so that losses on the bond are compensated by gains on the futures (depending on the efficiency of the hedge), but profits on the bond would then be offset by losses on the futures. An alternative is to buy a put option on the bond. If the bond price falls, the put can be exercised, eliminating further losses. If the price rises, the owner can still benefit from that rise. However, the option costs premium.
- *Zero-cost collars.* Institutional investors dislike paying premium because it affects the performance of the fund. The owner of a bond who is concerned about a fall in price can buy an out-of-the-money put and sell an out-of-the-money call. If the strikes are set appropriately then the premiums cancel out and there is zero net premium to pay. The owner is protected if the bond price falls below the strike of the long put. Unfortunately gains on the bond are capped if the price rises above the strike of the written call.
- *Covered call writing.* An investor who owns a bond can generate additional income by writing an out-of-the-money call on the asset. The premium received will enhance investment performance. If the bond price rises above the strike and the call is exercised, the investor is covered, since he or she can deliver the bond.
- *Leveraged position taking.* A trader who thinks that interest rates are set to fall can buy an out-of-the-money or at-the-money call on a fixed-coupon bond. This is much cheaper than buying the bond. If rates do fall the bond price will rise as its coupon (fixed rate of interest) becomes more attractive. The call will also increase in value and it can then be sold at a profit. The return on capital is greater than would have been achieved if the actual bond had been purchased.

Exchange-traded bond options

In Chapter 4 we looked at a number of bond futures contracts traded on the Chicago Board of Trade and other exchanges. Table 12.1 sets out the specification of the 10-year Treasury note option contract traded on the CBOT. The underlying here is a futures, so that if a long call is exercised the holder acquires a long position in one 10-year US Treasury note futures contract. If a long put is exercised the holder acquires a short position in a futures contract. Premiums are quoted per $100 in points and sixty-fourths of a point rather than in decimal format.

Table 12.1 CBOT option on 10-year US Treasury note futures

Trading unit:	Each option contract is based on one CBOT US 10-year Treasury note future with a specified delivery month. The underlying futures is based on US Treasuries with a face value of $100 000
Contract months:	Next three consecutive months plus the next two months in the cycle March, June, September and December
Last trading:	In the month before the delivery month of the underlying futures contract
Exercise style:	American. Options that expire in-the-money are automatically exercised

Reprinted by permission of the Board of Trade of the City of Chicago, Inc. copyright 2004, ALL RIGHTS RESERVED

Suppose that a trader is anticipating future cuts in interest rates, which will increase the value of Treasury notes and bonds. The futures prices, which are derived from those in the cash market, will follow suit. The trader buys a March call on the CBOT with the following details:

Contract type	Strike	Expiry	Premium
10-year Treasury note call	113	March	1-16

The underlying March futures is trading at $111 \frac{23}{32}$, which in decimal format is 111.71875 per $100 par value. Therefore the call is out-of-the money since it confers the right to buy a September futures contract at a higher price of $113. The premium is $1 \frac{16}{64} = \$1.25$ per $100 par value. On the contract size of $100 000 this amounts to $100 000 \times 1.25\% = \$1250$.

Suppose that the futures price rises to 115 on the exchange, driven upwards by falling interest rates. Then the trader could exercise the call, buy a futures at 113 and sell it into the market at 115. The profit from exercising the option is its intrinsic value, which is $115 - 113 = \$2$ per $100 par value. On the contract size of $100 000 this is $2000. The net profit for the trader is therefore $2000 less the initial premium of $1250, which comes to $750. Alternatively, assuming there is some time remaining to expiry, a better alternative might be to sell the call back into the market.

Bund and gilt bond options

The government bond options traded on the European exchanges are similar to the US Treasury contracts on the CBOT. The most important contract is the German government bond (or bund) option on Eurex, the combined Swiss–German exchange. The unit of trading is one bund futures contract. A call is the right to buy a specific futures contract at the strike price. A put is the right to sell a specific futures at the strike price.

- If a call option is exercised this results in a long position in the futures for the owner of the option and a short position for the writer.
- If a put option is exercised this results in a short futures position for the owner and a long position for the writer.
- The contract can be exercised on any exchange trading day.

As we saw in Chapter 4, the bund futures is based on €100 000 par value of a notional German government bond with between 8.5 and 10.5 years to maturity and a coupon rate of 6% p.a. The price is quoted in euros per €100 par value to two decimal places. The tick size (minimum price movement) is 0.01 per €100 par value, so that the value of each tick movement on the €100 000 contract size is €100 000 × 0.01% = €10. The premiums on the bund option contracts are quoted in the same way. Suppose that a trader buys one 114 strike Euro bund call option contract at a premium of 0.50 per €100, i.e. 50 ticks. The premium payable in cash terms is calculated as follows.

$$\text{Premium cost} = 50 \text{ ticks} \times €10 = €500$$

If the contract is exercised then the trader acquires a long position in the futures at a price of €114 per €100. The futures would have to be trading at 114 + 0.50 = 114.50 to break even on the deal (ignoring brokerage and funding costs). The trader has the right to buy one contract at 114. If this right is exercised and the futures is worth 114.50 then the profit from exercise is 50 ticks or €500, which recovers the initial premium paid. If the futures is trading above this level then the profit from exercise exceeds the premium.

The option on the long gilt futures on LIFFE is also an American-style contract and can be exercised on any business day. Exercise results in a long or short position in a gilt futures. The underlying futures is based on £100 000 par value of a notional 6% p.a. coupon gilt. Like the US Treasury contract on the CBOT, delivery against the futures can take place on any business day in the delivery month at the choice of the seller. The tick size on both the futures and the options is 0.01 per £100 and the value of each tick is £100 000 × 0.01% = £10. If a trader buys an option and the value of the option rises by (say) 20 ticks, then the trader can sell the contract back and realize a profit of 20 × £10 = £200 less transaction costs.

One feature of gilt options that is different to the LIFFE stock options we considered in Chapter 10 is that the premium is not paid in full at the time an option contract is purchased. Instead, like a futures contract, the buyer deposits initial margin at the outset, followed by a series of variation margin payments and receipts depending on the changing value of the option contract. If the buyer decides to exercise a contract the original premium cost must be paid to the clearing house, which credits the account of the seller.

CHAPTER SUMMARY

An interest rate option is a contract whose value depends on future interest rates. An OTC interest rate option is a call or a put on a forward rate agreement (FRA). An OTC interest rate call is also known as a caplet. If at expiry the actual interest rate for the period covered by the contract is above the strike the holder of the call is compensated in cash. Otherwise the contract expires worthless. The snag is that the caplet costs premium. An interest rate cap is a series or strip of caplets all with the same strike. The premium is the sum of the premiums of the constituent caplets. A borrower who is concerned about rising interest rates can buy a cap and at the same time sell a floor to offset some or all of the premium cost. This is called a collar and establishes a maximum and a minimum rate of interest. A European swaption is the right but not the obligation to enter into an interest rate swap on a future date as the payer or as the receiver of the fixed rate.

An OTC bond option conveys the right but not the obligation to buy or to sell a bond at a fixed strike price. Exchange-traded contracts on the CBOT and on LIFFE are options on bond futures. If an option is exercised it results in a long or short position in a futures contract. Bond options can be used to take speculative trading positions, to hedge against changes in interest rates and bond prices, and to generate additional premium income for a fund invested in fixed-income securities.

13

Option Valuation Concepts

INTRODUCTION

Option premium consists of intrinsic value, which is either zero or positive, plus time value. Intrinsic value cannot be negative because the holder is never obliged to exercise a contract that is out-of-the-money. Even if an option has zero intrinsic value it will still have some time value, assuming that it has not yet expired and the price of the underlying can fluctuate to any extent. The time value reflects the chance or possibility that the option *may* become in-the-money before expiration. Generally speaking, this chance is greater:

- the longer the time remaining until the expiry of the option;
- the greater the volatility of the price of the underlying asset.

Taken together these factors – time to expiry and volatility – represent opportunities for the buyer of an option and risks for the seller or writer of the contract. Time value is the price of that opportunity and that risk. Calculating intrinsic value is easy, but it is more difficult to calculate time value. The problem is that unlike (say) a US Treasury bill, the future cash flow arising from an option is inherently uncertain and depends on what happens to the price of the underlying over the life of the contract. To value an option we need a pricing methodology that is based on probability – taking into account the *possible* future cash flows that *might* result from buying or selling an option, and the probabilities that those will occur. This is the conception that underlies the models used to value option contracts.

The model for pricing European options on shares was developed by Black, Scholes and Merton in the 1970s. Myron Scholes and Robert Merton were awarded the Nobel prize for their work in 1997, Fischer Black sadly having died two years before. It is beyond the scope of an introductory text such as this to explain the mathematics behind the Black–Scholes model (as it is commonly known) in detail. Appendix A shows how it can easily be set up on an Excel spreadsheet, and Appendix C has some suggestions on further reading for anyone wishing to explore the mathematics of the subject.

The aim here is to provide an intuitive understanding of how the model operates in practice. The focus is on the inputs, and how changing those inputs affects the value that is calculated. In the financial markets relatively few people work through all the mathematics underlying the pricing of options, especially the techniques used in the later-generation models that have been developed since Black–Scholes. Nevertheless many people rely on pricing models in their day-to-day business activities and need to develop a reasonable working understanding of the inputs and outputs, the key assumptions, and the practical limitations.

THE CONCEPT OF EXPECTED PAYOUT

Option valuation starts from the idea of expected payout or payoff. Some readers will be familiar with this concept from economics or from business decision theory – or perhaps from

Table 13.1   Possible share prices at expiry and probabilities

Possible share price ($)	Probability (%)
120	25
100	50
80	25

personal experience when weighing up whether or not to make a risky investment or place a bet. The first step is to weight all the possible payouts (outcomes) from an investment or a bet by the chance or probability of achieving each outcome. The average or expected payout is the sum of all the weighted payouts.

As a very simple example, suppose that an investor is offered a deal with the following terms. The initial stake is $100. The investor reckons that there is a 35% chance of being repaid $220, a 25% chance of being repaid $150 and a 40% chance of getting nothing back at all on the deal. The question is: Is this a good proposition or not? By working out the expected payout we can help to provide an answer.

$$\text{Expected payout} = (\$220 \times 35\%) + (\$150 \times 25\%) + (\$0 \times 40\%)$$
$$= \$114.50$$

The stake is $100 but the expected payout is higher at $114.50, so the deal is a good one (assuming the probabilities have been correctly assessed and the investor is prepared to put any capital at risk in the first place). In theory, the investor should be prepared to stake up to just under $114.50 to take part in the deal. The basic concept of expected payout is very simple indeed but has real-world applications. For example, a company is likely to prosper if it always takes on projects whose expected payouts (in today's money) exceed the initial amounts invested.

An option is a financial instrument that offers a range of possible payouts depending on what happens to the price of the underlying. It follows that the expected payout from an option is the sum of all the possible payouts, each weighted by the probability of attaining that payout. The value of the contract is its expected payout; if it can be purchased for less than this, then it represents a good deal. A person who trades options and (over some sustained period) always buys contracts for less than their expected payout values will be successful.

To illustrate the idea, let us suppose that a share is trading in the cash market at $100. A trader is offered a one-year European call on the share struck at-the-money, i.e. with an exercise price of $100. How much should he or she pay for the contract? To keep things simple, we assume that interest rates are zero and the share pays no dividends. Therefore, its one-year forward price is also $100. The share is also rather unusual in that it can only take one of three possible values in one year. Table 13.1 sets out these values and the probabilities that each will be attained.

The greatest likelihood is that the share price after one year will still be $100. However there is a 25% chance that it will have increased by $20 and a 25% chance that it will have fallen by $20. The expected value of the share in one year's time is the sum of all the possible values weighted by their probabilities.

$$\text{Expected share value} = (\$120 \times 25\%) + (\$100 \times 50\%) + (\$80 \times 25\%)$$
$$= \$100$$

If today the trader entered into a *forward* contract to buy the share in one year's time at a fixed price of $100, then the expected payout on the deal is zero. If the share is worth $120 at the point of delivery the trader would make $20. However, the trader has an equal and opposite chance that the share will only be worth $80 at that time.

$$\text{Expected payout on forward} = (\$20 \times 25\%) + (\$0 \times 50\%) + (-\$20 \times 25\%)$$
$$= \$0$$

Since the expected payout on this deal is zero, the trader should not pay a premium to enter into such a contract. However, if the trader buys an at-the-money call the situation is totally different. This is the right but not the obligation to purchase the underlying share in one year's time at a strike of $100. If the share price is above $100 at expiry the call will be exercised, otherwise it will expire worthless. The trader buying the call has a *positive* expected payout.

$$\text{Expected payout from long call} = (\$20 \times 25\%) + (\$0 \times \$50) + (\$0 \times 25\%)$$
$$= \$5$$

Equally, the expected loss to the writer of the call is $5. Therefore in order to restore equilibrium (and fairness) the trader should pay a premium of $5 to the writer. That is the fair value of the at-the-money call. In this example we assumed that interest rates are zero. If rates are positive then the expected payout would have to be discounted back to the day when the option was purchased and the premium paid.

INPUTS TO THE BLACK–SCHOLES MODEL

The Black–Scholes model, adapted for a share that pays dividends, requires only five inputs to price a European-style option. (Appendix A explains how to set the model up on an Excel spreadsheet.) The value of option – the theoretical premium that should be paid for the contract – is the expected payout at expiry discounted back to the day the option is purchased and the premium paid. The inputs to the model are as follows:

- The spot or cash price of the underlying share
- The strike or exercise price of the option
- The time to expiry of the option
- The volatility of the underlying share
- The cost of carry on the underlying share – the interest rate to the expiry of the option less any dividend income received on the share over that period.

The purpose of the first two of these inputs is quite straightforward. They establish whether or not the option has any intrinsic value. They also help to determine how likely or otherwise it is that the option will be exercised. If a call has a strike of $100 and the cash market value of the share is also $100, the option has zero intrinsic value but we could say that there is a good chance – perhaps an even chance – that the share price *will* be trading above $100 at expiry and that the option will expire in-the-money. However, if the spot price is $100 and the strike is $200 it is far less likely that the call will ever be exercised. Assuming they both have the same expiration date, the value of an out-of-the-money option will generally be less than that of an at-the-money contract on the same underlying.

We discussed previously why time to expiry is important in valuing an option. There is a greater chance that the price of a share will change substantially over the course of a year than during a single day. Other things being equal, therefore, a longer-dated option tends to be more valuable because it provides greater profit opportunities for the buyer of the contract – the expected payout is higher.

Input number five to the model – the cost of carry – is also quite straightforward. A European option can only be exercised at expiry, which is in the future. Therefore it is priced in relation to the *forward* price of the share – its expected value on the expiration date. As we saw in Chapter 2, the forward price of a share is calculated from the spot price plus the net cost of carrying the share for delivery on the forward date, i.e. the funding rate less any dividends earned over the carry period. Therefore we need these inputs to the model. Another way to look at this is to appreciate that writers of options take very substantial risks, and normally expect to hedge or cover those risks. The writer of a call option is at risk if the share price increases. To hedge this exposure he or she buys a quantity of the underlying. To do this the writer borrows money, and has therefore to factor into the premium charged for the option the funding cost less any dividends earned on holding the shares.

The model also requires an estimate of the volatility of the underlying. The measurement of volatility is discussed in more detail in the next section, but the reason why it requires such an input is quite clear. All other things being equal, an option on a highly volatile share is more expensive than an option on an asset that trades in a narrow range. The chance of an extreme movement in the price of the underlying is greater, and so the option has a higher expected payout.

HISTORICAL VOLATILITY

Of the five inputs to the model only the volatility assumption is really problematical. The spot price is available from the stock exchange; nowadays the figure is likely to be broadcast widely and continuously updated on electronic data sources such as Reuters or Bloomberg. So too is the market interest rate. The strike of a contract is a matter of agreement between the various parties, as is the time to expiry. It is not too difficult to forecast the dividend income on a share if the option expires in a few weeks or months (although with longer-dated contracts forecasting dividends becomes increasingly speculative). The most difficult question is: Where can we find the correct volatility assumption?

A useful starting point is to look at the past price behaviour of the underlying share and calculate its *historical volatility*. This is measured statistically, as the standard deviation of the percentage returns (price changes plus dividends) on the share over a historical time period. The calculation is based on percentage returns rather than the dollar price of a share to produce a measure that is comparable across different assets that trade at different price levels. Essentially, however, the concept is simple. The more extreme the fluctuations in the share price over the historical time period, the greater the volatility value that will be calculated.

Standard deviation is a measure of dispersion from an average value and is widely used in many practical applications, not just in finance and business. As an example, Figure 13.1 is a histogram showing the distribution of heights in a sample group (it was actually based on a sample of 1000 adult women in the UK). On the horizontal axis heights have been grouped into ranges. The vertical axis shows the proportion of the sample that fell into each height range. If narrower and narrower ranges were taken, the graph would increasingly begin to resemble the famous bell curve or normal distribution, as illustrated in Figure 13.2. The shape of the curve tells us that the majority of the sample is grouped around the mean or average value – i.e. most people are at or around average height, and far fewer are at the extremes at either end. A bell curve has certain defining characteristics.

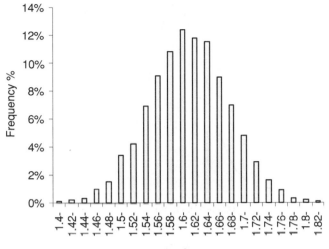

Figure 13.1   Histogram based on a sample of heights

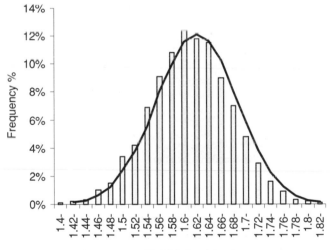

Figure 13.2   Histogram with bell curve plotted

- It has a single peak at the exact centre. The mean or average is also the value that appears most frequently in the distribution of values. Half the curve is above the mean and half below.
- The curve is symmetrical about the mean and falls off smoothly in either direction. It moves closer and closer to the horizontal axis but never actually touches it. For practical applications this is a little unrealistic. It is unlikely that any members of a human population fall into the category of being over 10 metres tall.
- In fact there is not just one but a whole family of bell curves. The shape of a curve is defined by the mean value and the standard deviation, which measures the extent to which the values tend to deviate from the mean.

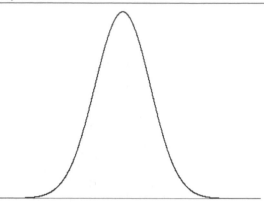

Figure 13.3   Distribution with lower standard deviation

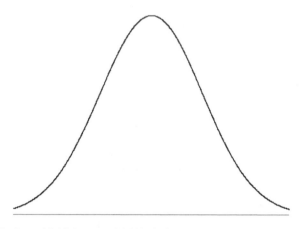

Figure 13.4   Distribution with higher standard deviation

Measuring the historical volatility of a share follows the same process as calculating the standard deviation for a sample of heights. (The method is given in Appendix A.) The first step is to find a sample of prices of the underlying share over some historical period. For example, we could use one month of daily closing prices on the stock exchange. The next step is to calculate the daily percentage price changes and the average of these values. This is the mean or the middle point of the bell curve. Volatility is measured by calculating the standard deviation – the extent to which the percentage price changes in the sample diverge from the average value. Graphically, a small standard deviation value produces a bell curve for the returns on the share that is tall and bunched around the mean (Figure 13.3). A larger standard deviation value will generate a curve that is much more spread out (Figure 13.4).

Applied to the option pricing model, what this means is that (other inputs being equal) an option on a share whose returns are assumed to follow the distribution in Figure 13.4 will be appreciably more valuable than one whose performance is assumed to follow the curve in Figure 13.3. The greater the volatility of a share, the greater the chance of an extreme price movement. This increases the expected payout to the buyer of the option, and hence the initial premium he or she will be required to pay to the writer of the contract.

IMPLIED VOLATILITY

The advantage of using historical volatility to price an option is that (normally) the sample data are readily available and the method of calculation is quite straightforward. In fact all the necessary functions required to work out the mean and the standard deviation for a set of data are included in spreadsheet packages such as Excel. However, there are serious practical and theoretical problems when using historical volatility to price options.

- *The sample data.* What is the correct historical time period on which to base the sample of price data? Perhaps it is best to use data from the last few months, since this is likely to be most representative of the current behaviour of the underlying. However, this runs the risk of not capturing the more extreme price movements that happen infrequently and at longer time intervals. We may be underestimating volatility by not incorporating such events. On the other hand, we do not wish to include data that are old and stale; the nature of the underlying share may have altered fundamentally since the data were collected.
- *The past and the future.* An even more serious problem is that historical volatility is by its very nature based on what happened to the underlying in the past. What we really need to know when pricing an option is how volatile the underlying *is going to be* over the life of the contract. This is what will really determine the expected payout to the buyer and the expected loss to the seller.

Unfortunately, in the absence of a crystal ball, there is no way of directly observing how volatile an asset will be in the future. We can only make a forecast. To some extent at least this is likely to be based on what has happened in the past – on the historical volatility – but we also need to incorporate reasonable expectations on the future events that are likely to affect the level of volatility. For example, we might observe that a share price has suffered a period of extreme turbulence in recent months, perhaps driven by factors that are specific to the company such as a boardroom crisis; or perhaps the result of general instability in the stock market caused by political or macroeconomic events. We might conclude that matters are now likely to settle down a little (possibly because the issues causing the uncertainty look likely to be resolved) and that the level of volatility over the next few months is set to decline. In a different case we may foresee future events that are likely to *increase* the volatility of a share – such as rising takeover speculation.

When options are freely traded on exchanges and in the over-the-counter market, it is quite easy to obtain data on the premiums at which they are currently being dealt. This can be used to calculate the *implied volatility* of an option. Implied volatility is the volatility assumption built into the actual dollar price of an option. It is obtained by 'operating the model backwards'. In other words, rather than use a volatility assumption to determine the dollar value of an option, we use the dollar price at which it is trading in the market to determine the volatility assumption that would generate such a price. All the other inputs to the pricing model – spot price, strike, time, carry – are kept constant. The volatility assumption is adjusted by trial-and-error until the model produces a value equal to the actual market dollar price of the option.

Implied volatility is used by dealers, by risk managers in banks and also by the buyers of options who are attempting to determine the contracts that represent good value and those that are overpriced. There are a wide range of practical applications.

- *Establishing market consensus.* Options on shares such as Microsoft and on indices such as the S&P 500 are very widely traded. From the general level of premiums being charged for such options on the market, we can extract the market's consensus expectation on what the volatility of the underlying asset is likely to be over the time to expiry of the contracts. Assuming it is a fair and efficient market with many participants, we can say that implied volatility provides us with an unbiased estimate of future volatility. It builds in the market's consensus expectations on all the future events that are likely to affect the future price behaviour of the underlying asset, based on currently available information.

- *Establishing relative value.* Since buyers and sellers can normally agree on the other inputs to valuing an option, the key issue when setting the price of a contract is deciding which volatility assumption to use. A trader who is considering buying an option can contact a dealer, ask for a price, and insert that value into the option model. This will tell the trader the volatility assumption used by the dealer to derive the option premium. If he or she believes that the share is going to be more volatile than the dealer predicts, then the trader should seriously consider buying the option. Its expected payout is likely to be greater than the premium charged by the dealer.

SHARE PRICE SIMULATIONS

The Black–Scholes model takes into account the fact that there is a very large number of possible payouts from an option contract, each of which has to be weighted according to its probability. The probabilities it uses are called *risk-neutral* probabilities. In simple terms, this means that it is assumed that the writer of an option manages the risks involved by trading in the underlying shares (this is called delta hedging and is explained in Chapters 14 and 15). The methodology is based on the assumption that the returns on a share follow a normal distribution – the famous bell curve. There is a method of replicating the result of the model using simpler calculations, although it does take a great deal longer, by setting up a so-called *Monte Carlo simulation*.

Figure 13.5 shows a histogram with the results of a Monte Carlo simulation used to price a short-dated at-the-money European call on a share struck at $100. The first step was to

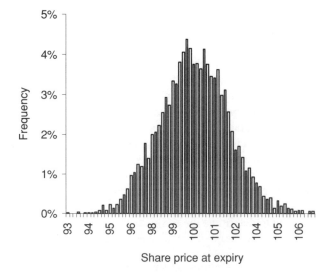

Figure 13.5   Histogram from a Monte Carlo simulation

produce a large set of random numbers. These were then used to generate a set of possible values for the underlying share at the expiry of the option, based on a starting level of $100 and incorporating a volatility assumption (and an assumption that the returns on the share follow a normal distribution). The resulting share values were grouped together into ranges on the horizontal axis. The height of the vertical bar indicates the frequency of occurrence in the simulation. The share prices that occurred most often in the simulation were in the ranges around $100. Very few values below $95 or above $105 were generated.

The call option we wish to price is a European call struck at-the-money at $100. All the share prices at $100 and below occurring in the simulation can be ignored since then the option would expire out-of-the-money with zero intrinsic value. Positive payouts occur if the share is trading above the strike at expiry. If the share value is $101 the payout is $1; if it is $102 the payout is $2; and so on. For any given share price, the histogram tells us the probability that the share will be trading at that level at the expiry of the option – this is measured on the vertical axis of the graph by the frequency of the occurrence of that value in the simulation. The European call can now be priced in four steps:

1. Take each possible share price at expiry (above the strike) and calculate the resulting payout from the option; this is simply its intrinsic value.
2. Weight each payout by the probability of receiving that payout, as measured by the frequency of the occurrence in the simulation.
3. Add up the probability-weighted payouts to calculate the average or expected payout from the option at expiry.
4. Discount the expected payout at expiry back to its present value. This establishes the value of the option.

One of the practical limitations of Black–Scholes is that the actual behaviour of shares in the real world appears not to conform to the pattern we would expect from a single bell curve. The problem is highlighted by extreme market events such as the 1987 crash, where some markets fell by over 20% in a day. These seismic events seem to occur more frequently than we would expect if the returns on shares actually followed a normal distribution.

One way to cope with this problem is to adjust the volatility assumptions used to price options in order to factor in the prospect of extreme market movements. These are often known as 'tail' events by option specialists, because they relate to share price movements at the extreme ends of the distribution curve. Another approach is to develop more complex models that alter or relax some of the assumptions of Black–Scholes – for example, models that use distributions other than the bell curve, or allow volatility to change during the life of an option.

VALUE OF A CALL AND PUT OPTION

This section firstly explores the relationship between the spot price of the underlying and the value of a call option. The example is based on a one-year option on a share struck at-the-money and valued using the Black–Scholes model adjusted for dividends. The details of the option contract are given in Table 13.2; the share price and the option premium are quoted in cents.

At a spot share price of 600, the option value, as given by the Black–Scholes model, is 13.93. Since the option is at-the-money it has zero intrinsic value and the 13.93 is all time value. What, however, will happen to the option if the spot price of the underlying changes? Table 13.3 illustrates the effects for a range of spot prices (shown in the first column) from

Table 13.2   Details of the contract

Underlying share:	XYZ
Spot/strike price:	600
Type of option:	Bought call
Time to expiry:	30 days
Volatility:	20% p.a.
Net carry:	1% p.a.
Call value:	13.93

Table 13.3   600 strike call option intrinsic and time value at different spot prices

Share price	Call value	Intrinsic value	Time value
550	0.96	0	0.96
560	1.90	0	1.90
570	3.48	0	3.48
580	5.90	0	5.90
590	9.35	0	9.35
600	13.93	0	13.93
610	19.66	10	9.66
620	26.46	20	6.46
630	34.18	30	4.18
640	42.64	40	2.64
650	51.65	50	1.65

550 up to 650. The second column shows the option value according to the model at that spot price; the third column shows how much of this is intrinsic value, and the fourth column shows the various time values.

A few examples from Table 13.3 should help to explain the figures.

- *Share price = 550*. The model values the call at 0.96. The contract is out-of-the-money and has zero intrinsic value. Therefore all the value must be time value.
- *Share price = 650*. The model values the call at 51.65. The contract is quite deeply in-the-money. Intrinsic value is 50, so time value is 1.65.

The results from Table 13.3 are graphed in Figure 13.6. The dotted line in the graph shows the total value of the option. The solid line represents intrinsic value, which is either zero or positive. The difference between the dotted line and the solid line is time value.

The graph illustrates the fact that when the share price is low and the call is deeply out-of-the-money it has zero intrinsic value and very little time value. An out-of-the-money call is rather like a bet with long odds. The stake (time value) is not very great but there is also little chance of success. As the share price increases towards the strike, the expected payout improves and the time value of the option rises.

Time value peaks around the at-the-money level – in this example, when the share price is 600 – at which point the contract behaves rather like an even bet. The graph in Figure 13.7 depicts the time value of the option against the different spot price levels, showing the peak around the 600 price level (and also looking like a bell curve). As the call moves in-the-money its value continues to rise, as it acquires more and more intrinsic value. However, the time

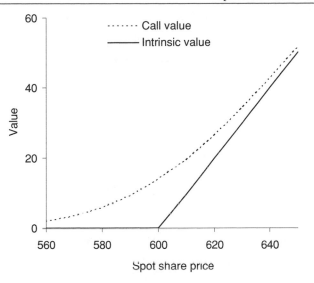

Figure 13.6   Value of 600 strike call for a range of different spot prices

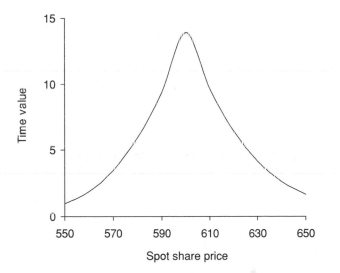

Figure 13.7   Time value of 600 strike call for a range of spot prices

value component fades away. Time value for an out-of-the-money or at-the-money call can be thought of as 'betting value'. It is a relatively small amount of money compared to the cost of buying the actual share, and the profit potential may be substantial.

However, the story starts to change when an option is in-the-money. A very deeply in-the-money long call resembles a long position in the underlying share. It is more or less certain that the contract will be exercised. However, a buyer of such a contract will have to pay a great deal of intrinsic value, which is all at risk if the share price falls, and so will not be prepared to pay much more on top by way of time value. The intrinsic value is close to what it would cost to buy the underlying share in the first place.

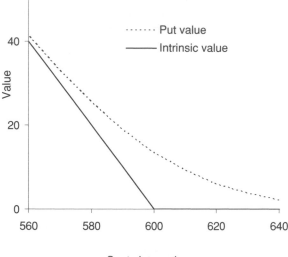

Figure 13.8   Value of 600 strike put option for a range of spot prices

Figure 13.8 shows the total value and the intrinsic value of a long European put option with similar terms to the call explored previously. The value of the option increases (decreases) as the share price falls (rises). Again intrinsic value is either zero or positive, but this time it is positive when the share price is below the strike (when the put is in-the-money). Time value is at its highest when the option is around the at-the-money level. As it moves further into the money, the long put increasingly resembles a short position in the stock. It is highly likely that it will be exercised.

PRICING CURRENCY OPTIONS

A European FX option can be valued using the variant of the Black–Scholes pricing model that is adapted for a share that pays a continuous dividend yield. (See Appendix A.) We saw that this version of the model requires five inputs:

- The spot or cash price of the underlying share
- The strike or exercise price of the option
- The time to expiry of the option
- The volatility of the underlying share
- The cost of carry – the interest rate (in effect LIBOR) less the share's dividend yield.

Take the case of a three-month European-style FX option which confers the right to sell euros and to receive US dollars in return. This is a euro put/dollar call. The spot rate €/$ is 1.15 and the strike of the option is also 1.15, i.e. 1 euro buys 1.15 US dollars. The volatility of the spot rate is 8% p.a. The 'interest rate' required by the model is the US dollar rate and the 'dividend yield' is the euro interest rate. Suppose the values are 1.15% p.a. and 2.2% p.a. respectively. The complete values are:

- Spot exchange rate = 1.15
- Strike = 1.15

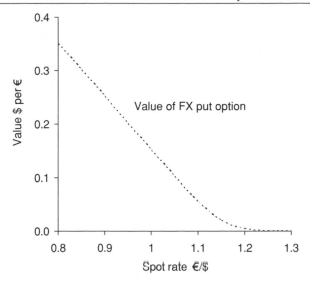

Figure 13.9   Value of long FX option (euro put/dollar call) for different spot rates

- Time to expiry = 3 months = 0.25 years
- Volatility of the spot rate = 8% p.a.
- Interest rate = 1.15% p.a.
- Dividend yield = 2.2% p.a.

Using these inputs, the option value calculated by the model is $0.0198 per €1. The volatility assumption of 8% p.a. may seem low but is quite typical for an option involving major currencies. Equity index options on the other hand can be priced at volatilities of 20% p.a. and more. It is an interesting fact that while equity markets have generally become more volatile over the past 15 years or so, the volatilities of the exchange rates between major currencies have generally declined. The explanation lies partly with the increased openness and transparency of currency markets, partly with the effects of globalization, which mean that major world economies and their currencies tend to be more closely aligned than in the past.

Figure 13.9 shows how the value of the 1.15 strike currency option is affected by changes in the spot exchange rate, all other factors remaining constant. As the spot rate falls (rises) the value of the option increases (decreases). As the spot rate falls the option starts to behave much like a short position in euros (long position in dollars). The probability of exercise is getting closer and closer to 100%.

PRICING INTEREST RATE OPTIONS

The Black–Scholes model was originally developed to price equity options. We have just seen that it can be modified to price FX or currency options. Since a bond is just another type of financial asset, it might seem reasonable to extend the methodology still further to price options on bonds.

To see where the dangers lie with this approach, consider the following case. The underlying is a one-year Treasury bond trading at $98 in the cash market. It pays no interest (it is a zero-coupon bond) but when it matures in one year the government will repay the face value of $100. We wish to value a one-year European call on the asset struck at $101. An analysis of past changes in the price of the bond suggests that the historical volatility is 5% p.a. and we decide to use this to price the option. The value of the call is quite clearly zero, since it confers the right to buy an asset for $101 in one year that can only ever be worth $100 at that point. Yet, with the above inputs (in particular the 5% volatility assumption), the Black–Scholes model will calculate a positive value.

What has gone wrong? The model assumes that over a period of time there is a chance that the price of an asset will stray from its initial spot price. Generally speaking, the longer the time to expiry, the greater the volatility of the asset, the more that is likely to happen. This is a reasonable assumption in the case of shares, whose values can theoretically rise to any level. The problem with a bond (especially a Treasury bond) is that its value tends not to deviate very far from par. Also, it does have a maximum value, the sum of all the future cash flows. Furthermore, the price of a bond tends to pull towards its par value as it approaches maturity. In the market this is sometimes known as the *pull-to-par* effect. No one is going to pay much more than $100 for a bond that redeems at par in a few days' time. As it approaches maturity the volatility of the price of a bond tends to decline. The value at maturity is fixed, and as it approaches maturity there is increasingly less uncertainty about the price at which it should be trading.

The mistake in the bond option pricing example was to use a volatility assumption based on the *historical* behaviour of the asset. Since it is a European option it can only be exercised at expiry, which is in one year's time, when the bond matures. The volatility of the bond at that point is actually zero because its maturity value is fixed at $100. This way of thinking is the basis for Black's model, developed in 1976 and still widely used, for pricing European interest rate and bond options. The model prices bond options in relation to the *forward price* of the bond at the expiry of the option. The volatility used is that of the forward price, to help to correct for the fact that volatility tends to decline as a bond approaches maturity.

The Black model is also used to price European short-term interest rate options. It prices these in relation to the forward interest rate at the expiry of the option rather than the cash market interest rate. Therefore, the volatility assumption that matters in this case is the volatility of the forward interest rate. The methodology still makes assumptions about the behaviour of interest rates over time that are open to challenge. More complex pricing methods are based on modelling the evolution of interest rates, in a way that is consistent with the forward rates that are actually observed in the market. Appendix C contains a list of references for those who would like to explore this subject further.

CHAPTER SUMMARY

The value of an option is determined by its average or expected payout. This is calculated by weighting all the possible payouts by the probability of attaining each value. The industry-standard Black–Scholes model can price options with (in effect) an infinite number of possible payouts. The model requires five inputs: the spot price of the underlying; the strike; time to expiry; the volatility of the underlying; and net carry – the cost of borrowing money less any income earned on the underlying. All other things being equal, the expected payout from a longer-dated option tends to be greater than from a shorter-dated contract. The most problematical input is the volatility of the underlying. This cannot be directly observed and must be estimated. Historical volatility is based on past movements in the price of the underlying and may not reflect the future. Implied volatility is the volatility assumption built into the dollar price of an option and incorporates expectations about the future.

An option that is deeply out-of-the-money has little time value, and the probability of exercise is low. Time value is at its highest around the at-the-money level when the probability of exercise is around 50%. As an option moves increasingly in-the-money it acquires more and more intrinsic value but the time value steadily reduces. A deeply in-the-money call closely resembles a long position in the underlying. A deeply in-the-money put is like a short position in the underlying. Currency or FX options can be priced using a modification to the Black–Scholes methodology. Interest rate options are more complex because interest rates and bond prices tend not to stray too far from their initial values. In addition, the volatility of a bond tends to reduce as it approaches maturity and its market price pulls back towards its redemption value.

14

Option Sensitivities: The 'Greeks'

INTRODUCTION

In Chapter 13 we saw that, according to the standard pricing model, the value of an option on a share is determined by five factors. (Appendix A shows how to set the model up on an Excel spreadsheet.)

- The spot or cash price of the underlying
- The strike or exercise price of the option
- Time to expiry
- The volatility of the underlying share
- The cost of carry – the interest rate to the expiry of the option less any dividend income received on the share over that period.

Dealers and investors in options are also interested in the *sensitivities* of the model. In other words, they are concerned with how changes to the inputs will affect the output value that is calculated. The sensitivities most commonly used in the market are known collectively as the 'Greeks': delta, gamma, theta, vega and rho. As vega is not actually a Greek letter, kappa is occasionally used instead. Technically speaking these are *partial derivatives* of the option pricing model. This means that they measure the change in the calculated option value for a given change in one of the inputs, all other inputs remaining constant.

The most important of the 'Greeks' is the *option delta*. This measures the sensitivity of the option value to a given small change in the price of the underlying. A bought call has positive delta. This means that the value of the contract increases as the share price rises. To that extent it is rather like a long or 'bull' position in the underlying. A bought put has negative delta. The value of the contract increases as the share price falls. This is similar to a short or 'bear' position in the underlying.

However, delta is not simply a sensitivity value. It also tells an option dealer how much of the underlying stock can be traded if he or she is to manage or hedge the risks involved in writing options. These concepts are explored in more detail in the remainder of the chapter and also in Chapter 15.

DELTA

Delta (Δ or δ) is defined as the change in the value of an option for a small change in the price of the underlying, with all the other inputs to the model remaining constant. In this and the following sections we take a specific example to help to explore the behaviour of the delta and the other 'Greeks' in more detail. The case taken throughout is that of a one-month European at-the-money call on a share. The option is valued using Black–Scholes adapted for a share that pays a continuous dividend yield. The share price and the option value are both quoted in cents. The full details of the contract are given in Table 14.1.

Table 14.1 Full details of contract

Underlying share:	XYZ
Spot price and strike price:	600
Type of option:	Long European call
Time to expiry:	30 days
Volatility:	20% p.a.
Interest rate – dividend yield:	1%
Call value:	13.93

Table 14.2 Change in call value for a small change in the underlying price

Spot share price	Call value	Absolute change
600	13.93	
599	13.42	0.51
601	14.46	0.53
	Average:	0.52

Table 14.3 Value of the delta

Long call is ...	Its delta is ...
out-of-the-money	less than 50% and converges on zero the more deeply out-of-the-money it becomes. The option is unresponsive to small changes in the underlying price. It is unlikely to be exercised.
at-the-money	around 50%. For a small change in the share price the value of the call moves (in the same direction) by about half as much.
in-the-money	above 50% and converges on 100% the more deeply in-the-money it becomes. Increasingly the call behaves like a long position in the underlying, and its value moves in line with that of the underlying.

The value of the option according to the table is 13.93 cents, but what happens to this value if the spot price of the underlying share changes? Since the contract is a long call it has *positive delta*. As the share price rises, the value of the option will also increase (all other factors remaining constant). The contract will lose value if the share price falls. Table 14.2 shows the actual effect on the value of the call for a 1 cent rise or fall in the price of the underlying.

The average of the two absolute price change values is 0.52 cents. This is the option delta. The delta tells us that for a 1 cent rise (fall) in the price of the underlying, the call will increase (decrease) in value by approximately 0.52 cents. In practice this tends to be a good approximation for small changes in the price of the underlying but increasingly inaccurate for large movements. We look at the consequences of this fact later in this and the next chapter. The 0.52 value is actually a ratio. It could also be expressed as a percentage value, i.e. 52%. This means that for a small increase (decrease) in the share price we expect the option to rise (fall) in value by approximately 52% of that change. Some market practitioners drop the percentage sign and would simply say that the option delta is 52.

The delta of a long or bought call is positive. It varies between zero and +1 or +100%. The value depends on whether the option is in-, at-, or out-of-the-money (see Table 14.3). The

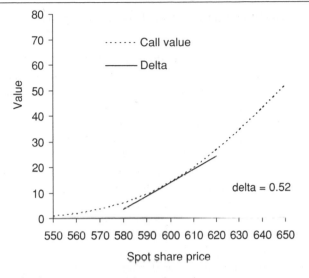

Figure 14.1   Delta as the slope or tangent on the option value curve

contract considered in the above example is at-the-money in relation to the spot price of the underlying. The spot and the strike are both 600. In effect it is rather like an 'even bet', meaning that there is roughly a 50:50 chance that it will expire in-the-money. So the call transmits about a half (in fact 52%) of a small change in the spot price of the underlying.

The delta of an out-of-the-money call is less than 50%. It is a 'longer odds' bet and is less responsive to small changes in the spot price. If a call is deeply out-of-the-money the probability of exercise is low and its delta is close to zero. The share price has to rise by a substantial amount before the option has any real chance of success. A small change of (say) 1 cent will not make any difference. If the contract moved in-the-money the delta would increase, to a limit of +1 or +100%. A deeply in-the-money long call behaves like a long position in the underlying and its price moves in line.

Figure 14.1 shows how the value of the long call option from the previous paragraphs will change for a range of possible spot prices of the underlying, all other inputs to the pricing model remaining constant. A similar graph appeared in Chapter 13 and the main difference is that Figure 14.1 also shows the slope or tangent on the option value curve at the point at which the option is at-the-money. The slope is the option delta. In this example it is about 0.52. For a 1 cent change in the spot price (shown on the horizontal axis of the graph) the call will change in value by about 0.52 cents. Because it is a long call the change in value is in the same direction: the delta is positive.

Because it is calculated as the slope on the option value curve, delta assumes a *linear relationship* between the spot price and the option value. The advantage is that it is easy to estimate from the delta the predicted change in the option value for a larger change in the spot price. It is just a matter of some basic multiplication.

- If the share price rises by 1 cent, delta predicts that the option will increase in value by about 0.52 cents.
- If the share price rises by 10 cents, delta predicts that the option will increase in value by about 5.2 cents.

- If the share price rises by 100 cents, delta predicts that the option will increase in value by about 52 cents.

The problem is that the graph in Figure 14.1 quite clearly shows that the actual relationship between the share price and the option value is non-linear. The option value describes a curve. This means that delta is just a first-order approximation of the change in the value of an option for a change in the spot price of the underlying. It works well for small changes but for larger movements it becomes increasingly inaccurate in its predictions. In this example, according to the model, the *actual* change in the value of the call for a 10 cent rise in the spot is 5.7 cents. The *actual* change for a 100 cent rise in the spot is 86.4 cents.

This might not seem like much of a problem if we bought the call at the outset at a premium of 13.93. If the spot price rises the increase in the option value is actually *greater* than that predicted by the delta. There is therefore an acceleration effect on our profit, which is shown by the positive curvature in the option value curve in Figure 14.1. If the spot falls, the value of the call will decrease, but because of the positive curvature it will fall by less than the delta prediction. There is therefore a deceleration effect on losses. This curvature is sometimes known as positive convexity, but more often in the options world it is called *positive gamma*. It is positive for bought calls and for bought puts. Gamma is covered in detail in the next section.

GAMMA

The curvature of the option value line in Figure 14.1 shows that delta, the slope on the option value curve, is not a constant. The slope is 0.52 when the option is at-the-money, but much less when the call is out-of-the-money and much more pronounced when it is in-the-money. Because of this phenomenon, and because the delta is the key to managing the risks on options, we also need a measure of the sensitivity of the delta. This is gamma (Γ or γ).

Gamma measures the change in the delta for a small change in the spot price of the underlying. It is actually a second-order Greek, since it measures the 'change in a change'. It can be observed in the graph in Figure 14.1 as the curvature on the option value line. The curvature (the gamma) is highest when the option is near the at-the-money level. When the call is deeply out-of- or in-the-money, the relationship between the spot price and the option value is almost linear (the gamma is low). In Figure 14.1 the delta of the long call when it is at-the-money is 0.52. The gamma value at that point is actually just over 0.01. This means that for a 1 cent change in the share price the delta will change by roughly 0.01.

Delta at spot price 600 cents = 0.52 or 52%
Delta at spot price 599 cents = 0.52 − 0.01 = 0.51 or 51%
Delta at spot price 601 cents = 0.52 + 0.01 = 0.53 or 53%

To help to see the effects of gamma in more detail, Figure 14.2 shows a graph of the change in the delta of the call option as the price of the underlying changes. All the other inputs to the pricing model were kept constant – the strike, the time to expiry, the volatility and the net carry. The graph illustrates what we would expect – namely, that delta moves from zero to 1 or 100% as the share price rises. When the option is at-the-money the delta is around 0.5 or 50%.

Figure 14.2 also shows that the rate of change in delta – the gamma – is highest when the option is around the at-the-money point (in this example, when the spot price is 600). When

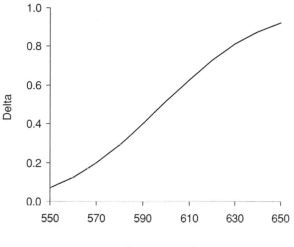

Figure 14.2 Delta of a one-month call for a range of spot prices

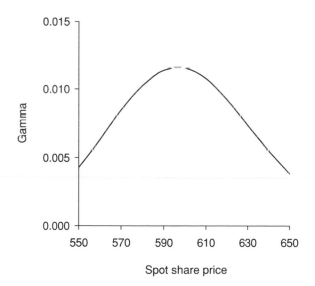

Figure 14.3 Gamma of a one-month call for a range of spot prices

the call is deeply out-of-the-money, the delta is close to zero and will not be affected by small changes in the share price. The gamma is low. When the option is deeply in-the-money the delta is close to 1 or 100%. The call is behaving rather like a long position in the share, and a small change in the spot price will not affect this fact. The delta is insensitive to small changes in the spot price, and the gamma is low, but when the option is at-the-money, the gamma is at its highest and the delta is most unstable. Figure 14.3 graphs the gamma of the call for a range of spot prices of the underlying. It is highest around 600, the at-the-money point.

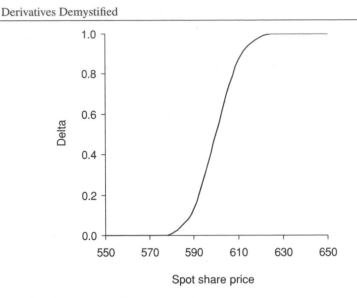

Figure 14.4   Delta of a two-day call for a range of spot prices

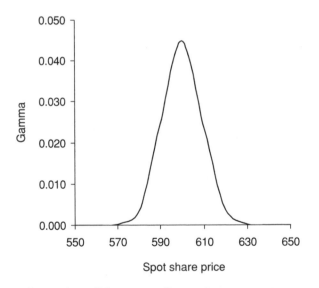

Figure 14.5   Gamma of a two-day call for a range of spot prices

Delta, gamma and expiry

What happens to delta and gamma as an option approaches expiry? Figures 14.4 and 14.5 together show the effects on the call option in the previous sections struck at 600. The data for the option are unchanged, except that it is now assumed that there are only two days remaining to expiry rather than 30.

The graphs show that if the call is deeply out-of-the-money the delta is close to zero, as before. However, the gamma has reduced considerably compared to the situation with 30 days to expiry. With only two days remaining it has become increasingly clear that the call is not going to be exercised, the delta is close to zero and is more or less rooted at that level. A similar principle would apply if the contract was deeply in-the-money. It would behave like a long position in the underlying share, and a small change in the spot price would not make any difference. As it approaches expiry the delta of an in-the-money option tends to become increasingly stable and the gamma begins to fall.

However, if the option is still at-the-money as it approaches expiry, the delta (still around 0.5) starts to become increasingly unstable. The gamma gets higher and higher. In response to a small rise in the share price, the delta of the call will suddenly rise towards 100% and the call will behave rather like a long position in the share. However, if the spot price falls even a little below the strike, the delta will collapse back towards zero. The gamma is high and the delta is extremely unstable.

THETA

Theta (Φ or ϕ) measures the change in the value of an option (all other inputs to the model remaining constant) for a given change in time to expiry. It shows the decay in an option's time value over a day or some other time period. The 30-day at-the-money long call explored in the previous sections of this chapter was worth 13.93 cents at the outset. The spot was 600 and the strike was 600. With 30 days to expiry the option has a theta per day of -0.24. This means that if one day elapses (all other factors remaining constant) the value of the call will fall by approximately 0.24 cents.

Usually theta is negative for a long (bought) option, whether it is a call or a put. Other things being equal, options tend to lose time value each day throughout their life. Figure 14.6 illustrates what happens to the long 30-day call as it approaches expiry. All the other inputs to pricing the option have been kept constant and the only factor that is changed is the time remaining to expiry. In particular, the option remains at-the-money throughout and so has zero intrinsic value.

The graph shows that the time value of the long call decays with every day that elapses toward expiry. With zero days elapsed (30 days to expiry) the option is worth about 13.93 cents. With

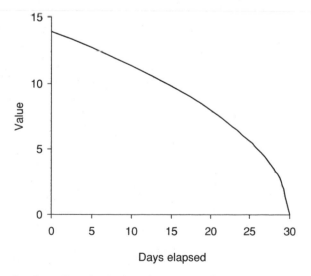

Figure 14.6   Time value decay for a 1-month at-the-money call

one day elapsed (29 days to expiry) the call is only worth about 13.69. The one-day theta is −0.24. As each day passes, the expected payout on the option falls, because for any given movement in the share price, the change is less likely to occur over 29 days than over 30 days, and is less likely still over 28 days.

Graphically, theta can be represented as the slope or tangent at a particular point on the curve in Figure 14.6. This clarifies one important issue: the theta is not a constant value – in fact the slope becomes much more pronounced as the option approaches expiry. The rate of time decay accelerates. In this example the theta value with 30 days to expiry is −0.24; with 20 days to expiry it is −0.29; and with two days to expiry it is −0.89. One simple and intuitive way to think of this phenomenon is in terms of proportions of time. A change from 30 to 29 days to expiry is a small proportional change in the remaining life of the option, and has only a small effect on time value. However, a change from two days to one day to expiry is half the remaining life of the option, and the decay in time value is much more pronounced.

VEGA

Vega (occasionally stated as kappa, κ) measures the change in the value of an option (all other factors remaining constant) for a given change in volatility, typically 1%. Vega is positive for a long call and a long put. An increase in the assumed volatility of the underlying increases the expected payout from a bought option, whether it is a call or a put. The 1% vega of the long 600 strike call considered in the previous sections is 0.68. This means that for a 1% increase (decrease) in volatility the value of the option will increase (decrease) by approximately 0.68 cents.

Call value at 20% volatility = 13.93 cents
1% vega = 0.68
Call value at 21% volatility = 14.61 cents

Figure 14.7 shows the relationship between the volatility assumption used to price the long call and (on the vertical axis) the value of the option. It is a positive relationship that is also

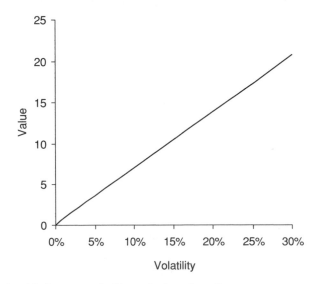

Figure 14.7   Relationship between volatility and value of a call

almost linear. As a very rough rule of thumb, doubling volatility tends to double the value of an at-the-money option.

RHO

Rho (ρ) measures the change in the value of an option for a given change in the interest rate (all other factors remaining constant). In practice, dealers normally use LIBOR as the rate concerned since they tend to fund their positions at or around LIBOR. The 1% rho for the long call explored in previous sections is 0.24. This means that for a 1% p.a. rise (fall) in rates the option value will increase (decrease) in value by about 0.24 cents.

> Call value at 4% p.a. interest rate = 13.93 cents
> 1% rho = 0.24
> Call value at 5% p.a. interest rate = 14.17 cents

Rho is positive for a long call. The purchaser of a call can invest the strike price until the expiry of the option. At higher interest rates, the benefit is that much greater than at lower interest rates, and the value of the call is higher. The phenomenon can also be explained from the perspective of the writer of the call. He or she can hedge the risk by borrowing money and buying a quantity of the underlying. If interest rates rise then the cost of borrowing will also rise and writers of calls will have to pass this on to buyers in the form of higher premiums. Figure 14.8 shows the positive (and linear) relationship between interest rates and the value of the long call.

A long put option has negative rho as its value is inversely related to interest rates. Again, one way to think about this effect is from the perspective of a dealer writing a put. He or she is exposed to a fall in the value of the asset. To hedge this risk the dealer can short the underlying and deposit the proceeds. If interest rates rise the interest earned on the deposit will also rise. The dealer can afford to pass on the additional gains to a buyer of the put in the form of a lower premium.

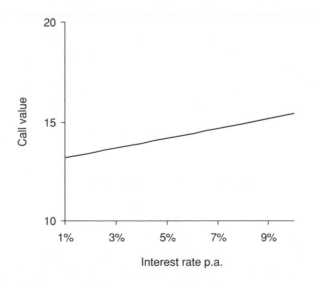

Figure 14.8   Relationship between the interest rate and call value

Table 14.4   Greeks for four basic option strategies with European options

Strategy	Delta	Gamma	Vega	Rho
Long call	+	+	+	+
Long put	−	+	+	−
Short call	−	−	−	−
Short put	+	−	−	+

SIGNS OF THE 'GREEKS'

The previous sections in this chapter have explored the 'Greeks' on a long 30-day European call option. The values and 'signs' of the 'Greeks' can be summarized as follows:

- *Delta 0.52 or 52%.* For a 1 cent rise (fall) in the spot price the value of the long call position will increase (decrease) by about 0.52 cents. The spot price and the option value move in the same direction, i.e. the relationship is positive.
- *Gamma 0.01 or 1%.* For a 1 cent rise (fall) in the spot price the option delta will increase (decrease) by about 0.01. The relationship is also positive.
- *Theta −0.24.* As one day elapses, the value of the option will fall by about 0.24 cents. The relationship between time passing and option value is negative or inverse.
- *Vega 0.68.* If volatility rises (falls) by 1% p.a., the value of the long call will increase (decrease) by about 0.68 cents. The relationship is positive.
- *Rho 0.24.* If interest rates rise (fall) by 1% p.a., the value of the long call position will increase (decrease) by about 0.24 cents. The relationship is positive.

Table 14.4 sets out the 'signs' of the Greek letters for a long call and for three other basic option strategies using European options. Theta is not included as it is generally negative for a bought option and positive for a written option, although there are some exceptions, often involving quite deeply in-the-money contracts.

The table shows that gamma is positive for long option positions. This means that for larger movements in the spot price the profits tend to exceed those predicted by delta while the losses are lower than predicted. This is the effect of the positive curvature (positive convexity) in the relationship between the spot price and the value of the option position. The table also shows that gamma is negative for short (written) calls and puts. Negative curvature (convexity) can be extremely dangerous as losses on positions tend to accelerate beyond that predicted by delta, and profits tend to decelerate. The next chapter is devoted to exploring these effects.

CHAPTER SUMMARY

The 'Greeks' are sensitivity measures. They show the change in the value of an option for a given small change in one of the input values to the pricing model, all other inputs being held constant. Delta measures sensitivity to a small change in the spot price of the underlying; gamma measures the stability of delta; theta measures the change in the value of an option as time passes; vega measures the sensitivity to changes in volatility; and rho to changes in interest rates.

The delta of a bought call is positive. Its value increases (decreases) as the share price rises (falls). The gamma is also positive. If the underlying price rises (falls) the delta will become more (less) positive. This means that profits tend to accelerate and losses to decelerate. A long put has negative delta and positive gamma. Its value increases (decreases) as the price of the underlying falls (rises). The positive gamma means that profits tend to accelerate and losses to decelerate; the most money that can be lost is the initial premium that was paid.

15

Managing Trading Risks on Options

INTRODUCTION

This chapter discusses how the 'Greeks' and in particular delta and gamma are used to measure and manage the risks on a short option position. It considers these risks from a trading perspective and from the viewpoint of the seller or writer of a contract operating in the dealing room, rather than that of the end-user of the product working in a company or investing institution. Certain concepts reappear in the next chapter which investigates a number of key option strategies used by professional traders and dealers. Those who are not likely to be concerned with trading and risk management issues as they affect option portfolios may wish to move on to Chapters 17 and 18. These chapters explore convertible and exchangeable bonds and a range of structured securities assembled using derivative products.

Delta is not just a sensitivity measure, although that is an important application. It is also the number that tells an option trader how to cover or hedge the risks on an option position. The problem is that the delta of an option is not stable. It changes as the spot price moves; the extent of its instability is measured by the option gamma. This fact poses serious problems for the writers of options. If a short option position has high gamma the writer will have to consider readjusting his or her hedge at frequent intervals. The result can be very expensive indeed, as the extended case study in this chapter demonstrates.

DELTA RISK ON A SHORT CALL

We return to the call option investigated in the previous chapter. This time, however, the contract is considered from the perspective of the writer rather than the purchaser. Also, to make the example more realistic, the contract will be based on 10 000 shares rather than a single share. The other data are as before. The spot and the strike are both 600 cents and the option is sold at a premium of 13.93 cents per share – the fair value calculated in the previous chapter using the pricing model. The buyer of the contract has the right but not the obligation to purchase 10 000 XYZ shares and to pay $10\,000 \times \$6 = \$60\,000$ for those shares.

The total premium payable is $10\,000 \times \$0.1393 = \$1393$. This is paid by the buyer of the contract at the outset. In fact, it is the maximum profit the writer can ever make on the deal. The full details of the contract from the perspective of the writer are set out in Table 15.1.

The delta of the short call is -0.52 per share or -52%, where the minus sign means that, for the writer of the option, the profit and loss on the position moves *inversely* with the value of the underlying share. If the spot price of the underlying increased by 1 cent, then the value of the call would rise by 0.52 cent per share. Unfortunately this would be a loss for the writer, who is short the option. If the share price fell by 1 cent, then the call would move out-of-the-money, resulting in a profit for the writer, who could repurchase the option for 0.52 cent per share less than the premium at which it was sold.

Table 15.1   Written call option contract on 10 000 shares

Underlying:	XYZ share
Spot price:	600 cents
Strike price:	600 cents
Contract type:	Short call
Number of XYZ Shares:	10 000
Time to expiry:	30 days
Exercise type:	European
Premium received	$1393

The delta on the short call can also be expressed in terms of the total number of shares on which it is written. This is the *position delta*. Here the contract is based on 10 000 shares, so it is calculated as follows:

$$\text{Position delta} = -10\,000 \text{ shares} \times 0.52 = -5200 \text{ shares}$$

This value tells us that for a 1 cent rise (fall) in the spot price, the loss (profit) on the short call is roughly the same as that on a short position in 5200 shares (assuming that all other inputs to pricing the option are held constant). To see why this is the case, recall that the initial premium received for selling the contract was $1393. To close out the short option position the writer would have to buy back the contract. If the spot price increased by 1 cent to 601 then the value of the call (according to the pricing model) would be 14.45 cents per share. On 10 000 shares this is $1445. So if the writer bought back the call the loss would be $52.

$$\text{Contract sale price} - \text{Repurchase price} = \$1393 - \$1445 = -\$52$$

On the other hand, if the share price fell by 1 cent, all other factors remaining constant, then the writer of the option would be in profit to the extent of about $52. The option contract could be repurchased for $52 less than the initial sale premium received. These are the same profits and losses we would expect on a short position in 5200 shares. The position delta is in fact a very useful value for the option writer. It also shows that for small movements in the spot price, the profits and losses on the contract can be balanced out by a long position in 5200 XYZ shares, that is, by buying 5200 shares in the underlying. Suppose, for example, that the spot price increased by 1 cent, then the writer would lose about $52 on the call but make about $52 on the 5200 shares.

$$\begin{aligned} \text{Loss on option} &= \text{Contract sale price} - \text{Repurchase price} \\ &= \$1393 - \$1445 = -\$52 \\ \text{Profit on shares} &= 5200 \text{ shares} \times \$0.01 = \$52 \end{aligned}$$

This also works in reverse. If the spot price fell by 1 cent then a loss of $52 on the 5200 shares would be balanced by a $52 profit on the short option contract, which would become less expensive to repurchase. Balancing out the risks on an option position in this way is called *delta hedging*. A trader who has hedged out the risk on an option position by delta hedging is said to have a position that is *delta neutral*. There is no exposure to small changes in the spot price of the underlying. However, as we will see in the next section, this does not mean that all the risks have been managed.

DELTA HEDGING AND GAMMA

Delta hedging works well for small movements, such as 1 cent, in the spot price of the underlying. What if the movement in the spot price is more substantial? The answer is that the delta hedge would not be as efficient. The reason is because the option has gamma; in other words, the delta is not stable. As the spot price changes, the delta of the option contract will also change. If the movement is substantial then the original delta hedge (in our example the purchase of 5200 shares) would no longer match the risk on the option contract.

To illustrate this point, suppose that the underlying share price suddenly jumped from 600 to 610 cents. The pricing model values the option now at 19.66 cents per share or $1966 on the contract. It is more expensive than formerly because it has moved in-the-money. The writer sold the contract at the outset for a total premium of $1393, so repurchasing the contract to close out would result in a loss.

$$\text{Loss on option} = \$1393 - \$1966 = -\$573$$

Unfortunately, the profit on the shares purchased in the delta hedge would not be sufficient to balance this out, resulting in a net loss of about $53. The hedge consisted of 5200 shares and in this scenario the share price has risen by 10 cents or $0.1.

$$\text{Profit on shares} = 5200 \text{ shares} \times \$0.1 = \$520$$

The problem is illustrated graphically in Figure 15.1. The dotted line shows the profit and loss to the writer of the call option in dollars if the spot moves in a range between 550 and 650 cents. The straight line shows the profit and loss on the 5200 shares purchased in the delta hedge. All the other inputs to valuing the option are held constant. There is still 30 days to expiry, volatility has not changed and the net cost of carry is the same.

The profit and loss profile for the shares is linear. However, the option exhibits negative curvature or convexity, better known in the options business as negative gamma. In simple terms,

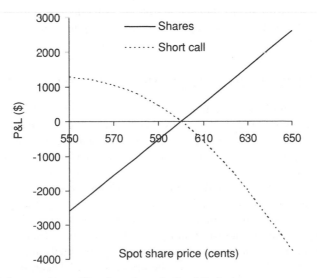

Figure 15.1   Profit/loss on short call and on shares in the delta hedge

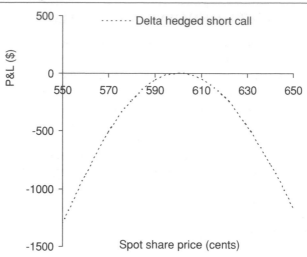

Figure 15.2   Net profit/loss on delta hedged short call option

this means that for large increases in the spot price the losses on the option contract accelerate. For large falls in the spot price the profits decelerate and 'pull back' towards a maximum of $1393. For very small movements in the price of the underlying, profits and losses on the option and on the shares more or less cancel out. The curvature in the option value line does not have any real effect. However, for large changes it does, and there is a substantial discrepancy between the profits and losses on the option and on the shares.

This is a problem for the writer of the call regardless of whether the spot price rises or falls. If it rises then the loss on the option accelerates because of the negative curvature (gamma), while the gains on the shares are linear. If the spot price falls the losses on the shares linear, but the profit on the option pulls back towards the initial premium – the maximum profit on a short option position is the premium received at the outset. Figure 15.2 illustrates this fact graphically by showing the *net profit and loss* on the delta hedged position – short the call option, long the 5200 shares – for a range of possible spot prices. Again, the other inputs to the pricing model are kept constant.

PROFIT FROM A SHORT CALL POSITION

An impartial observer looking at the graph in Figure 15.2 might easily conclude that writing the option is not much of a deal. It is so risky that it was hedged by buying a quantity of the underlying stock. However, it seems that the best that can happen is that the net profit and loss on the delta hedged position is zero! If the movement in the spot price is substantial then in theory the potential losses are infinite.

The point of course is that the graph looks at the position at a specific moment in time, and with all the inputs to pricing the option other than the spot price remaining constant. It is not surprising that the deal seems to lose money if the share price moves sharply in either direction – the writer of an option has a negative vega (volatility) position. In other words, the position tends to lose money if the underlying is more volatile than predicted when the option was sold.

What kind of market would the writer of the option prefer? The answer is, one in which the share price trades in a narrow range. If at the expiry of the call the share is still trading at

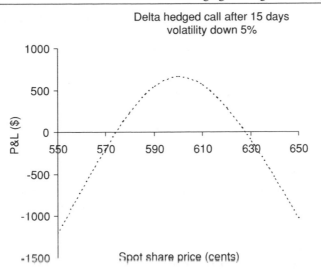

Figure 15.3   Profit/loss on hedged short call after 15 days and with a decline in volatility

600 cents then the contract would expire worthless with zero intrinsic value. The 5200 shares purchased in the delta hedge could then be sold off at zero profit or loss. Overall, the writer would have made a profit of $1393, the initial premium received by selling the option contract (less transaction costs).

The delta hedged position could also be closed out *before* expiry, by repurchasing the call option and selling the 5200 shares in the delta hedge. Figure 15.3 shows the net profit and loss that would result from doing this, for a range of possible spot prices, but this time it is assumed that 15 days has elapsed since the option was sold. It is also assumed that volatility has declined by 5% p.a. The graph shows that provided the spot price of the underlying has remained in a range somewhere between 575 and 628 cents, the delta hedged position could be closed out at a profit (by repurchasing the call and selling the shares).

CHASING THE DELTA

To go right back to the beginning of the story, suppose the writer of the call has just sold the contract for a premium of $1393 and bought 5200 shares to manage the delta risk. There is still 30 days to expiry. We saw previously that if the share price then suddenly jumped to 610 the losses on the short call would exceed the profits on the shares in the delta hedge by about $53. However, unless the writer of the option actually closed everything out at that point by repurchasing the call and selling the shares, this would be an unrealized loss (also called a marked-to-market loss). Nevertheless, the option writer would have some difficult decisions to make. There are at least three choices.

- *Do nothing.* Leave the position as it is, with the option hedged with the initial purchase of 5200 shares. The problem is that if the share price continued to rise then the discrepancy between the losses on the call and the profits on the shares would get worse. In theory the potential net loss is infinite.

- *Close out.* Repurchase the option contract, sell the 5200 shares and actually realize the net loss of $53.
- *Adjust the hedge.* Readjust the delta hedge to protect against further increases in the spot price.

Here we explore the third possibility in a little more detail, sometimes known as 'chasing the delta'. Writing a call option is not only a negative delta position, it is also a negative gamma position, which means that if the spot price rises the delta becomes even more negative. In this particular case if the spot price rose to 610 cents then the delta on the short call would no longer be −5200 shares. It would actually be about −6300 shares, i.e. the short call would behave rather like a short position in 6300 shares. The problem is that the option writer only bought 5200 shares in the first instance to manage the delta risk, and the position is no longer delta neutral. However, it could easily be restored to delta neutrality by buying a further 1100 shares.

> At share price = 610 cents
> Short call delta now = −6300 shares
> Shares currently in hedge = 5200 shares
> Additional shares required = 1100 shares

The purchase price would be 610 cents per share. Adopting this strategy would give the writer additional protection against further increases in the share price. However there is a sting in the tail. Let us assume that the share price rose to 610 cents and the writer of the option bought the extra 1100 shares to restore delta neutrality. Let us also assume that the share price then suddenly dropped back again to 600 cents. This would create a real problem as the option delta would fall back to −5200 shares and the writer would have 1100 too many shares in the delta hedge. Selling off these shares at 10 cents below the purchase price of 610 cents would crystallize a loss.

> Realized loss = 1100 shares × −$0.1 = −$110

This is almost 10% of the premium at which the contract was initially sold and there are still 30 days remaining to expiry! The lesson is that while it is possible for the writer of an option to adjust or 'chase' the delta continually when the spot price moves, the result might well be a series of crystallized or realized losses.

Some option traders have a very simple and useful way of looking at the premium received from selling an option. It is a sum of money that can be used to readjust the delta hedge from time to time. As long as the price of the underlying stays within the volatility assumption used to price the option contract, the delta can be readjusted periodically and there will still be some of the premium remaining at expiry. But if the underlying is much more volatile than initially forecast, then losses on readjusting the delta hedge will exceed the initial premium collected. As ever with options, the key to success lies with an accurate forecast of the volatility of the underlying over the life of the contract.

PRACTICAL CONSTRAINTS ON HEDGING

There are a number of practical issues with the delta hedging methodology that will impact on the premium that dealers actually charge for writing options. This is because the Black–Scholes model makes a number of simplifying assumptions that may not always be realistic in practice.

- *Transaction costs.* It ignores transaction costs such as commissions and the spreads between bid (buy) and offer or ask (sell) prices. A dealer who is delta hedging an option will normally have to suffer such costs and this has to be factored into the premium charged for the contract. The problem is acute with volatile assets in less liquid markets which can trade with very high bid/offer spreads.
- *Perfect liquidity.* The model assumes that the writer of an option can continually trade the underlying asset to manage the delta risk without difficulty and without affecting the price of the underlying. Again the option premium will have to be adjusted if this is not the case.
- *Continuous random path.* Black–Scholes assumes that the price of the underlying trades continuously and moves through all levels without sudden jumps. Illiquid assets do not trade very frequently and their prices can display discontinuous movements.
- *Constant volatility.* The model assumes that the volatility of the underlying is known and constant throughout the life of an option. In fact the volatility must be forecast, and volatility is not constant. In more extreme markets it can climb alarmingly.
- *Normal distribution.* The model assumes that the returns on the underlying follow a bell curve. In fact there is plenty of evidence that this is not completely accurate, particularly in equity markets. The actual distribution of the returns on a share tends to exhibit what is sometimes called a 'fat tail'. The probability of extreme movements in the stock price is greater than can be modelled on a single bell curve.

We saw three or four major stock market crashes in the twentieth century, depending on the definition used. If the returns on shares were normally distributed on a single bell curve, these events should not come round nearly as often – perhaps some should never occur in the entire history of the planet! The Black–Scholes assumptions are not too difficult to accept in normal market conditions and with certain assets (such as major currency pairs) which are extremely actively traded. However, if a dealer feels that there may be difficulty in managing the delta hedge in practice, then he or she will load this into the premium quoted for an option.

The problem is extreme in the case of options on the shares of smaller companies, where it may be difficult to buy and sell the underlying and any significant purchases or sales are likely to affect the market price. In addition, information about the company may be sparse and unreliable, and the share price may be subject to sudden jumps rather than moving continuously through ranges.

The good news about trading options is that there are real advantages to scale. A dealer who buys and sells significant quantities of call and put options on the same underlying will normally find that many of the risks (as measured by the Greek letters) offset each other. Only the residual risks need be monitored and potentially hedged out, which can save heavily on transaction costs. The dealer will always be charging a spread between the price at which he or she sells and buys contracts. In addition, the dealer may not run the book on a completely delta neutral basis, i.e. overall he or she takes a long or a short position in the underlying. This can generate additional and welcome profits, providing of course the price of the underlying moves in the desired direction.

CHAPTER SUMMARY

Writers of options can manage risk on their short positions by buying and selling quantities of the underlying. A position that is not exposed to small movements in the spot price of the underlying is said to be delta neutral. The problem is that delta is not a constant. The rate of change in delta is measured by gamma. A option writer who trades in the underlying to match the delta risk will find that the profits and losses do not cancel out if the movement in the price of the underlying is substantial. The writer can readjust the delta hedge from time-to-time but runs the risk of realizing a series of losses if the underlying proves to be more volatile than predicted. If the underlying behaves as predicted, the writer should be able to manage the delta risk and achieve an overall profit on the option transaction.

In practice there are a number of constraints on delta hedging. Transaction costs mean that it is not possible to readjust the delta hedge continually as the pricing model demands. Less liquid stocks may be difficult to trade without moving the spot price, and the spot price may be subject to sudden jumps. Volatility can change over the life of an option, and there is a danger of extreme movements in the price of the underlying. Option writers have to take these constraints into account when deciding on the premium they charge for options. However, there are advantages of scale in running a book or portfolio of options since the risks can net out.

16

Option Trading Strategies

INTRODUCTION

A long call is a straightforward 'bull' strategy – if the price of the asset rises the call also increases in value. Similarly, a long put is a straightforward bear position and profits from a fall in the value of the underlying. However, these are far from being the only possibilities on offer. Options are extremely flexible tools that can be employed in many combinations to construct strategies with widely differing risk and return characteristics.

Nowadays even more tools are available due to the creation of exotic options – products such as barriers and compound options encountered previously. In this and subsequent chapters further new instruments are introduced: average price or Asian options; digital or binary options; forward start options; choosers; and cliquet or ratchet options which are designed to lock in intervening gains resulting from movements in the price of the underlying asset.

The structuring desk of a modern securities firm is the place where these various products are brought together. The firm's sales and marketing staff speak to a client about trading and hedging requirements, map out the problem, and ask their colleagues in the structuring desk to help to design a solution appropriate for that client. As the available tools become more varied and sophisticated, there is considerable opportunity for creativity in the process. Progress towards a solution tends to be iterative. The first set of ideas may not be very appealing to the client because the premium cost is too high, or there are unattractive currency exposures, or there are tax implications, or the levels at which the strategy makes and loses money do not coincide with the client's opinion on where the market is moving. There are, however, many ways of adjusting the structure. Strikes can be changed or additional options incorporated that affect the premium or the overall risk/return characteristics. Eventually a solution is assembled that the sales people agree is appropriate for the client. The various components – the individual options and other derivative products from which it is constructed – are priced ultimately by the firm's traders. Once the solution is agreed and signed, the traders manage the various risks that the house acquires as a result of doing the deal with its client.

This chapter continues the investigation of structuring solutions using derivatives, and discusses some key trading strategies. Some of these are used to implement directional views on the movement in the price of an underlying asset; others are concerned with profiting from changes in the volatility of an asset. They all have in common, however: That there is no overall solution that is correct for all circumstances. The trade could be done in many different ways to suit different market conditions and forecasts.

BULL SPREAD

As the name suggests, a bull spread is a bet that the price of the underlying asset will increase. If the price falls the loss is restricted, but the potential profit is capped. To illustrate how this works, suppose a trader believes that the spot price of XYZ share (currently 100) is very

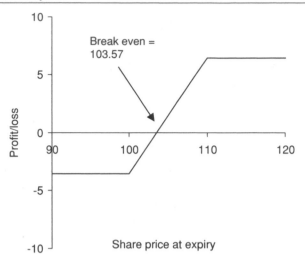

Figure 16.1   Bull spread expiry payoff profile

likely to increase over the next few months, although within a tightly defined range. The trader contacts an option dealer and constructs a bull spread with the following components. The net premium payable on the trade is 3.57. (The currency units are not important here, they could be pence, cents or any other unit.)

Contract	Expiry	Strike	Premium
Long call on XYZ share	3 months	100	−6.18
Short call on XYZ share	3 months	110	+2.61

Figure 16.1 shows the payoff profile of the bull spread at the expiry of the options. The maximum loss is the net premium. The potential profit is capped at 6.43 when the share price is trading at 110, the strike of the short call. The break-even point is reached when the stock is trading at 103.57. The advantage of this strategy compared to buying the 100 strike call on its own is that the net premium payable is reduced.

Figure 16.2 takes a rather different perspective on the deal. It looks at the value of the strategy on the day it is put in place, not at expiry, and assumes that the spot price changes on that day in the range 70–130, with all the other inputs to pricing the option being constant. If the share price increases then the trade can be unwound by selling the 100 strike call and buying back the 110 strike call. The maximum profit is still 6.43 (ignoring the time value of money effects).

The bull spread can also be constructed using put options. In this case it would involve selling an in-the-money put struck at 110 and buying an out-of-the-money put struck at 100. The advantage here is that net premium would be received rather than paid at the outset, although taking the time value of money fully into account there is actually no difference in the ultimate payoff.

BULL POSITION WITH DIGITAL OPTIONS

An alternative to the bull spread is to buy a digital or binary call option on the underlying share XYZ. The net premium payable on the bull spread in the previous section was 3.57. At roughly the same cost a dealer could offer a three-month *cash-or-nothing* (CON) digital call

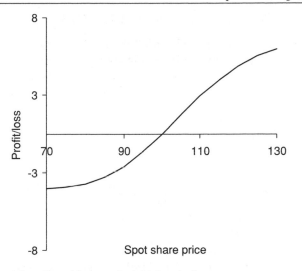

Figure 16.2 Bull spread profit and loss on the initial trade date

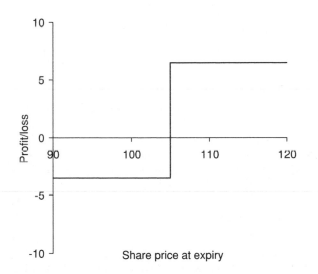

Figure 16.3 Profit/loss at expiry on digital call option with strike 105 and cash payout 10

option on the share struck at 105 and with a cash payout of 10. The CON call works as follows: if at expiry the share price is above 105 and the option is in-the-money then the payout is 10; otherwise it is zero. Figure 16.3 illustrates the position at expiry. The net profit and loss is the payout (either 0 or 10) less the premium. The maximum profit is 10 less the premium while the maximum loss is simply the premium.

In this case the premium on the digital option is roughly the same as for the bull spread, the maximum loss and the maximum profit at expiry are about the same, but the nature of the bet is a little different. The digital option is for someone who is convinced that the share price is going to be trading above (but not much above) 105 at expiry. If it is in the range 100 to 105 the CON call pays out nothing at all – unlike the bull spread – but if the spot is higher than

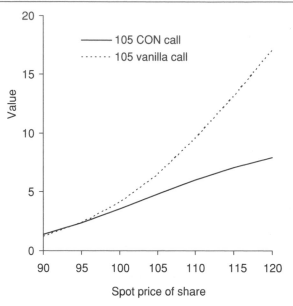

Figure 16.4   Value of a cash-or-nothing call for different spot prices

105 the entire cash payout of 10 is due. The payout on the CON call could be increased, but at the expense of additional premium. For example, a cash-or-nothing call with similar terms but a payout of 20 would cost about twice as much in premium.

The behaviour of a digital option in response to changes in the spot price of the underlying is interesting. This is illustrated in Figure 16.4. The dotted line in the graph shows the value of a 105 strike standard or vanilla call option. The solid line is a 105 strike cash-or-nothing call with a payout of 10. In both cases there are three months to expiry. As the share price increases, the value of the vanilla call continues to rise and begins to behave rather like a long position in the underlying. However, the value of the CON call converges on the cash payout (actually its present value). The probability of exercise is approaching 100% but the payout is fixed at 10 and cannot be any higher regardless of the value of the underlying in the spot market.

There are many other variants available. For example, an asset-or-nothing (AON) option pays out the value of the underlying asset if it expires in-the-money, otherwise nothing. In other cases binary options are structured such that they only pay out if the underlying has hit a threshold or barrier level during a defined period of time.

BEAR SPREAD

A bear spread gains from a fall in the value of the underlying but with limited profit and loss potential. In the following example the strategy is assembled using European puts on the same underlying share considered in the previous sections with a spot price of 100. The net premium payable on the trade is 2.22, which is also the maximum loss. The maximum profit is achieved when the underlying share is trading at 95. Below that level any gains on the long 100 strike put are offset by losses on the short 95 strike put. The expiry payoff profile is shown in Figure 16.5.

Contract	Expiry	Strike	Premium
Long put	3 months	100	−5.68
Short put	3 months	95	+3.46

Table 16.1   Greeks for the bear spread

Option	Delta	Gamma	Theta (1day)	Vega (1%)	Rho (1%)
Long 100 put	−0.455	0.026	−0.029	0.197	−0.128
Short 95 put	0.325	−0.024	0.027	−0.179	0.090
Net: bear spread	−0.130	0.002	−0.002	0.018	−0.038

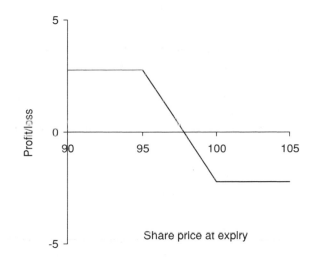

Figure 16.5   Bear spread expiry payoff profile

It is not necessary, of course, to maintain a position like this all the way to the expiry of the two options. It could be closed out at any point by selling a 100 strike put and buying a 95 strike put on the same underlying with the same time to expiry. Whether this realizes a profit or a loss depends on what has happened to the share price in the meantime, and to changes in the other factors that determine the values of the two options.

To give an idea of the exposures that are involved, Table 16.1 shows the values of the 'Greeks' for the long 100 put, the short 95 call, and the net of these values. (For more information on the Greeks and how they are used by traders see Chapters 14 and 15.)

The Greeks for the bear spread are the sums of the values of the components of the strategy. As always, the assumption is that all other inputs to the pricing model remain constant. For example, the delta assumes that the time to expiry, volatility and net carry remain the same, and only the spot price of the underlying is changed. The vega assumes that the spot, the time to expiry and the carry are held constant and only the volatility is changed. The values in Table 16.1 are interpreted as follows (again, the units might be pence, cents or some other small unit):

- *Delta −0.13.* For a small rise (fall) in the price of the underlying of 1 unit the bear spread shows a loss (a profit) of approximately 0.13 units per share. The fact that delta is negative indicates that this is a bear strategy – it profits from a fall in the share price.
- *Gamma 0.002.* For a small rise of 1 unit in the price of the underlying the delta will change from −0.13 to −0.13 + 0.002 = −0.128. For a fall of 1 unit in the underlying the delta will move to −0.13 − 0.002 = −0.132.

- *Theta −0.002.* If one day elapses (all other factors remaining constant) the bear spread will lose approximately 0.002 units in value. The strategy will suffer a little from time value decay though not to any great extent. It consists of a long and a short three-month option and the theta effects more-or-less cancel out.
- *Vega 0.018.* If volatility increases (decreases) by 1% p.a. the bear spread will increase (decrease) in value by 0.018 units. The strategy is not particularly sensitive to changes in volatility.
- *Rho −0.038.* If interest rates rise (fall) by 1% p.a. the bear spread will decrease (increase) in value by 0.038 units. Again the rho is not high. The values on the short and long puts just about cancel out.

The key exposure with this trade is the negative delta. It tells us that this is indeed a bear strategy. The other Greeks are not high values, although the slightly positive gamma may be a small benefit. When the gamma on an option strategy is positive this is an example of what is sometimes called a 'right-way' exposure. This means that if the price of the underlying falls the strategy either becomes more of a short position or less of a long position, and if the price rises it becomes more of a long position or less of a short position. However, the gamma effect is rather limited in this example since one option was bought and another was sold.

A more clear-cut example of a positive gamma trade would consist of buying a call that is at-the-money and approaching expiry (a put would display similar characteristics). The delta of the call will be around plus 0.5 and the gamma positive. It will behave rather like a position in half a share. But if the spot price falls the delta will be less positive, to the limit of zero, at which point there is no effective exposure to the share price, and if the spot rises the delta will become more positive, to the limit of 1 or 100%, at which point the call will behave like a long position in the share. Later examples in this chapter show that negative gamma positions are 'wrong way' exposures. Whether the underlying rises or falls, the exposure to changes in the price of the underlying tends to move in exactly the wrong direction.

PUT OR BEAR RATIO SPREAD

In the spread trades examined so far in this chapter, a long call or put on one share is balanced out by a short call or put also on one share. It is possible to construct spread trades using different ratios. The ratio spread trade shown below uses European put options. The underlying is the same as before and the spot price is 100. The net premium payable is 0.8 (again, the units could be pence, cents or in some other currency).

Contract	Expiry	Strike	Premium per share	Total premium
Long put on 1 XYZ share	3 months	100	−5.68	−5.68
Short put on 2 XYZ shares	3 months	92	+2.44	+4.88

Figure 16.6 shows the expiry payoff profile. At a spot price of 100 and above, all the options expire worthless. The overall loss is the net premium. Below 100 the long 95 strike put is in-the-money. The maximum profit of 7.2 is reached when the share price is at 92. It consists of 8 intrinsic value on the long 100 strike put, less the net premium. Below 92 the short put comes into effect. However, since it is written on two shares in this case, the line does not flatten out but falls at a 45 degree angle.

The bear ratio spread is a useful strategy when a trader believes the share price is likely to fall, but to a limited extent. The loss is restricted if the share price actually rises. However the

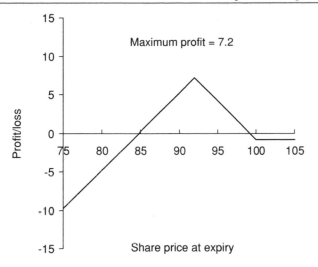

Figure 16.6   Bear ratio spread expiry payoff profile

potential losses if it crashes are quite considerable. At a share price of zero the loss on the strategy is 84.8. The rate of loss depends on the ratio of options bought and sold. For example, the trader could increase the proportion to 1:3. This is a much more risky trade, although in this example net premium would be received at the outset.

LONG STRADDLE

A long straddle is essentially a bet on rising volatility levels. It consists of a long call and a long put on the same underlying with the same strike and the same time to expiry. The strike is often set around the at-the-money level, as in the following example, which uses the same underlying share from previous sections, trading at 100 in the spot market.

Contract	Expiry	Strike	Premium
Long call	3 months	100	−6.18
Long put	3 months	100	−5.68

The disadvantage of the trade is that two lots of premium have to be paid, totalling 11.86. On the other hand, this is the maximum loss. Figure 16.7 shows the expiry payoff profile. The break-even points are reached when the underlying is trading at 88.14 or at 111.86. As long as the price has broken out of that range, in either direction, the strategy shows a profit. The trade is suitable for someone who considers that the share is set to rise or fall sharply over the next few months, but is not sure of the direction the movement will take. The stimulus could be the immanent release of financial results that are likely to impact on the share price, positively or negatively; or simply a period of uncertainty ahead, which will move the price out of its current trading range.

A long straddle is *long volatility* trade – the vega is positive. In other words (all other factors remaining constant), if the volatility assumption used to price the two options rises, they will increase in value and the long straddle will move into profit.

The delta at the outset, with at-the-money options, is normally quite close to zero. The gamma is positive which means that it is a 'right-way' exposure. If the spot price continues to

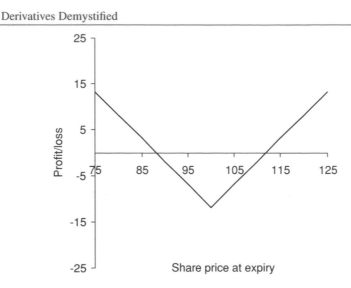

Figure 16.7   Long straddle expiry payoff profile

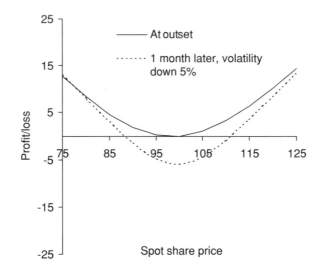

Figure 16.8   Profit/loss on straddle in response to changes in the spot price

rise, the straddle will become delta positive, i.e. it will behave increasingly like a long position in the underlying. If the spot continues to fall, it will become delta negative, i.e. it will behave increasingly like a short position. Unfortunately the strategy is normally also theta negative so that it tends to suffer from time value decay.

The solid line in Figure 16.8 shows how the profit and loss on the strategy is affected by changes in the spot price of the underlying on the day it is put in place. Other factors are held constant – there is still three months to expiry, the volatility and the carry have not changed. The effects of bid–offer spreads are also ignored. At a spot price of 100 the profit is zero. The long straddle could be sold back into the market for exactly the same premium at which it was purchased. But if the spot price rises, the call will move increasingly in-the-money. The put will lose value, but the maximum loss is the initial premium paid. Similarly, if the spot falls the put will move in-the-money but the loss on the call is restricted to the premium paid.

The dotted line in Figure 16.8 shows the profit and loss on the straddle after one month has elapsed and with the assumption that volatility has declined by 5%. The curve has shifted downwards because the two options have lost time value. Roughly speaking, the spot price of the underlying would have to have risen or fallen by about 11 to compensate for the losses resulting from falling volatility and time decay (the vega and the theta effects).

CHOOSER OPTION

The problem with the long straddle is that premium has to be paid on both the call and the put. The strategy tends to suffer from time value decay and is sensitive to declining volatility. The time decay effect will become more exaggerated if the options are still around the at-the-money level as the expiry date approaches. One way to reduce the net premium is to buy a *chooser option*. Here the buyer has the right to decide, after a set period of time, whether it is to be a call or a put. The example in this section is based on the same underlying used previously, trading at 100 in the spot market. The details of the contract are as follows:

Contract	Expiry	Strike	Time to choose	Premium
Long chooser	3 months	100	1 month	−9.40

After one month the owner must decide whether it is to be a call or a put. In either case the strike will be 100 and the time remaining to expiry at that point will be two months. Figure 16.9 shows the profit or loss profile for this chooser option on the day it is purchased, in response to immediate changes in the spot price, with all the other factors that determine its value held constant. The curve is similar to that for the long straddle.

The value of the long chooser at any time is the value of the call or the put option it can become, whichever is the greater of the two. If the spot rises (falls) from the initial level it will behave like a long call (put) since it is most likely that that will be selected. The gamma (the

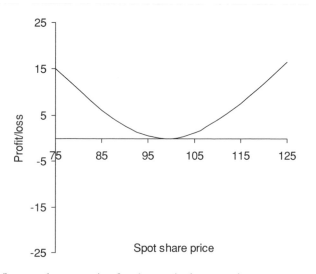

Figure 16.9 Profit/loss on chooser option for changes in the spot price

curvature in the graph) is positive. This tells us that we have a 'right-way' exposure. The more the spot price rises (falls) the more the chooser will behave like a long (short) position in the underlying and its delta will move towards $+1$ (-1).

The chooser might sound like an extremely exotic structure, although in fact it can be assembled from quite standard components and is therefore quite easily priced. Ignoring the complications of carry, the chooser just considered could be replicated by buying a three-month put and a one-month call, both struck at 100.

SHORT STRADDLE

A short straddle consists of a short call and put on the same underlying with the same strike and the same time to expiry. It is a *short volatility* (short vega) trade, since if volatility declines then (all other factors remaining constant) both options will fall in value. The short straddle can then be closed out by repurchasing the options for less than the premium at which they were sold. To illustrate the nature of the strategy, we will take the exact reverse of the long straddle deal previously discussed. The underlying is the same and is trading at 100.

Contract	Expiry	Strike	Premium
Short call	3 months	100	+6.18
Short put	3 months	100	+5.68

Figure 16.10 shows the expiry payoff profile. The maximum profit is the combined premium, achieved when the underlying is trading at 100. The seller of the straddle is looking for a dull market in which the underlying trades in a narrow range around the original spot price of 100. As long as the underlying is trading in a range somewhere between 88 and 112 the strategy will make a profit at expiry.

Next, the solid line in Figure 16.11 shows the profit and loss on the short straddle at the outset, when it has just been sold, in response to *immediate* changes in the spot price of the underlying. When the underlying is trading at 100 the strategy is approximately delta neutral, which means

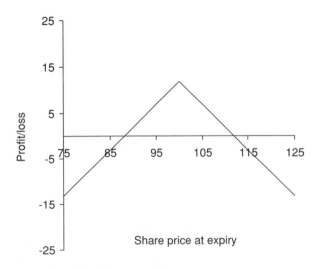

Figure 16.10   Expiry payoff profile of short straddle

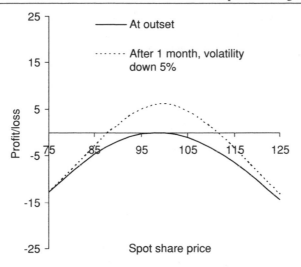

Figure 16.11   Profit/loss on short straddle for changes in the spot price

that for small movements in the spot the profits and losses net out to approximately zero. There is no directional exposure to small changes in the price of the underlying. If the share price rises a little, the short call will move into loss; it would cost more to repurchase than the premium at which it was sold. However, the put option will move out-of-the-money and become slightly cheaper to repurchase. Similarly, if the share price falls a little, then losses on the short put are offset by gains on the short call.

However, the shape of the curvature in the graph reveals the fact that this is a negative gamma position. This is a classic 'wrong-way' exposure. If the share price rises sharply the delta will become negative and the losses on the short call will greatly exceed the profit on the short put (the maximum of which is the initial premium at which it was sold). If the share price continues to rise the delta of the strategy will become increasingly negative and converge on −1 or −100%. At that point the straddle behaves just like a short position in the underlying. Similarly, if the share price falls, the delta of the straddle will become increasingly positive. The losses on the put will exceed the gains on the call. Eventually the straddle will behave just like a long position in the underlying.

Figure 16.11 shows clearly that the trade loses money if the market moves in either direction, except if the movement is very small. How, then, does it make money? The answer is provided by the dotted line in the graph, which shows the profit and loss profile after one month has elapsed, assuming a 5% drop in volatility. As long as the spot price has not changed by more than about 11 in either direction, the short straddle is in profit, since it can be repurchased for less than the premium at which it was sold. A short straddle is usually theta positive and as time goes by both options become cheaper to repurchase. It is also vega negative; if volatility declines both options lose value.

MANAGING THE GAMMA RISK

The major risk involved in selling a straddle is the negative gamma. As we have seen, this is a 'wrong way' exposure. The higher the gamma, the more quickly the delta neutrality will break down, and the faster the strategy will lose money as the spot price of the underlying fluctuates.

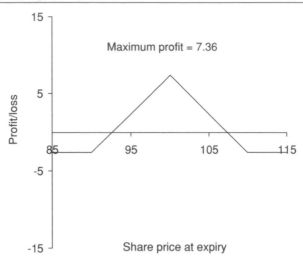

Figure 16.12   Limiting the potential losses on a short straddle

One way to reduce the risk is to sell a straddle and at the same time buy out-of-the-money call and put options. Figure 16.12 shows the expiry payoff profile of the short straddle struck at 100 combined with a long call struck at 110 and a long put struck at 90. The straddle is sold for a premium of 11.86. The premium paid on the long call and put combined is 4.5. Therefore, the net premium received this time is only 7.36, which is also the maximum profit that can be achieved on the strategy.

The effect of buying the out-of-the-money call and put is to limit the potential losses on the combined strategy. It also has the effect of reducing the negative gamma, which means from a trading perspective that the trade will stay approximately delta neutral for fairly large swings in the spot price of the underlying. The problem with this solution is that it costs premium to buy the two options, which reduces the available profit. (The strategy is sometimes called an *iron butterfly*.)

Another way to try to combat the negative gamma on a short straddle is to monitor the position and manage the risk dynamically. For example, if the spot price of the underlying rises, the short straddle will become delta negative and the losses on the position will accelerate, as Figure 16.11 illustrates. This can be combated by 'buying delta', e.g. buying some of the underlying. This helps to neutralize losses arising from further increases in the share price. There is, however, a potential difficulty. If the spot price subsequently falls back again, the shares that were purchased to achieve delta neutrality will no longer be required. They would have to be sold for less than the purchase price, realizing a loss.

The same thing would happen in reverse, if the underlying share price fell. The short straddle would become delta positive, like a long position in the stock. One way to combat this is to short the underlying, but if the spot price subsequently increased then the short position would have to be closed out at a loss. As we saw in Chapter 15, chasing the delta in this way can be extremely costly. The lesson is that a trader who sells a straddle has to be confident about the volatility forecast. If the underlying trades in a narrow range then the risks on the trade can be managed at reasonable cost and overall a profit will be realized. However, if the underlying turns out to be much more volatile than forecast, then the losses realized by managing the delta exposure will exceed the premium charged at the outset.

CALENDAR OR TIME SPREAD

A calendar spread is designed primarily to take advantage of the different rates of time decay on options with different expiry dates. It is not based on a view on which direction the share price is likely to move. The delta – the exposure to small changes in the price of the underlying – is normally quite close to zero. In the following example a three-month call is purchased and a one-month call is sold on the same underlying, both European-style and struck at-the-money. The spot price of the underlying is currently 100 and the net premium paid is 2.62.

Contract	Expiry	Strike	Premium
Long call	3 months	100	−6.18
Short call	1 month	100	+3.56

The positive and negative deltas from the long and the short call will cancel out. However the theta, the rate of time decay, will be different on the two options. The one-month call will lose value more quickly since it is closer to expiry than the three-month contract. This is beneficial, since to close out the trade the one month call has to be repurchased and the three-month call sold. In this example, with the same input values for the underlying used throughout this chapter, the net theta on the strategy is about 0.024. This means that if one day elapses (all other factors remaining constant) the strategy will gain in value by roughly 0.024 units.

However, the rate of time decay on an option is non-linear, so the daily profit increases as time goes by. For example, if five days elapse the profit is not $5 \times 0.024 = 0.12$. It is in fact 0.13. To illustrate this effect, Figure 16.13 shows the decay in the time value of each option over the course of one month starting from the date the strategy is first established. This assumes that all other inputs are held constant, and in particular that the spot price and volatility are unchanged throughout.

There are of course drawbacks to the calendar spread strategy. It is gamma negative, because the negative gamma of the short-dated option exceeds the positive gamma of the longer-dated

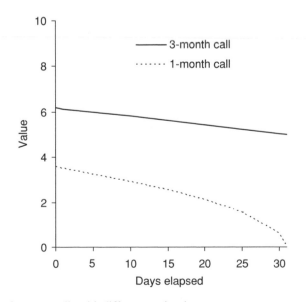

Figure 16.13   Time decay on calls with different expiry dates

option. In practical terms this means that the delta neutrality may break down if the spot price changes to any significant extent, and the position would then be exposed to directional movements in the value of the underlying.

CHAPTER SUMMARY

Options can be used to take trading positions in the underlying with a wide variety of risk/return characteristics. A bull spread is a trade with a maximum loss if the price of the underlying falls and a capped profit if it rises. A bear spread gains from a fall in the price of the underlying but the profits and losses cannot exceed defined levels. Options can also be combined in different ratios. Digital or binary options add to the trading strategies available. A cash-or-nothing digital option pays out a fixed amount of money if it expires in-the-money, otherwise it pays nothing.

Some strategies are designed to take advantage of changes in volatility or the passage of time rather than directional movements in the underlying. A long straddle profits if volatility rises. It also tends to suffer from time value decay and costs two lots of premium. A long chooser option has a similar profile; the buyer has the right to decide after a period of time whether it is a call or a put. A short straddle gains if volatility declines, all other factors remaining constant. It is often set up such that there is little exposure to small movements in the price of the underlying. However, if the price move is substantial the strategy will move into loss. A calendar spread is designed to exploit the different rates of time decay on options on the same underlying that have different expiry dates.

17

Convertible and Exchangeable Bonds

INTRODUCTION

A convertible bond (also known as a *convert* or *CB*) is a bond that can be converted into a fixed number of (normally) ordinary shares, at the choice of the investor. The shares are those of the issuer of the bond. Often conversion can take place during the whole life of the bond with the exception of short periods. The number of shares it can be converted into is called the *conversion ratio*. The current value of those shares is known as the *parity* or conversion value of the CB.

An investor in a convertible has the right to return the bond to the issuer and receive shares according to the conversion ratio. The bond has embedded within it a call option on the underlying shares, which will increase in value if the share price performs well. The option is embedded in the sense that it cannot be split off and traded separately from the convertible bond. It can only be exercised through conversion. When a convertible bond is first issued the investors do not pay a premium to the issuer for the embedded option. Instead, they receive a lower coupon or interest rate on the CB than they would on a standard or straight bond from the same issuer, i.e. one without the conversion feature.

The first cousin of the convertible is the *exchangeable bond*. This is exchangeable for shares of a company other than the issuer of the bond. Issuers include companies that hold significant stakes in other firms (known as cross-shareholdings) who wish to dispose of those stakes in an orderly and effective manner. They borrow at a relatively cheap rate by selling exchangeable bonds and, assuming exchange takes place, are spared the need to redeem the bonds for cash. Other deals are based on the privatization of assets. For example, in July 2003 the German state-owned development bank KfW issued €5 billion of bonds exchangeable into Deutsche Telekom shares. The deal was led by Deutsche Bank and JP Morgan.

In some respects an exchangeable bond is the easier of the two to analyse. An investor in a convertible has two types of exposure to the issuing company. Firstly, he or she is exposed to changes in the company's share price, since this will affect the value of the bond. Secondly, the CB will lose value if the credit rating of the issuing company is cut and/or the market becomes increasingly concerned about the prospects of a ratings downgrade or outright default. In practice these factors are likely to be quite closely related. A collapse in a company's share price may well be accompanied by a reduction in its credit rating, and the convertible bond will suffer twice over. The advantage of an exchangeable is that changes to the credit rating of the issuer are unlikely to be quite so closely correlated with movements in the price of the shares, since they are those of a separate organization.

One other problem with a CB is that normally upon conversion the issuing company creates the new shares to deliver to the investors. This has the effect of diluting the value of the existing equity, since the profits of the company are now distributed more widely. The advantage of an exchangeable bond is that it is exchangeable for existing shares and there is no dilution as such. However, this does not mean that there will be no effect at all on the price of the underlying share when an exchangeable bond issue is announced. The market might regard the bond as a means of disposing of a large block of shares, albeit deferred to a later date, and this could depress the share price on the market. In practice the effect can be rather muted, which is one reason why a company might decide to dispose of surplus cross-shareholdings by issuing exchangeable bonds rather than through an outright sale of the shares on the stock market.

Collectively, securities such as convertible and exchangeable bonds are known as *equity-linked* issues, because their values are tied to the value of a single share or (sometimes) to a basket of shares. The equity-linked market is now very big business indeed. According to research firm Dealogic, global convertible issuance reached $165 billion in 2001.

INVESTORS IN CONVERTIBLE BONDS

Buyers of CBs tend to fall into two main categories. The first consists of hedge funds and traders searching for arbitrage and relative value transactions. If a CB is relatively cheap then arbitrageurs can buy the bond (thereby acquiring an inexpensive embedded call option) and hedge out the directional exposure to the underlying by shorting the stock, using the delta hedging technique explained in Chapter 15. Essentially what remains is a 'long volatility' position, i.e. one that profits from significant swings in the price of the underlying share in either direction, somewhat like the long straddle trade explored in Chapter 16. A CB is also sensitive to changes in market interest rates and to the credit rating of the issuer. However, these can be hedged using interest rate and credit default swaps. It is not uncommon for more than 50% of a CB issue to be taken up by arbitrageurs.

The second category of buyers of CBs are the more traditional or 'outright' investors. These include fund managers who are seeking to generate additional returns by taking an equity exposure but who also wish to ensure that the value of the capital invested in the fund is not placed at undue risk. Convertibles offer clear advantages for the more risk-averse investors.

- *Capital protection.* There is no obligation to convert a CB. If the share performs badly a CB can always be retained as a bond, earning a regular coupon stream and with the principal or par value repaid at maturity. On a day-to-day basis, even if the value of the embedded call option has collapsed, a CB will not trade below its value considered purely as a straight bond. In the market this is sometimes called the CB's *bond floor.*
- *Upside potential.* On the other hand, if the share performs well then the investor in a CB can convert into a predetermined quantity of shares at a favourable price. In the jargon of the market, a CB offers upside potential (because of the embedded call option) but also downside protection (because of the bond floor).
- *Income enhancement (versus equity).* The coupon or interest rate on the CB may be higher than the dividends an investor could receive if he or she bought the underlying shares, at least for a period of time. If so, the investor will earn an enhanced income until conversion. However, if the embedded call is particularly attractive this may not be the case. Some CBs pay no interest at all.
- *Higher ranking than equity.* CBs are higher ranking than straight equity (ordinary shares or common stock). A company must make interest and principal payments to bond investors before the ordinary shareholders are paid anything.
- *Equity-like bond.* Professional investors managing fixed-income funds can face restrictions on purchasing ordinary shares. The advantage of a CB is that it is structured as a bond

although it has an equity-linked return. If the share price rises the convertible will also increase in value.

Research notes issued by CB analysts in investment banks and aimed at the more traditional investor group normally discuss the 'equity story'. In other words, they explain why the analyst believes that the share price has the potential to increase over some defined investment horizon. Since the value of the CB is linked to the share price, such an investor will not buy the convertible unless he or she feels positive about the issuing company and is convinced that its shares have profit potential.

Typically, the note will also explain the kind of return the investor can expect to achieve on the CB for given changes in the price of the underlying share. This is often called the *participation rate*, and the concept will be explored further in a later section of this chapter. The research note may also discuss the level of capital protection investors can expect from the CB and compare this with the potential losses that could be suffered if the underlying shares are purchased. Techniques for valuing convertible bonds are now more widely understood than previously and the note will probably also refer to the fair value of the call option embedded in the CB (established using a pricing model).

ISSUERS OF CONVERTIBLE BONDS

Historically CB issuance in the USA was dominated by high-growth companies with lower credit ratings, especially in the technology and biotechnology sectors. In recent times more highly-rated issuers have been attracted to the market as the appetite among investors for equity-linked bonds has increased. Something of the reverse process has occurred in Europe, with increased sub-investment grade issuance in recent years.

A lower rated corporate may find it difficult to obtain an acceptable price for selling its shares. The stock may be perceived by investors as too risky. On the other hand, if it issued regular or straight bonds the coupon rate demanded by investors may be too high. Or there may be no takers at all. If so, the company might find that it can raise capital more effectively by tapping the convertible bond market. A CB provides investors with a good measure of capital protection in the shape of the bond floor, while offering the prospects of attractive returns if the share price performs well. In addition, if the issue is keenly priced, it will attract hedge funds and other traders seeking to construct arbitrage strategies. In summary, CBs can provide a useful source of capital for companies. There are a number of potential advantages for the issuer compared to selling shares or regular straight bonds.

- *Cheaper debt.* Because investors have an option to convert into shares, the coupon paid by the issuer of a CB will be less than the company would have to pay on regular or straight bonds (without the conversion feature). In addition, issuance costs are usually lower and it is not normally essential to obtain a credit rating.
- *Selling equity at a premium.* The conversion price of a CB is what it would cost an investor to acquire a share by purchasing and then converting the bond. When a CB is issued the conversion price can be set at a premium of 25% and more to the price of the share in the cash market. (Recently there has been a trend towards very high premiums, sometimes over 50%.) Investors accept this because they believe there is a good chance that the share price will rise by at least this percentage over the life of the bond. For the issuer this is equivalent to selling shares substantially above the level of the share price at issue (assuming the bonds are converted).

- *Tax deductibility.* Usually companies can offset interest payments against tax, but not dividends. A corporate that issues a CB can have the benefit of this so-called tax shield until such time as the investors decide to convert and the company issues them with shares.
- *Weaker credits.* The CB market can help lower credit-rated corporates tap the capital markets. In such cases the share price is often highly volatile which increases the potential payout from the embedded call and can make the CB attractive to hedge funds.

CB MEASURES OF VALUE

In order to explore the nature of convertible bonds further we will take a simple example and consider some valuation issues, in particular the relationship between the value of a CB and the price of the underlying share. The CB we will consider was issued some time ago at par, i.e. $100, and now has five years remaining until maturity. Further details are given in Table 17.1.

When the CB was first issued, the coupon rate was set below that for a straight bond. So its value at issue considered as a bond (i.e. the present value of the interest and principal cash flows) was actually less than $100. However, investors were prepared to buy the CB at par because of the value of the embedded call option. At issue, typically somewhere around 75% of the value of a CB consists in bond value and the rest is option value.

In this example, we are looking at the value of the CB not at issue, but some time later and with five years remaining to maturity. We will assume that the required return on the market for straight debt of this credit rating is now 5% p.a., exactly the same as the coupon rate on the CB. This means that the bond value of the CB is now exactly par, i.e. $100. The CB should not trade below its bond value (also known as its bond floor) since this represents the value in today's money of the future interest and principal cash flows. Does this mean that the CB now is *only* worth $100? The answer depends on the current share price. Suppose that the market cash price of the share is now $5. This allows us to calculate the bond's *parity* or conversion value.

$$\text{Parity or conversion value now} = \$5 \times 25 = \$125$$

Parity measures the equity value of the CB. In other words, it measures the current value of the package of shares into which the bond can be converted. Just as a CB should not trade below its bond value, it should not be possible to purchase a CB for less than its parity value, assuming that immediate conversion is permitted. The reason once again is the possibility of arbitrage. If we could buy the bond for less than $125 and immediately convert into shares worth $125 we would make a risk-free profit. Market forces should prevent this from happening and the CB should trade for at least its parity value. Parity is related to the modern concept of intrinsic value. The CB should not trade below its parity value in the same way that an American-style call option should not trade below its intrinsic value.

Table 17.1   Details of the bond

Issuer:	XYZ inc.
Par or nominal value:	$100
Conversion ratio:	Convertible into 25 XYZ shares
Coupon rate:	5% p.a.
Conversion dates:	Any business day up to maturity

Does this mean that the XYZ convertible should *only* trade at its parity value? No, for at least two reasons. Firstly, unlike an investment in the underlying shares, the CB offers capital protection in the shape of the bond floor. Secondly, the CB still has five years to maturity and there is a good chance that the share price will increase over that time, which would drive the value of the CB up still further. The CB contains an embedded call option on 25 underlying XYZ shares with five years to expiry, which has significant time value. The amount that investors are prepared to pay over the parity or conversion value of a convertible bond is called *conversion premium* or premium-over-parity. Suppose the XYZ share price is $5 and the parity value of the convertible bond is $125. If the CB is trading for (say) $156 in the market then its conversion premium is calculated as follows:

Conversion premium = $156 − $125 = $31
Percentage conversion premium = $31/$125 = 24.8%
Conversion premium per share = $31/25 shares = $1.24

If an investor buys the CB for $156 and immediately converts, then the cost of buying the equity through this means is $6.24 per share. This is $1.24 or 24.8% more than it would cost to buy the share in the cash market. It also means that the share price would have to rise by at least 24.8% before it would make any sense for the investor to convert the bond into shares. Note that the term 'conversion premium' does not quite mean the same thing as the modern expression 'option premium' though it is related, as we will see in more detail in the next section.

CONVERSION PREMIUM AND PARITY

To help to explore these issues further, Figure 17.1 illustrates the basic relationship between bond value, parity and conversion premium for the XYZ bond. The bond value (bond floor) is

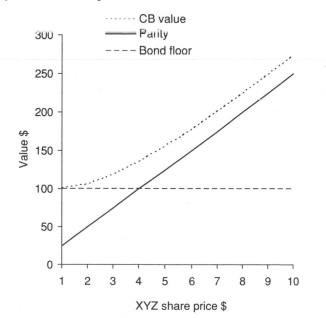

Figure 17.1   CB value, parity and bond floor

assumed to be $100 and there are now five years to maturity. The CB has been priced assuming a 30% p.a. volatility for the underlying shares and assuming that they pay no dividends. Since the CB has a 5% coupon this means that an investor has an income advantage in holding the convertible bond. In the graph parity is shown as a solid diagonal line. Since the bond is always convertible into exactly 25 shares the relationship between the share price and parity is perfectly linear. If the share price is very low at (say) $1, then the parity or equity value of the bond is only $25. At a share price of $10 parity is $250. The bond floor is shown as a horizontal line; the bond value of the CB is taken to be $100 whatever the current share price level. The total CB value is a curved dotted line.

The difference between the total CB value and the parity value of the bond at a given share price is the conversion premium. There are two main factors that determine the conversion premium for this bond, and the one that predominates depends on where the share price is trading.

1. *Bond floor.* At very low share prices the value of the CB reverts to its bond floor. It is extremely unlikely that it will ever be converted and the value of the embedded call option is almost zero. It is deeply out-of-the-money. At this level conversion premium is largely determined by the fact that the holder of the CB is not obliged to convert and has the comfort of being able to retain the security as a pure bond investment. If the investor owned shares instead, then the value of those shares would be sliding down the diagonal parity line.
2. *Embedded call.* At very high share prices the value of the CB converges on its parity value. The CB starts to trade like a package of 25 shares since it is almost 100% certain that it will be converted. There is very little uncertainty about the eventual outcome. The embedded call is deeply in-the-money and (as is the case with such options) the time value component is very low.

OTHER FACTORS AFFECTING CB VALUE

It is often said in the markets that 'a CB is just a bond with an option'. This is a good enough definition when explaining the basic structure of the instrument, but it can be a little misleading in practice and needs a few words of qualification. Firstly, a CB can normally be converted over a period of time and not just at maturity. The pricing methodology has to take into account the fact that it should not trade at less than its parity value, otherwise arbitrage opportunities would be created.

Secondly, when a CB is converted the issuing company normally creates new shares. This has the unfortunate effect of diluting the value of the equity. Thirdly, we assumed in constructing the graph in Figure 17.1 that the bond floor of the CB (its value considered purely as a straight bond) is unaffected by changes in the share price. In practice this is unlikely. A CB is issued by a company and the bond is convertible into the shares of the same company. If the share price collapses we might well expect the bond floor to shift downwards because of fears that the company might default on its debt or declare bankruptcy. In assessing the value of the CB we should properly make some assumptions about the relationship between movements in the share price and the value of the bond floor.

We noted before that an exchangeable bond is in some ways easier to analyse. The bond is issued by one company but is exchangeable for the shares of another. This means that the credit risk on the bond and the value of the shares are not quite so intimately related. An investor who is weighing up the 'equity story' on the shares and considering whether they offer profit potential can assess this possibility quite separately from any questions about the credit or default risk on the bond. Exchangeables are often issued by highly-rated organizations that wish to sell off and 'monetize' the value of stakes in other businesses that were acquired for historical reasons that are no longer relevant.

As a final valuation issue, it is important to understand that many CB issues incorporate complex early redemption provisions. The issuer may have the power to 'call' the bond back early at par or just above if it is trading above a certain trigger level for a period of time. To return to our example, suppose that XYZ company has the right to retire the CB at par if it trades above $175 for a period of two weeks. This would occur if the XYZ share price had risen sharply and driven up the parity value of the CB. By putting out the 'call' or early retirement notice the company is effectively forcing investors to convert. It could then issue new convertible bonds at a conversion price set above the current share price. The call feature is obviously an advantage to the issuer and a disadvantage to the investor and this fact should be reflected in the market value of the CB.

The position on early retirement of CBs tends to be quite complex and to require some fairly sophisticated valuation. A convertible may incorporate a number of separate call features, some of which allow the issuer to 'call' the bond back early after a period of time whatever its value in the market; and others which are only triggered when the CB trades above a certain level for a period of time. In addition, the terms of the bond may grant the investor the right in certain circumstances to 'put' or return the bond back to the investor for cash. This is obviously an advantage to the investor, who can have his or her capital returned early if the CB is found to be a poor investment. As such, the put feature should be reflected in the market value of the security.

PARTICIPATION RATES

The participation rate of a CB tells an investor the rate of return he or she might expect to achieve for a given change in the share price, other factors remaining constant. To explore this concept further, we return to the XYZ convertible bond analysed in the previous sections. The details of the bond were as given in Table 17.2 (there are no call or put features).

If we imagine that the XYZ share price is currently $5, then the parity value of the CB is $125. However, the bond still has five years to maturity; it offers a 5% coupon while the underlying share pays no dividends; and unlike an investment in the share the bond offers capital protection. For all these reasons the CB will be worth more than its parity value.

Suppose that the CB is in fact trading at $156 in the market. Table 17.3 shows what would (in theory) happen to the value of the CB if the share price suddenly jumped to $6 or fell to $4. The method employed here was to revalue the embedded call assuming that the only variable that changes is the underlying share price. The table also shows the percentage change in the share price starting from $5 and the resulting percentage change in the value of the CB.

Table 17.2   Details of the bond

Issuer:	XYZ inc.
Par or nominal value:	$100
Conversion ratio:	Convertible into 25 XYZ shares
Coupon rate:	5% p.a.
Remaining maturity:	5 years
Conversion dates:	Any business day up to maturity

Table 17.3 Participation rate calculations for convertible bond

Share price ($)	Change (%)	CB value ($)	Change (%)	Participation (%)
4	−20	136	−13	64
5	0	156	0	0
6	20	178	14.1	71

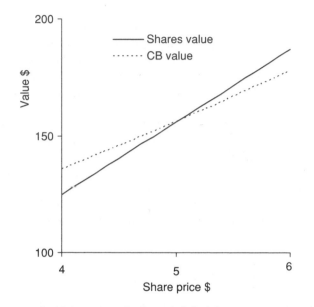

Figure 17.2 CB compared with investment in the underlying shares

The table also shows that if the share price rises from $5 to $6 (an increase of 20%) the percentage rise in the value of the CB is about 14%. An investor who bought the CB at $156 would only achieve 71% of the gains that he or she would have achieved if the money had been used instead to buy XYZ shares. This is the upside participation rate, the rate at which the CB investor would participate in the rise in the share to a target level of $6.

Upside participation rate = 14.1%/20% = 71%

On the other hand, if the share price falls to $4 then an investor in the CB would only suffer 64% of the losses he or she would have made on the underlying shares; and if the share price collapses, the value of the CB will revert to its bond floor. The dotted line in Figure 17.2 illustrates how, in theory, the CB will change in value for a given change in the underlying share price. The solid line shows what would happen if, rather than investing in the CB, an investor used the money to buy XYZ shares in the cash market at $5 each.

MANDATORILY CONVERTIBLES AND EXCHANGEABLES

A mandatorily convertible (MC) is, as the name suggests, a bond which the investor *must* convert on a future date. As an example, Deutsche Telekom launched a €2.3 billion MC bond in February 2003 in order to reduce its debt burden, which then amounted to over €60 billion. The deal was successful and about three times over-subscribed.

Table 17.4   The terms of the ME bond

Bond issue price:	$100
Maturity:	1 year
Exchange ratio:	Each bond is mandatorily exchangeable into one share at maturity.
Coupon rate:	0%

A mandatorily *exchangeable* (ME) might be issued by a company that has a cross-holding of shares in another business which it definitely wishes to dispose of on some future date. In effect the bond is a deferred or forward sale of the shares but with the cash proceeds received up front. There are many reasons why the company might wish to dispose of the shares in this way rather than by simply selling them in a cash market transaction.

- It may be more tax efficient.
- The market impact may be lower – announcing a cash market sale of a large block of shares could seriously affect the market price. This would be particularly painful if the company intended to retain some of its holding.
- There may be legal or regulatory restrictions on selling the shares until some period of time has elapsed.

A very simple example may help to explain the basic idea. A more detailed (and realistic) example is given in the next section. Let us suppose that a company owns a block of shares it wishes to dispose of in one year's time. The current share price is $100, the annual dividend is $1 per share and the one-year interest rate is 5% p.a. The one-year fair forward price, established using the cash-and-carry method explained in Chapter 2, is therefore $100 + $5 − $1 = $104.

The company could go to a dealer and agree to sell the shares forward in an over-the-counter transaction. If it contracts the forward deal at $104 per share then it could borrow money today against the future cash flow guaranteed by this transaction. It is due to receive $104 per share in one year's time so, at an interest rate of 5% p.a., it could borrow just over $99 per share today. Alternatively, rather than agree the forward, the company might get a better deal by selling a mandatorily exchangeable bond to investors through the public markets. The terms of the bond might be as shown in Table 17.4.

In this structure, investors buy a bond for $100 and one year later they receive (without any choice) one share per bond. In effect, the company is selling the shares to the bond investors in a year's time but receiving the proceeds up front. The advantage is that it is receiving $100 per share up front rather than the $99 that could be borrowed against a forward sale of the shares. In practice mandatorily convertible and exchangeable bonds can be constructed such that investors have some protection against a fall in the share price. Alternatively, there is no capital protection as such, but investors receive an attractive coupon in compensation for the requirement to exchange the bond for shares. An example is explored in the next section.

STRUCTURING A MANDATORILY EXCHANGEABLE

The advantage of these types of deals is that they can be packaged in different ways to make them more attractive to investors. One technique used by investment banks is to issue a ME bond with a coupon rate that is appreciably higher than the dividends investors would receive if they bought the underlying shares in the cash market. However, investors are obliged to exchange

Table 17.5   The bond structure

Bond issue price:	$100
Maturity:	3 years
Mandatorily exchangeable for:	ABC shares
ABC share price at issue:	$100
Share dividend yield:	0% p.a.
Exchange ratio:	If the ABC share price is below $100 at maturity the investor receives one share per bond. At share prices between $100 and $125 the investor receives a quantity of shares worth $100. At share prices above $125 the investor receives 0.8 shares per bond
Coupon rate:	5% p.a.

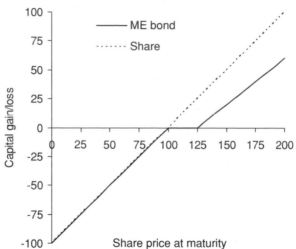

Figure 17.3   Capital gains/losses on a mandatorily exchangeable at maturity

the bond for shares at maturity, using an exchange ratio formula that can produce a lower rate of participation in any rise in the share price compared to purchasing the actual shares in the first instance. For example, a deal might be structured along the lines shown in Table 17.5.

The solid line in Figure 17.3 shows the capital gain or loss an investor would make on this ME at maturity for a range of different possible share prices. The assumption is that the investor has purchased a bond for $100 when it was issued. The dotted line shows the capital gains and losses the investor would have achieved if he or she had used the $100 to buy one ABC share in the first instance. A few examples will help to explain the ME bond values in the graph.

- *Share price at maturity = $75.* The investor receives one share worth $75 and the capital loss on the bond is $25.
- *Share price at maturity = $100.* The investor receives one share worth $100 and there is no capital gain or loss on the bond.
- *Share price at maturity is between $100 and $125.* The investor receives shares to the value of $100. The capital gain on the bond is zero.
- *Share price at maturity = $150.* The investor receives 0.8 shares worth $120 and the capital gain on the bond is $20. This is $30 less than the gain would have been if the investor had purchased one ABC share for $100 in the first instance.

- *Share price at maturity = $200.* The investor receives 0.8 shares worth $160 and the capital gain is $60. This is $40 less than it would have been if the investor had purchased one ABC share rather than the bond at the outset.

At share prices higher than $125 the investor in the ME bond begins to participate in further increases in the share price, but to a lesser extent than if he or she had bought shares in the first instance. Also the bond does not offer the kind of capital protection afforded by a traditional convertible or exchangeable bond. However it does pay a high coupon rate of 5% p.a. while the underlying share pays no dividends. The investor has the benefit of this income advantage for three years and then the bond has to be exchanged for shares. In a flat share market with little opportunities for capital growth this may be a major plus point. The coupon income also provides some offset against a possible fall in the value of the shares over the three years.

CHAPTER SUMMARY

A convertible bond (CB) can be converted into a fixed number of shares of the issuer, at the decision of the holder. The number of shares acquired is determined by the conversion ratio. The parity value of a CB is its value considered as a package of shares, i.e. the conversion ratio times the current share price. The bond floor is its value considered purely as a bond. A CB should not trade below its bond floor or its parity value, assuming that immediate conversion is possible. Its value over-and-above parity is called conversion premium.

Conversion premium is affected by the value of the call option that is embedded in a CB. At a low share price it is unlikely that the bond will be converted and it trades close to its bond floor. Conversion premium is high. At a high share price conversion is likely and the bond will trade close to its parity value. Conversion premium is low.

CBs are bought by investors who wish to profit from increases in the share price but who do not wish to suffer excessive losses if it falls. They are also bought by hedge funds as a means of acquiring relatively inexpensive options. In practice, valuing a CB can be complex. It often incorporates 'call' features that allow the issuer to retire the bond before maturity, sometimes to force conversion. An exchangeable bond is issued by one organization and is exchangeable for shares in another company. They are sometimes issued by an organization that has acquired an equity stake in another business; rather than sell the shares outright it raises cheap debt by selling bonds exchangeable for those shares. An investor who buys a mandatory convertible or exchangeable bond is obliged to acquire shares at some future point in time. The bond may be structured such that the investor receives a high coupon or has some level of capital protection.

18

Structured Securities: Examples

INTRODUCTION

One of the strengths of derivatives is that they can be combined in many ways to create new risk-management solutions. Similarly, banks and securities houses can use derivatives to create new families of investments aimed at the institutional and retail markets. Products can be developed with a wide range of risk and return characteristics, designed to appeal to different categories of investors in different market conditions. The choice is no longer limited to buying bonds, investing in shares or placing money in a deposit account. Derivative instruments can create securities whose returns depend on a wide range of variables, including currency exchange rates, stock market indices, default rates on corporate debt, commodity prices – even electricity prices or the occurrence of natural disasters such as earthquakes.

Some structured products are aimed at the more cautious or risk-averse investor. They incorporate features that protect at least some percentage of the investor's initial capital. Others actually increase the level of risk that is taken, for those who wish to achieve potentially higher returns. A classic (and infamous) example is the 'reverse floater' whose value moves inversely with market interest rates. The problem is that it may also incorporate a significant amount of leverage, so that if interest rates rise the potential losses are enormous. In 1994 Orange County in California lost over $1.6 billion through such investments.

Derivatives also allow financial institutions and corporations to 'package up' and sell off risky positions to investors who are prepared to take on those risks for a suitable return. Chapter 17 gave an example of the technique. A company that owns a cross-holding in another firm's equity can issue an exchangeable bond. The company benefits from cheaper borrowing costs and (assuming exchange takes place) will never have to pay back the principal value. The bond could be structured as a mandatorily exchangeable, such that the shares are definitely sold off on a future date at a fixed price but with the proceeds from the sale received up front.

There are literally thousands of ways in which derivatives can be used to create structured securities and only a few examples can be explored in an introductory text such as this. The first sections in this chapter discuss a very typical structure, an equity-linked note with capital protection. We look at a number of different ways in which the product can be constructed to appeal to different investor groups, and at the actual components that are used in its manufacture. The final sections explore structured securities whose returns are linked to the level of default on a portfolio of loans or bonds. This is one of the largest growth areas in the modern financial markets.

CAPITAL PROTECTION EQUITY-LINKED NOTES

We begin with an equity-linked note (ELN) – a product that offers investors capital protection plus some level of participation in the rise in the value of a portfolio or basket of shares. When sold into the retail market the return on these products is usually linked to the level of a well-known stock market index such as the S&P 500 or the FT-SE 100. An index like this simply tracks the change in the value of a hypothetical portfolio of shares. The notes can also be given a 'theme' selected to be attractive to investors at a particular moment in time. For example, the payoff might depend on the value of an index of smaller company shares or of technology stocks. The notes we will assemble in this chapter are based on a portfolio of shares currently worth €50 million. The total issue size is €50 million, the notes mature in two years' time and their maturity value will be calculated as follows:

$$\text{Maturity value of notes} = (\text{Principal invested} \times \text{Capital protection level})$$
$$+ (\text{Principal invested} \times \text{Basket appreciation} \times \text{Participation rate})$$

For example, suppose we issue the notes with 100% capital protection and 100% participation in any increase in the value of the portfolio over two years. If at maturity the basket of shares is worth €40 million, then the investors get back their €50 million and suffer no loss of capital. But if the basket has risen in value by (say) 50%, then the investors are paid €75 million.

$$\text{Maturity value} = (\text{€50 million} \times 100\%) + (\text{€50 million} \times 50\% \times 100\%)$$
$$= \text{€75 million}$$

The first step in assembling the notes is to guarantee the investors' capital. The strategy here is to take some proportion of the €50 million raised by selling the notes and invest the money for two years, so that, with interest, it will grow to a value of exactly €50 million at maturity. Suppose we identify a suitable fixed-rate investment that pays 5.6% p.a. with interest compounded annually. If, in that case, we deposit about €44.84 million the investment will be worth €50 million at maturity in two years. This can be used to guarantee the €50 million principal on the structured notes.

How can we also pay the investors a return based on any appreciation in the value of the portfolio? Clearly we cannot buy the actual shares since most of the money collected from the investors has been used to guarantee the capital repayment.

The answer is that we buy a European call option that pays off according to the value of the basket of shares in two years' time, the maturity of the structured notes. The strike is set at-the-money at €50 million. Suppose the portfolio at maturity is worth €75 million, a rise of 50% from the starting value. Assuming 100% capital protection and 100% participation, we would then have to pay the investors €75 million at maturity. However, we are covered. We have €50 million from the maturing deposit and the intrinsic value of the call would be €75 million − €50 million = €25 million.

The next step is to contact our option dealer and purchase a two-year at-the-money European call on the basket of shares. Suppose that the dealer quotes us a premium of €8.6 million for the contract. Then it is clear that we cannot offer investors 100% capital protection and 100% participation in any rise in the value of the portfolio. We collected €50 million from investors and deposited €44.84 million, which leaves only €5.16 million. If the investors demand the full capital guarantee, we will need to spend less money on the option contract. In fact the premium we are able to pay determines the participation rate we can offer to the investors in the notes. We know that €8.6 million buys 100% participation; therefore our budget will only buy a maximum participation rate of 60%.

$$\text{Maximum participation rate} = \text{€5.16 million} / \text{€8.6 million} = 60\%$$

EXPIRY VALUE OF 100% CAPITAL PROTECTION NOTES

Table 18.1 shows the value of the equity-linked notes at maturity in two years' time, on the basis that they are offered with 100% capital protection and a 60% participation rate. The first column shows a range of possible values the basket may take at maturity; the second shows the percentage change starting from €50 million. The final three columns show the value of the notes and the capital gain or loss investors in the notes have made at maturity.

Some examples from the table will help to explain the figures. Let us suppose that the basket at maturity is worth €50 million or €60 million.

- *Basket Value €50 million.* The notes offer 100% capital guarantee, so investors get back their original €50 million. As the change in the value of the basket is zero, investors receive no additional payment. Their capital gain/loss is zero.
- *Basket value €60 million.* Investors are repaid their €50 million. The basket has risen in value by 20%, the participation rate is 60% so they are also paid an additional €50 million × 20% × 60% = €6 million. The capital gain for the investors is 60% × 20% = 12%.

The solid line in Figure 18.1 shows the percentage capital gains or losses on the notes over the two years to maturity, for a range of different values of the basket at that point. The dotted line shows the percentage rise in the basket. If the basket at maturity is worth (say) €80 million then an investor who had purchased the underlying shares in the first instance would have achieved a capital gain of 60%.

Table 18.1 Maturity value of 100% capital protection equity-linked note

Basket value at maturity (€)	Basket change (%)	ELN maturity value (€)	Capital gain/loss (€)	Capital gain loss (%)
40 000 000	−20	50 000 000	0	0
50 000 000	0	50 000 000	0	0
60 000 000	20	56 000 000	6 000 000	12

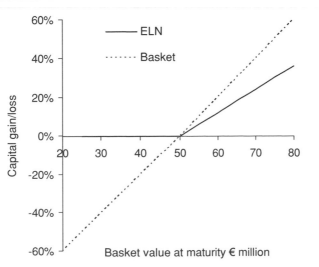

Figure 18.1   Capital gain/loss on 100% capital guarantee note

An investor in the equity-linked notes would have made 60% of this, i.e. 36%. On the other hand, if the basket is only worth €20 million at maturity then an investor in the shares would have lost 60% of their capital while a purchaser of the notes would have lost none. Note that this analysis only considers capital gains and losses; the notes do not pay any dividends or interest. Potential investors could buy the underlying shares and earn dividend income, or deposit the cash with a bank and earn interest.

100% PARTICIPATION NOTES

Some investors prefer to have a lower level of capital protection but a higher degree of participation. Suppose that we decide to offer a 100% participation rate. We saw before that this requires an expenditure of €8.6 million to purchase a call option. From this we can calculate how much there remains from the €50 million to place on deposit, and the proceeds in two years' time at a return of 5.6% p.a. This calculation shows that we can only afford to guarantee a repayment of €46.2 million at maturity, which is roughly 92% of the initial capital provided by the investors.

Figure 18.2 shows capital gains and losses on 92% capital protection and 100% participation notes for a range of possible basket values at maturity. If the shares are worth €50 million investors are repaid 92% of their capital (a loss of 8%). If an investor had bought the actual shares the capital loss would have been zero. On the other hand, the maximum loss on the notes is 8% while 100% could potentially be lost on the shares.

If the basket is worth more than €50 million at maturity, the advantage of the higher participation rate becomes apparent. For example, if it is worth €80 million these notes produce a capital gain of 52%. This compares favourably with 36% on the 100% capital protection notes (though unfavourably with a direct investment in the basket which would have returned a 60% capital gain).

One possibility, of course, is to offer different classes of notes aimed at different purchasers, some with higher capital protection aimed at the more risk-averse and 100% participation notes

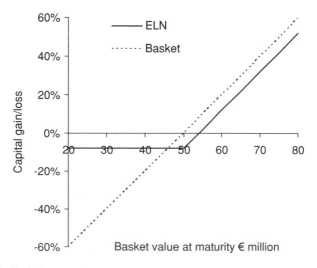

Figure 18.2   Capital/gain loss on 100% participation equity-linked note

aimed that those who are prepared to take a little more risk for potentially higher rewards. Note that the securities we have been structuring so far in this chapter function in essence rather like exchangeable bonds. There is a level of capital protection plus an equity-linked return.

CAPPED PARTICIPATION NOTES

It is possible to offer investors 100% capital protection and at the same time 100% participation in any rise the value of the basket of shares, at the cost of capping the profits on the notes. How can we establish the level of the cap? The strategy involves selling an out-of-the money call on the basket and receiving premium. This increases the amount of money available to buy the at-the-money call on the basket. The other side of the coin is that the profits on the notes must be capped at the strike of the call that is sold. We know how much money has to be raised from selling such an option.

Cash raised from issuing notes = €50 million
Deposited for 100% capital protection = €44.84 million
Premium cost of long call for 100% participation = €8.6 million
Shortfall = €3.44 million

This tells us that we must write a call on the basket of shares with a strike set such that the buyer is prepared to pay us a premium of €3.44 million. Suppose we contact an option dealer and agree to write a call on the basket struck at a level of €67.5 million, which raises exactly the required amount of money. The strike is 35% above the spot value of the basket.

The overall effect is that we can promise 100% capital protection and 100% participation in any rise in the basket, but the capital gain on the notes must be limited to €17.5 million, or a 35% return based on the initial capital of €50 million. We purchased a call on the basket struck at €50 million. However, any gains on the shares beyond a value of €67.5 million will have to be paid over to the buyer of the €67.5 million strike call.

Figure 18.3 compares the capital gains and losses on the capped equity-linked notes to what investors would have achieved if they had invested the money in the actual shares. To see how

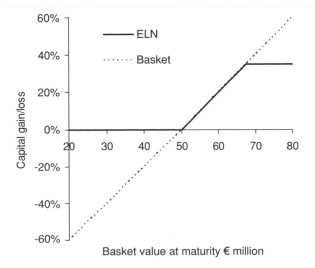

Figure 18.3 Capital/gain loss at maturity on capped equity-linked note

this works out for investors, we can take some values from the graph. These are based on different possible values of the basket at the maturity of the notes.

- *Basket value €40 million.* As the notes offer a 100% capital guarantee, investors are repaid €50 million. The capital loss is zero. On the other hand, if they had bought the actual shares they would have lost €10 million or 20% of their capital.
- *Basket value €60 million.* The investors are repaid their €50 million initial capital. The basket has risen by 20% and the participation rate is 100%, so they are also paid an additional €10 million for the rise in basket. The capital gain for the investors is 20%, as it would have been if they had purchased the actual shares.
- *Basket value €80 million.* The investors are repaid their €50 million capital. The basket has risen in value by 60%. However the capital gain on the notes is capped at 35%. The total amount repaid to investors at maturity is €67.5 million.

The capital gain on the notes is capped here at 35%, but the potential gains if the actual shares had been purchased by the investors is unlimited. On top of this, of course, the shares would pay dividends which can be re-invested, whereas the notes pay no interest at all. They could be structured to include interest payments, but some other feature would have to be adjusted. For example, the capital protection level could be reduced, or the level of the cap lowered.

AVERAGE PRICE NOTES

One concern that investors might have about purchasing the equity-linked notes is that the basket could perform well for most of the two years to maturity, and then suffer a serious collapse towards the end. This sort of problem is illustrated in Figure 18.4. The portfolio is worth €50 million at the outset and, with some ups and downs, is trading comfortably above that level with only a few months to the expiry of the notes. However, it then suffers a slump. In all of the versions of the equity-linked notes considered so far in this chapter, the investors

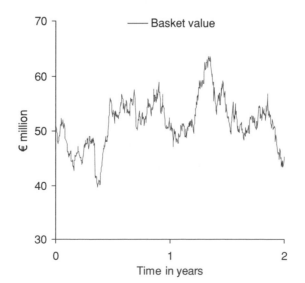

Figure 18.4   Potential price path for the basket over two years

would not benefit from those interim price rises. The payout is based solely on the value of the basket at maturity.

One way to tackle this problem is to use an *average price* or Asiatic call option when assembling the notes. The value of a fixed strike average price call option at expiry is zero, or the difference between the *average* price of the underlying and the strike, whichever is the greater. These contracts are specifically designed to help with the sort of concerns investors may have about the equity-linked notes, since the payout would not be based on the value of the basket at a specific moment in time, the expiry date, but its average value over some defined period of time. This could be the three- or the six-month period leading up to expiry, or even the whole life of the option contract. The averaging process can be based on daily or weekly or monthly price changes.

Average price options have another advantage of great practical importance to structurers assembling products such as equity-linked notes. All other things being equal, an average price option tends to be cheaper than a standard vanilla option. The reason, again, relates to volatility. The averaging process has the effect of smoothing out volatility. To put it another way, the average value of an asset over a period of time tends to be relatively stable, more so than the cash price over the same period. (This assumes that the movements follow a random path, so that price rises and falls tend to cancel out to some extent.) The more frequently the averaging process is carried out, the better the smoothing effect. All other things being equal, an average price option with daily averaging is cheaper than one with weekly averaging.

We know that to structure the notes with 100% capital protection we must deposit €44.84 million. Using vanilla call options, we need €8.6 million to offer a 100% participation rate. The reason for adjusting the notes in various ways – e.g. lowering the participation rate or capping the profits – is that there is not enough cash available to do both. However, with the same values used to price the vanilla option the cost of buying an average price option from a dealer could actually come in within budget. We could offer a 100% capital guarantee plus 100% participation in any increase in the *average value* of the basket.

LOCKING IN INTERIM GAINS: CLIQUET OPTIONS

Average rate options are very useful but they are not likely to help if the shares first perform well and then very badly indeed for a sustained period of time leading up to maturity. The chances are that the average price would be below the strike. One solution to this problem, although it is likely to be expensive, is to use a *cliquet* or ratchet option when assembling the notes. A cliquet is a product that locks in interim gains at set time periods, which cannot subsequently be lost. Suppose, this time, that when assembling the equity-linked notes we buy a cliquet option, consisting of two components:

1. A one-year European call starting spot with a strike at the current spot value of the basket €50 million. This is a standard call option.
2. A one-year European call, starting in one year, with the strike set at the spot value of the basket at that point in time. This is known as a forward start option.

To help to explain the effect of the cliquet, Figure 18.5 shows one potential price path for the basket of shares over the next two years. The value starts at €50 million. At the end of one year it is worth approximately €55 million. The first option in the cliquet, the spot start call, will expire at that point and will be worth €5 million in intrinsic value. This cannot be lost.

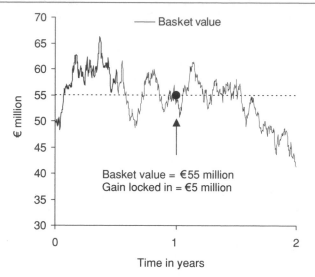

Figure 18.5   Possible price path for the basket and locked-in gain

Now the strike for the second option in the cliquet, the forward start option, will be set at €55 million. At the expiry of that option the basket in this example is worth less than €55 million, so it expires worthless. If the basket at expiry was worth more than €55 million then gains would be achieved in addition to the €5 million locked in.

The problem with the cliquet is of course the cost of the premium. It actually consists of two call options each with one year to maturity, one starting spot and the other starting in one year's time. This is more expensive than a standard two-year call option because it provides additional flexibility. The result is that if the cliquet is used, the capital protection level on the notes would have to be lowered, or the participation rate cut, or the returns capped.

SECURITIZATION

In these final examples we look at structured bonds whose returns are linked to the level of default on a pool of assets. Generally, *securitization* is the process of packaging up assets such as mortgages and bank loans and selling them off to capital markets investors in the form of bond issues. The bondholders are paid out of the cash flow stream from the underlying assets. The growth in securitization has been one of the most significant developments in finance over the past decade. Issuance in the European market in 2002 totalled €157.7 billion, according to the European Securitization Forum – a body formed of major participants in the business.

Investment bankers have become increasingly creative about the types of assets that are given the securitization treatment. It seems that almost anything that generates future cash flows that can be forecast with a reasonable degree of accuracy can be packaged up and sold into the public bond markets. Bonds have been issued that are backed by the royalty and copyright payments due to rock stars (so-called *Bowie bonds*). Italy has issued bonds backed by future ticket sales at art galleries and by future collections of unpaid tax. Soccer clubs have borrowed against receipts due from season ticket sales. Even whole companies have been securitized, notably in the UK chains of managed pubs.

The basic process of securitization usually tends to fall into a fairly standard pattern. Firstly, a set of assets is identified that will generate a stream of future cash flows. Secondly, the assets are sold by their owner to an entity known as a special purpose vehicle (SPV). The purpose of the SPV is to issue bonds, and with the proceeds purchase the assets from the original owner. The cash flow stream from the assets is used to service the interest and principal payments due on the bonds.

The bonds are usually rated by one or more of the major ratings agencies. If the underlying assets are of poor quality and there is risk that the cash flow stream may not be sufficient to pay back the bondholders, then it is necessary to use what are known as *credit-enhancement* techniques to make the bonds more attractive. A common method is to issue different classes or *tranches* of bonds with different risk-return characteristics.

For example, there may a tranche with the highest credit rating AAA, which means that investors have a very high probability of being paid. Further tranches will have lower credit ratings but will pay high coupons in compensation. If the assets do not generate sufficient cash flows then the lowest-rated bonds suffer first. Often at the bottom of the pile there is a so-called equity investor who earns a return if there is anything left after all the other classes of investors have been paid.

Figure 18.6 shows a typical securitization structure. The underlying assets are bank loans originated by a commercial bank. The bank would like to sell off the assets, partly because it wishes to free up capital to create further loans; and partly because it wishes to reduce the level of credit or default risk it retains on its balance sheet. A bank that holds loans that carry the risk of default has to set aside capital to cover this eventuality. This can adversely affect important performance ratios such as return on equity. So the bank sells the loan portfolio to a company (the SPV) specifically set up for the purchase, with the help of its investment banking advisers and lawyers. The SPV raises the cash to buy the loans from the bond investors, who are repaid via the SPV from the cash flows from the underlying loans.

Why would investors buy the bonds? Because the issue is set up in such a way that they receive a return they believe is attractive in relation to the risks being taken. Since the underlying assets in this example are bank loans, the main risk to the investors is that of a significant level

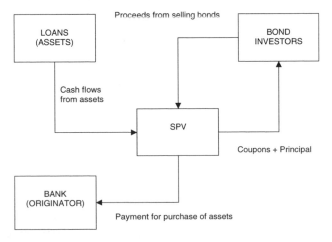

Figure 18.6   Securitization of bank loans

of default. This could mean that the SPV is unable to pay some coupons on the bonds, or even that the bondholders' capital is at risk.

The system of creating different tranches of bonds with different risk and return character-istics helps in such circumstances. The more risk-averse investors can buy the highest-rated tranche, making their investment very secure. Others may be prepared to buy the lower-rated tranches which pay higher coupons but suffer first if the underlying loans default. Another method often used in securitization is known as *over-collateralization*. In effect the loan assets transferred to the SPV are increased so that a certain level of default in the loan portfolio is allowed for.

The main advantage of using an SPV from the perspective of investors is that the assets are segregated and transferred from the ownership of the originator of those assets – in the example, from the commercial bank. The bond investors are only exposed to the credit or default risk on the assets, which may be easier to assess and monitor. If they purchased bonds issued directly by the commercial bank rather than by the SPV they would be exposed to a much wider set of risks – for example, the risk that the bank as a whole is mismanaged and is unable to repay its debt.

SYNTHETIC SECURITIZATION

There are occasions, however, when a bank does not wish to sell a loan portfolio outright. It may consist of commercial loans to important corporate clients, and for relationship reasons it would be difficult to transfer the ownership to another party. There may be other tax, legal and regulatory constraints. However, if the bank retains the ownership of the loans on its balance sheet it is exposed to the risk of default and has to set capital aside against this risk. Derivative products can provide a range of alternative solutions; this time we will use a credit default swap (CDS). As we saw in Chapter 7, a CDS has two parties: the protection seller and the protection buyer.

- *Protection buyer.* The protection buyer pays a premium of so many basis points per annum to buy protection on a referenced bond or loan or portfolio of loans.
- *Protection seller.* If a defined credit event occurs during the life of the contract, the protection buyer either receives a cash compensation payment or delivers the asset to the protection seller in return for a defined payment.
- *Credit event.* A credit event is anything defined in the CDS contract that triggers the com-pensation payment or the delivery of the asset to the protection seller. Typical events include non-payment on due obligations and ratings downgrades.

Figure 18.7 illustrates a synthetic securitization deal involving a commercial bank. This time the bank does not physically sell the assets to an SPV, but instead buys protection from the SPV on the assets or some proportion of the assets using a credit default swap. It pays an annual premium to the SPV for the protection. The SPV issues bonds to investors and uses the proceeds to buy Treasury securities.

The investors in the bonds issued by the SPV earn a return in addition to the return on the Treasuries because of the premium paid to the SPV by the bank. The bank pays the premium for the protection it receives as the buyer of protection under the CDS contract. As the seller of protection, the SPV will have to make compensation payments to the bank if credit events are triggered, i.e. defaults on the portfolio of loans. Since it has no other assets it would have to sell some of its stock of Treasury bonds to achieve this, thus reducing the cash available to pay back the investors.

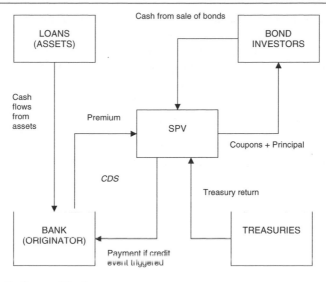

Figure 18.7 Synthetic securitization

This structure is called a *synthetic securitization* because the bank does not physically sell the assets. Instead it retains them on its balance sheet but purchases protection against default by entering into the credit default swap with the SPV. Normally some elements of credit enhancement will be incorporated into the structure to encourage investors to buy the bonds. The commercial bank may agree to suffer the first losses on the loan portfolio up to a certain level before any payment from the SPV is triggered under the terms of the CDS. In addition, the bonds issued by the SPV will normally be structured into different tranches, such that the lower rated bonds will suffer before the higher rated bonds are affected.

CHAPTER SUMMARY

Derivatives are not only used in risk management and in trading applications. They are also used to create a very wide range of so-called structured securities whose returns to investors depend on such factors as the value of a basket of shares, currency exchange rates or the level of interest rates over some period of time. Banks can also use derivatives to package up the risks they acquire as part of their business operations and 'sell them off' to investors who are prepared to assume the risks for a suitable return.

The equity-linked note, which goes by a variety of brand names, is a typical structured product and is now offered to retail investors as well as to institutions. Normally the investors are offered a level of capital protection plus participation in any rise in the value of an equity index or a specific basket of shares. The product can be assembled by depositing a sum of money to guarantee the principal repayment and buying a call on the index or basket. The gain on the note may be capped or based on the average value of the index or basket, or it may be structured such that interim gains are locked in.

Securitization is the process of assembling assets such as loans and selling bonds to investors that are repaid from the cash flows generated by the assets. Usually the assets are transferred into a special purpose vehicle which exists simply to collect cash and pay interest and principal to the bondholders. Typically, different tranches or 'slices' of bonds are sold with different risk-return characteristics and different credit ratings. Sometimes the assets used are existing bonds which are trading cheaply in the market because they are unpopular in some way. Securitization deals have also been based on the cash flows due from future trade receivables, ticket sales, taxation, royalty and copyright payments and the revenues from managed pub chains.

A bank that does not wish to sell a loan book physically can enter into a synthetic securitization deal. Here it buys protection against default on some proportion of its loan book from an SPV and pays a fee or premium. The SPV uses this premium to pay its bond investors a return above and beyond that on Treasury bonds. The downside is that investors will suffer losses if there is a significant level of default on the bank's loan book.

Appendix A
Financial Calculations

TIME VALUE OF MONEY

Time value of money (TVM) is a key concept in modern finance. It tells us two things:

- A dollar received today is worth more than a dollar to be received in the future.
- A dollar to be received in the future is worth less than a dollar received today.

The reason for this is because a dollar today can be invested at a rate of interest and will grow to a larger sum of money in the future. The cost of money for a specific period of time (its time value) is measured by the interest rate for the period. Interest rates in the financial markets are normally quoted on a nominal per annum basis. A nominal interest rate has two components:

- *Real rate.* This compensates the lender for the use of the funds over the period.
- *Inflation rate.* This compensates the lender for the predicted erosion in the value of money over the period.

Normally the inflation element is more subject to change than the real or underlying rate. The relationship between the two can be expressed mathematically (with the rates inserted in the formulae as decimals):

$$1 + \text{Nominal rate} = (1 + \text{Inflation rate}) \times (1 + \text{Real rate})$$
$$\text{Real rate} = [(1 + \text{Nominal rate})/(1 + \text{Inflation rate})] - 1$$

If the nominal interest rate for one year is 5% p.a. (0.05 as a decimal) and the predicted rate of inflation over the period is 3% p.a. (0.03 as a decimal) then the real interest rate is calculated as:

$$\text{Real rate} = (1.05/1.03) - 1 = 0.0194 = 1.94\% \text{ p.a.}$$

By convention, interest rates are usually expressed per annum, even if the borrowing or lending period is shorter than a year. To calculate the interest due on a loan or deposit that matures in less than one year the annualized rate must be reduced in proportion.

FUTURE VALUE (FV)

Suppose we deposit $100 for one year with a bank. The interest rate paid is 10% p.a. simple interest, that is, without compounding. The principal amount invested is called the present value (PV). The principal plus interest at the maturity of the deposit is called the future value (FV). The interest rate expressed as a decimal (10 divided by 100) is 0.1.

$$\text{Future value (FV)} = \text{Principal} + \text{Interest at maturity}$$
$$= 100 + (100 \times 0.1) = 100 \times 1.1 = 110$$
$$\text{Interest at maturity} = 100 \times 0.1 = 10$$

This is a simple interest calculation because there is no compounding or 'interest on interest' involved in the formula. Note that if we deposit $100 for one year and our account is credited with $110 at maturity, we could work out that the simple interest return earned on the investment is 10% p.a. Suppose now we invest $100, but this time for two years at 10% p.a. and interest is compounded at the end of each year. What is the future value (FV) after two years? At the end of one year there is $100 \times 1.1 = \$110$ in the account. Therefore, to work out the FV at the end of two years we multiply this by 1.1 again.

$$\text{Future value (FV)} = \text{Principal} + \text{Interest}$$
$$= 100 \times 1.1 \times 1.1 = 100 \times 1.1^2 = 121$$

Because of compounding we now have $21 in interest. The first year's interest was $10. The second year's interest is $11. In addition to interest on the original principal of $100, we have earned $1 interest on interest. The general formula for calculating present value when interest is compounded periodically is:

$$\text{FV} = \text{PV} \times (1 + r/m)^n$$

where   FV = future value
        PV = present value
        r = the interest rate p.a. as a decimal (the percentage rate divided by 100)
        m = the number of times interest is compounded per year
        n = the number of compounding periods to maturity = years to maturity $\times$ m

In the previous example interest was compounded only once a year and it is a two-year deposit, so the values are:

r $= 0.1$
r/m $= 0.1/1 = 0.1$
n $= 2$
PV $= 100$
FV $= 100 \times 1.1^2 = 121$

There are many types of investment where interest is compounded more than once a year. For example, the calculations for US Treasury bonds and UK gilts are based on six-monthly periods, known as semi-annual compounding. Other investments pay interest every three months. Credit cards often charge interest on unpaid balances on a monthly basis. Suppose we invest $100 for two years at 10% p.a. Interest is compounded every six months. What is the future value at maturity in this case?

$$\text{FV} = 100 \times (1 + 0.1/2)^4 = 121.55$$

The annual rate expressed as a decimal is divided by two to obtain a six-monthly rate. Compounding is for four half-yearly periods. The future value is higher than when interest was compounded annually. This illustrates a basic principle of TVM. It is better to earn interest sooner rather than later, since it can be re-invested and will grow at a faster rate.

ANNUAL EQUIVALENT RATE (AER)

Because interest rates in the market are expressed with different compounding frequencies it is important to be very careful when comparing rates. For example, suppose we are offered

Table A.1   Nominal rate 10% p.a.

Compounding frequency	Annual equivalent rate (% p.a.)
Annually	10.0000
Semi-annually	10.2500
Quarterly	10.3813
Monthly	10.4713
Weekly	10.5065
Daily (365 times per annum)	10.5156

two investments. The maturity in both cases is one year, but the first investment offers a return of 10% p.a. with interest compounded annually. The second offers a return of 10% p.a. with interest compounded semi-annually. Which should we choose?

The answer is the semi-annual investment, since the interest paid half-way through the year can be re-invested for the second half of the year. And yet the quoted or nominal interest rate (10% p.a.) looks exactly the same in both cases. This tells us that a nominal 10% p.a. interest rate with semi-annual compounding cannot be directly compared with a 10% p.a. rate with annual compounding. In fact 10% p.a. with semi-annual compounding is equivalent to 10.25% p.a. with annual compounding. This can be demonstrated using the future value formula. Suppose we invest $1 for a year at 10% p.a. with semi-annual compounding. The present value is $1. The future value at maturity is calculated as:

$$FV = \$1 \times (1 + 0.1/2)^2 = \$1.1025$$
$$\text{Interest at maturity} = \$1.1025 - \$1 = \$0.1025$$

This is same amount of interest we would receive if we invested $1 for one year at 10.25% p.a. with annual compounding. This calculation is the basis for what is known as the *annual equivalent rate* (AER) or the effective annual rate. A rate of 10% p.a. with semi-annual compounding is equivalent to 10.25% p.a. with annual compounding. Table A.1 sets out some other examples. For example, a nominal or quoted interest rate of 10% p.a. with daily compounding is equivalent to 10.5156% p.a. with interest compounded once a year.

The following formula will convert between nominal and annual equivalent rates:

$$r_{ann} = (1 + r_{nom}/m)^m - 1$$

where r_{ann} = the annual equivalent rate p.a. as a decimal
         r_{nom} = the nominal interest rate p.a. as a decimal
         m = the number of times interest is compounded a year.

Once potential source of confusion in the financial markets is the way that people refer to interest rates. A rate said to be '10% semi-annual' does not usually mean an interest rate of 10% every six months. It normally means a rate of 10% p.a. with semi-annual compounding. The rate every six months is actually half of 10% which is 5%.

As interest is compounded more and more frequently the annual equivalent rate approaches a limit. This is defined by what is known as *continuous compounding*, a method of calculating interest widely used in the derivatives markets. The effective annual equivalent rate where interest is compounded continuously can be calculated as follows (all rates are expressed as decimals in the formula):

$$r_{ann} = e^{rcont} - 1$$

where r_{ann} = the annual equivalent rate (AER) p.a.
            r_{cont} = the nominal rate of interest p.a. with continuous compounding
            e   = the base of natural logarithms $\cong 2.71828$.

A nominal 10% p.a. rate with continuous compounding is equivalent to approximately 10.5171% p.a. with annual compounding. The EXP() function in Excel calculates e to the power of the value in the brackets.

PRESENT VALUE (PV)

So far we have looked at calculating a future value given a present value and a rate of interest. It is also possible to calculate the value in today's terms of a cash flow due to be received in the future. The basic time value of money formula with periodic compounding is:

$$FV = PV \times (1 + r/m)^n$$

Rearranging:

$$PV = FV/(1 + r/m)^n$$

In this version of the formula r is known as the discount rate. This formula allows us to calculate the value in today's terms of cash to be received in the future. This has very wide applications in financial markets. For example, a debt security such as a bond is simply a title to receive future payments of interest and principal. The 'coupon' is the regular interest amount paid on a standard or 'straight' bond issued by a government or a corporate. A zero-coupon bond pays no interest at all during its life and trades at a discount to its par or redemption value.

Suppose you are deciding how much to pay for a 20-year zero-coupon bond with a par value of $100. The return on similar investments is currently 10% p.a. expressed with annual compounding. Applying the TVM formula, the fair value of the bond is calculated as:

$$PV = 100/1.1^{20} = \$14.8644$$

The discount rate is the return currently available on similar investments with the same credit (default) risk and the same maturity. This establishes a required rate of return and hence a fair value for the bond. Economists would call it the 'opportunity cost of capital' – the return that would be achieved on comparable investments if money is not tied up in the bond.

This methodology is extended to pricing coupon bonds, i.e. bonds that make regular interest payments during their life. Let us suppose that you buy a bond that pays an annual coupon of 10% p.a. The par or face value is $100 and the bond has exactly three years remaining to maturity. How much is it worth today, if the rate of return on similar investments in the market is currently 12% p.a. expressed with annual compounding? The traditional valuation methodology is to establish the cash flows on the bond, discount each cash flow at a constant rate, then sum the present values.

- The cash flow in one year is $10, an interest payment of 10% of the $100 face value. Its PV discounted at 12% for one year is $10/1.12 = \$8.9286$.
- The cash flow in two years is another interest payment of $10. Its PV discounted at 12% for two years is $10/1.12^2 = \$7.9719$.

- The cash flow in three years is a final $10 interest payment plus the payment of the bond's $100 face value, a total of $110. Its PV discounted at 12% for three years is $110/1.12^3 =$ $78.2958.

The sum of the PVs is $95.2, which establishes a fair market price for the bond. The bond is trading below its face value of $100 because it pays a fixed coupon of only 10% p.a. in a current market environment in which the going annual return for investments of this kind is 12% p.a. In economic terms, investors will tend to sell the bond and switch into the higher-yielding investments now available, until its price is pushed below its $100 face value and stabilizes at around $95.2.

Option pricing models tend to use continuously compounded rates to calculate future values and also to discount future cash flows, such as the exercise or strike price of a European-style call or put. Future and present values with continuously compounded rates are calculated as follows:

$$FV = PV \times e^{rt}$$
$$PV = FV \times e^{-rt}$$

where   FV = future value
        PV = present value
        r = the continuously compounded interest rate p.a.
        t = time in years
        e   = the base of natural logarithms $\cong 2.71828$.

For example, the future value of $100 invested for one year at a continuously compounded rate of 10% p.a. is calculated as follows:

$$FV = \$100 \times e^{rt} = \$100 \times e^{0.1 \times 1} = \$110.5171$$

The present value of $100 to be received in one year if the continuously compounded rate of interest for the period is 10% p.a. is calculated as follows:

$$PV = \$100 \times e^{-rt} = \$100 \times e^{-0.1 \times 1} = \$90.4837$$

YIELD OR RETURN ON INVESTMENT

The basic time value of money formula with periodic compounding is as follows:

$$FV = PV \times (1 + r/m)^n$$

Given a present value and a future value, it is also possible by rearranging the formula to calculate the periodic rate of return achieved on an investment:

$$\text{Rate of return p.a.} = [\sqrt[n]{(FV/PV)} - 1] \times m$$

where   FV = future value
        PV = present value
        m = the number of times that interest is compounded a year
        n = the number of compounding periods to maturity = years $\times$ m.

Suppose we invest a present value of $100 for three years. The future value to be received at maturity is $125. There are no intervening cash flows. The annualized rate of return expressed with different compounding frequencies is calculated as follows:

$$\text{Rate of return with annual compounding} = [\sqrt[3]{(125/100)} - 1] \times 1$$
$$= 7.72\% \text{ p.a.}$$
$$\text{Rate of return with semi-annual compounding} = [\sqrt[6]{(125/100)} - 1] \times 2$$
$$= 7.58\% \text{ p.a.}$$

The rate of 7.58% p.a. is a semi-annually compounded rate. Its annual equivalent rate, i.e. its equivalent expressed with annual compounding, is 7.72% p.a. A continuously compounded rate of return can also be calculated from a present and a future value. Where r is a continuously compounded rate, we have the following equation:

$$FV = PV \times e^{rt}$$

The continuously compounded return can be calculated as follows:

$$\text{Rate of return p.a. with continuous compounding} = \ln(FV/PV) \times (1/t)$$

where $\ln() = $ the natural logarithm of the number in brackets
       $t \quad = $ time to maturity in years.

To take the previous example, suppose we invest $100 for three years and are due to receive $125 at maturity. There are no intervening cash flows.

$$\text{Rate of return with continuous compounding} = \ln(125/100) \times (1/3)$$
$$= 7.44\% \text{ p.a.}$$

A rate of 7.44% p.a. with continuous compounding is equivalent to 7.72% p.a. with annual compounding. The Excel function used to calculate the natural logarithm of a number is LN(). It is the inverse of the EXP() function.

TERM STRUCTURE OF INTEREST RATES

In developed markets the minimum rate of return on an investment for a given maturity period is established by the return on Treasury (government) securities. It is sometimes called the risk-free rate because there is no risk of default. The term structure shows the returns on Treasury zero-coupon securities for a range of different maturity periods. Why not use coupon-paying securities? The problem is that the return on a coupon bond depends to an extent on the rate at which coupons can be re-invested during the life of the security. To calculate a return it is necessary to make assumptions about future re-investment rates. A zero-coupon bill or bond is much simpler. Because there are no coupons, no assumptions need be made about re-investment rates.

Zero-coupon rates are also known as *spot rates*, and working with spot rates has many advantages. Firstly, as stated previously, they can be used to calculate future values without making any assumptions about future re-investment rates. Secondly, they can be used as a reliable and consistent means of discounting future cash flows back to a present value. A one-year risk-free cash flow should be discounted at the one-year Treasury spot rate; two-year risk-free cash flows should be discounted at the two-year Treasury spot rate; and so on. A non-Treasury security such as a corporate bond is valued by discounting the cash flows at the appropriate Treasury spot rates plus a premium or spread that reflects the credit and liquidity risk of the bond. For example, if the bond pays a coupon in one year this should be discounted at the one-year Treasury spot rate plus a spread; if it pays a coupon in two years this should be discounted at the two-year Treasury spot rate plus a spread; and so on.

Just as importantly, spot rates can be used to calculate *forward* interest rates, which are used in the pricing of interest rate forwards, futures, swaps and options. In the next section we show how forward rates can be extracted from spot or zero-coupon rates.

CALCULATING FORWARD INTEREST RATES

Table A.2 shows spot or zero-coupon rates for different maturity periods, expressed with annual compounding. These are based on interbank lending rates rather than Treasuries, so they incorporate a spread over the risk-free Treasury spot rates. The first rate $Z_{0\times1}$ is the rate of return applying to a time period starting now and ending in one year. In our examples, cash flows that occur in one year will be discounted at this rate. The second rate $Z_{0\times2}$ is the rate of return that applies to a time period starting now and ending in two years. Cash flows that occur in two years will be discounted at that rate. The rate $Z_{0\times3}$ is the three-year spot or zero-coupon rate, the rate at which three-year cash flows will be discounted.

The forward interest rate between years one and two can be calculated from these values using an arbitrage argument. We will call that forward rate $F_{1\times2}$. It is the rate of return that applies to investments made in one year that mature two years from now. Also, if we were discounting a cash flow that occurs in two years back to a present value one year from now, then it should be discounted at $F_{1\times2}$. If we wished to discount *this* value back to a present value now, it should be discounted at the one-year spot rate $Z_{0\times1}$.

Suppose we borrow $1 now for two years at the two-year spot rate of 5% p.a. We take this cash and deposit the money for one year at 4% p.a., the one-year spot rate. Suppose further that we could agree a deal with someone that allowed us to re-invest the proceeds from this deposit in a year for a further year at (say) 8% p.a. with annual compounding. Our cash flows in two years' time would look like this.

- Principal plus interest repaid on loan $= \$1 \times 1.05^2 = \$1.1025$
- Proceeds from one-year deposit at 4% p.a. re-invested for a further year at 8% p.a. $= \$1 \times 1.04 \times 1.08 = \$1.1232$

This is an arbitrage. In two years' time we repay $1.1025 on the loan but achieve $1.1232 by investing the funds for a year and then rolling over the deposit for a further year. Since it is unlikely that such 'free lunches' will persist for long, this tells us that it is unlikely that anyone would enter into a deal that allowed us to re-invest for the second year at 8% p.a. The fair forward rate $F_{1\times2}$ is the rate for re-investing money in one year for a further year such that no

Table A.2   Spot or zero-coupon rates expressed with annual compounding

Spot rate	Value (% p.a.)
$Z_{0\times1}$	4.00
$Z_{0\times2}$	5.00
$Z_{0\times3}$	6.00

such arbitrage opportunity is available. For no arbitrage to occur the following equation must hold:

$$(1 + Z_{0\times2})^2 = (1 + Z_{0\times1}) \times (1 + F_{1\times2})$$

This equation says that the future value of the two-year loan at maturity at the two-year spot rate must equal the proceeds from investing that money for one year at the one-year spot rate re-invested for a further year at the forward rate that applies between years one and two. In our example the values are as follows:

$$1.05^2 = 1.04 \times (1 + F_{1\times2})$$

therefore:

$$F_{1\times2} = 6.01\% \text{ p.a.}$$

A similar argument can be used to calculate $F_{2\times3}$, the forward rate of interest that applies between years two and three. Suppose we borrow \$1 for three years now at $Z_{0\times3}$. We invest the \$1 for two years at $Z_{0\times2}$. For no arbitrage to be available the forward rate between years two and three must be such that the following equation is satisfied:

$$(1 + Z_{0\times3})^3 = (1 + Z_{0\times2})^2 \times (1 + F_{2\times3})$$
$$1.06^3 \qquad = 1.05^2 \times (1 + F_{2\times3})$$

therefore:

$$F_{2\times3} = 8.03\% \text{ p.a.}$$

Notice here that the forward rates are increasing with time. This is the typical situation where the term structure of interest rates shows the spot rates increasing with time to maturity. The market is building in expectations of rising interest rates in the future.

FORWARD RATES AND FRAs

Forward interest rates have to relate to the market prices of interest rate futures and forward rate agreements, otherwise arbitrage opportunities may be available. This is because interest rate futures and FRAs can be used to lock into borrowing or lending rates for future time periods. For example, suppose we could arrange the following deals (the example ignores the effects of bid/offer spreads and brokerage):

- Borrow \$100 000 for two years at the two-year spot rate 5% p.a.
- Deposit \$100 000 for one year at the one-year spot rate 4% p.a.
- Sell a 1 × 2 year FRA on a notional \$104 000 at a forward rate of 8% p.a.

The principal plus interest on the deposit in one year is \$104 000. The effect of selling the FRA on this amount is to lock in a re-investment rate of 8% p.a. for a second year. Table A.3 shows the proceeds from this strategy at maturity in two years, taking a range of possible re-investment rates up to 12% p.a.

- Column (1) is the principal plus interest on the initial \$100 000 loan at maturity in two years at a rate of 5% p.a. annually compounded.
- Column (2) is the proceeds from depositing that money for one year at 4% p.a.
- Column (3) has a number of possible levels the one-year rate could take in one year for re-investing the proceeds of the deposit.

Table A.3   Arbitrage constructed if FRA rate is not set at the forward interest rate

(1) Loan repayment end-year 2 ($)	(2) Deposit proceeds end-year 1 ($)	(3) Re-investment rate (% p.a.)	(4) Deposit proceeds end-year 2 ($)	(5) FRA payment end-year 2 ($)	(6) Net cash end-year 2 ($)
−110 250	104 000	4	108 160	4160	2070
−110 250	104 000	6	110 240	2080	2070
−110 250	104 000	8	112 320	0	2070
−110 250	104 000	10	114 400	−2080	2070
−110 250	104 000	12	116 480	−4160	2070

Table A.4   No arbitrage if FRA is transacted at the forward interest rate

(1) Loan repayment end-year 2 ($)	(2) Deposit proceeds end year 1 ($)	(3) Re-investment rate (% p.a.)	(4) Deposit proceeds end-year 2 ($)	(5) FRA payment end-year 2 ($)	(6) Net cash end-year 2 ($)
−110 250	104 000	4	108 160	2090	0
−110 250	104 000	6	110 240	10	0
−110 250	104 000	8	112 320	−2070	0
−110 250	104 000	10	114 400	−4150	0
−110 250	104 000	12	116 480	−6230	0

- Column (4) calculates the proceeds of the deposit re-invested for a further year at the rate in column (3).
- Column (5) is the payment on the FRA, either positive or negative. For example, suppose the one-year rate in one year is 4%. The FRA rate is assumed to be 8% and the notional $104 000. We will receive a compensation payment on the FRA of 8% − 4% = 4% applied to the notional of the FRA, which comes to $4160.
- Column (6) is the sum of columns (1), (4) and (5).

The values in column (6) are always positive, whatever happens to interest rates in the future, which shows that there is an arbitrage. It should not be possible for us to sell the 1×2 year FRA at 8% p.a. The fair rate for selling the FRA is the forward rate $F_{1\times2}$ which we calculated in the previous section as 6.01% p.a. Table A.4 assumes that the FRA is sold at 6.01% p.a., and the arbitrage profit disappears.

FORWARD RATES AND INTEREST RATE SWAPS

An interest rate swap (IRS) is an agreement between two parties to exchange cash flows on regular dates, in which the cash flows are calculated on a different basis. In a standard interest rate swap, one payment leg is based on a fixed rate of interest and the other is based on a floating or variable interest rate linked to a benchmark such as the London Interbank Offered Rate (LIBOR). The floating rate is reset at regular intervals, such as every six months. The notional principal used to calculate the payments is fixed.

It will be helpful in the following discussion to use discount factors. A discount factor is simply the present value of $1 at the zero-coupon or spot rate to the receipt of that cash flow.

Table A.5   Spot rates and discount factors

Spot rate	Value (% p.a.)	Discount factor	Value
$Z_{0\times1}$	4.00	$DF_{0\times1}$	0.96153846
$Z_{0\times2}$	5.00	$DF_{0\times2}$	0.90702948
$Z_{0\times3}$	6.00	$DF_{0\times3}$	0.83961928

Table A.6   Swap floating rate cash flows

Year	Notional ($m)	Rate	Value (% p.a.)	Floating cash flow ($m)
1	100	$Z_{0\times1}$	4.00	4.00
2	100	$F_{1\times2}$	6.01	6.01
3	100	$F_{2\times3}$	8.03	8.03

Table A.5 shows the discount factors based on the spot rates used in previous sections of this appendix. The one-year spot rate is 4% p.a. The one-year discount factor at this rate is:

$$1/1.04 = 0.96153846$$

The two-year spot rate is 5% p.a. So the two-year discount factor at this rate is:

$$1/1.05^2 = 0.90702948$$

One advantage of using discount factors is that the present value of a future cash flow can immediately be established by multiplying that cash flow by the discount factor for that time period.

We will now explore the relationship between swap rates, discount factors and forward rates. Let us assume that we are considering entering into an interest rate swap deal with the following terms:

Notional principal: $100 million
Maturity: 3 Years
We pay: Fixed rate, annually in arrears
We receive: Floating rate, annually in arrears
Interest calculations: annually compounded rates
First floating rate setting: 4% p.a.

Under the terms of the swap, we would pay a fixed rate of interest on a notional principal of $100 million annually in arrears for three years. Our counterparty would pay in return a variable rate of interest on $100 million annually in arrears for three years. The question is: What fixed rate of interest should we pay to make this a fair deal?

One answer to this question is to start by calculating the floating rate cash flows on the swap (see Table A.6). Since we are receiving the floating rate, these are positive cash flows. The first cash flow due at the end of Year 1 is based on the one-year spot rate of 4% p.a. The second cash flow will be based on the one-year rate in one year's time, which we assume is established by the forward rate $F_{1\times2}$. The third and final cash flow will be based on the one-year rate in two

Table A.7   Present value of floating rate cash flows

Year	Notional ($m)	Floating cash flow ($m)	Discount factor	Present value ($m)
1	100	4.00	0.96153846	3.85
2	100	6.01	0.90702948	5.45
3	100	8.03	0.83961928	6.74
			Sum:	16.04

Table A.8   Fixed rate cash flows on swap

Year	Notional ($m)	Fixed cash flow ($m)	Discount factor	Present value ($m)
1	100	−5.92	0.96153846	−5.69
2	100	−5.92	0.90702948	−5.37
3	100	−5.92	0.83961928	−4.97
			Sum:	−16.04

years' time, which we assume is established by the forward rate $F_{2\times3}$, which we calculated as 8.03% p.a.

The next step is to discount these cash flows at the zero-coupon or spot rates for each time period – or, to make the calculation easier, to multiply each cash flow by the discount factor for that time period. The results and the sum of the present values is shown in Table A.7.

A *par swap* is one in which the present value of the floating and fixed legs sum to zero. If a swap is entered into at exactly par the expected payout to both sides is zero and neither side pays a premium to the other. The fixed rate on a par swap is the single rate such that, if the fixed cash flows are calculated at that rate, the present value of the fixed cash flows completely offsets the present value of the floating rate cash flows. As a result, the net present value of the swap is zero.

In our example, assuming the swap is agreed at par, we need to find a fixed rate such that the present value of the fixed cash flows on the swap equals minus $16.04 million. (In our example, the fixed cash flows are negative because we are paying fixed on the swap.) At that rate the net present value – i.e. the sum of the PVs of the fixed and floating cash flows – is zero. A direct way to calculate the rate is shown below, but it can also be found by trial-and-error. Either way, as Table A.8 shows, the answer is 5.92% p.a. The fixed cash flows are minus $5.92 million each year for three years. The present values are established by multiplying each cash flow by the appropriate discount factor. The sum of the present values is minus $16.04 million, which offsets the present value of the floating leg cash flows. (There is some rounding in these values.)

The fixed rate can be established directly, using the forward rates and discount factors. It is a weighted average of the spot rate $Z_{0\times1}$ and the forward rates $F_{1\times2}$ and $F_{2\times3}$ weighted by discount factors $DF_{0\times1}$, $DF_{0\times2}$ and $DF_{0\times3}$ respectively.

$$\frac{(0.04 \times 0.96153846) + (0.0601 \times 0.90702948) + (0.0803 \times 0.83961928)}{0.96153846 + 0.90702948 + 0.83961928}$$

$$= 0.0592 = 5.92\%$$

BLACK–SCHOLES OPTION PRICING MODEL

For a European call option on a share with no dividends the Black–Scholes formula is:

$$C = [S \times N(d_1)] - [E \times e^{-rt} \times N(d_2)]$$

where S = the spot price of the underlying
       E = the exercise or strike price of the option

$$d_1 = \frac{\ln(S/E) + (r \times t) + (\sigma^2 \times t/2)}{\sigma \times \sqrt{t}}$$

$$d_2 = d_1 - (\sigma \times \sqrt{t})$$

and the terms are as follows:

$N(d)$ = The standard normal cumulative distribution function, i.e. the area to the left of d under a normal distribution curve with mean zero and variance one. The correct Excel function to use is NORMSDIST().

$\ln()$ = The natural logarithm of a number to base e $\cong$ 2.71828. The Excel function to use is LN().

σ = volatility per annum (as a decimal)

t = time to expiry (in years)

r = the continuously compounded interest rate (as a decimal). The Excel function for e to the power of the value in brackets is EXP().

The call value is the expected payout of the option discounted back to the time of purchase. The formula says that the value of a call is the spot price (S) minus the present value of the exercise price (E), where S and E are weighted by the factors $N(d_1)$ and $N(d_2)$ respectively. $N(d_1)$ is the option delta. $N(d_2)$ is the probability that the option will be exercised and the strike price paid. The model uses continuous compounding in the present value calculation.

Suppose we wish to use Black–Scholes to price a call with the following details.

> European call option on a non-dividend paying share XYZ.
> Spot $(S) = 100$
> Exercise price $(E) = 100$
> Time in years $(t) = 0.25$
> Annual volatility $(\sigma) = 20\% = 0.2$
> Interest rate p.a. $(r) = 5\% = 0.05$

The complete values used to price the call (using the appropriate Excel functions) are:

LN $(100/100) = 0.00$
$d_1 = 0.1750$
$d_2 = 0.0750$
NORMSDIST(0.1750) = 0.56946
NORMSDIST(0.0750) = 0.52989
$100 \times$ EXP$(-0.05 \times 0.25) = 98.7578$

Call value = $(100 \times 0.56946) - (98.7578 \times 0.52989) = 4.615$

The value P of a European put option on a stock that pays no dividends is calculated as:

$$P = [E \times e^{-rt} \times N(-d_2)] - [S \times N(-d_1)]$$

BLACK–SCHOLES WITH DIVIDENDS

The model can be adjusted to price European options on shares paying dividends. The following version assumes that dividends are paid out in a continuous stream, and is commonly used to price stock index and currency options:

$$C = [S \times e^{-qt} \times N(d_1)] - [E \times e^{-rt} \times N(d_2)]$$
$$P = [E \times e^{-rt} \times N(-d_2)] - [S \times e^{-qt} \times N(-d_1)]$$

where C = the value of a call
       P = the value of a put
       q = the continuous dividend yield on the underlying as a decimal
       $$d_1 = \frac{\ln(S/E) + [(r - q) \times t] + (\sigma^2 \times t/2)}{\sigma \times \sqrt{t}}$$
       $$d_2 = d_1 - (\sigma \times \sqrt{t})$$

This model can be used to price currency options. A sterling call/US dollar put, for example, is the right to buy pounds and pay, in return, a fixed amount of dollars. The inputs to the model are as follows:

- The spot price of the underlying becomes the £/$ spot rate.
- The volatility is the volatility of the spot rate.
- q is the sterling interest rate, the return on the currency that will be acquired by the holder and sold by the writer if the call is exercised.
- r is the dollar interest rate.

HISTORICAL VOLATILITY

The historical volatility of an asset is measured as the annualized standard deviation of the returns on the asset over some historical period of time. The percentage returns are calculated using natural logarithms. The Excel function to use here is LN(). Using natural logarithms rather than simple percentage price changes has the advantage that price changes are additive. This is not the case with simple percentages. For example, suppose a share is trading at 100, falls to 95 then rises to 104.

$\ln(95/100) = -5.1293\%$
$\ln(104/95) = 9.0514\%$
Total $= -5.1293\% + 9.0514\% = 3.9221\%$
$\ln(104/100) = 3.9221\%$

If we use simple percentages the fall in the price from 100 to 95 is -5%. The rise from 95 to 104 is 9.4737%. These do not add up to 4%, which is the simple percentage rise from 100 to 104. Table A.9 illustrates the calculation of historic volatility using natural logarithms. The price of the underlying security starts at 500 on Day 0. In column (2) we show the closing price of the stock over the next 10 trading days (covering two calendar weeks). Column (3) calculates percentages changes. For example, the percentage change in the share price between Day 0 and Day 1 is calculated as $\ln(508/500) = 1.59\%$.

The average daily percentage change in the share price is $+0.22\%$, and column (4) calculates the extent to which each daily percentage price change deviates from the average. For instance, 1.59% is 1.37% away from the average. The next number in the sequence -3.2% is -3.42%

Table A.9   Steps in the calculation of historic volatility

(1) Day	(2) Price	(3) % Price change	(4) Deviation (%)	(5) Deviation^2 (%)
0	500			
1	508	1.59	1.37	0.02
2	492	−3.20	−3.42	0.12
3	498	1.21	0.99	0.01
4	489	−1.82	−2.04	0.04
5	502	2.62	2.41	0.06
6	507	0.99	0.77	0.01
7	500	−1.39	−1.61	0.03
8	502	0.40	0.18	0.00
9	499	−0.60	−0.82	0.01
10	511	2.38	2.16%	0.05
		Average = 0.22		Sum = 0.33

away from the average. Column (5) squares the deviations and the sum of the squared deviations shown at the bottom of the column is 0.33%.

Sample variance is a statistical measure of the extent to which a set of observations in a sample diverges from the average or mean value. In Table A.4 we used 10 observations based on the change in the share price over two calendar weeks. The sample variance is calculated as follows:

$$\text{Variance } \sigma^2 = \frac{\text{Sum of deviations}^2}{\text{Number of observations} - 1}$$
$$= 0.33\%/9 = 0.0033/9 = 0.000367 = 0.0367\%$$

The reason we divide by one less than the number of observations is simply to adjust for the fact that we are using a sample of price changes (and a relatively small sample at that). Volatility is defined as the standard deviation of the returns on the share. It is the square root of the variance.

$$\text{Standard deviation } \sigma = \sqrt{\text{Variance}} = \sqrt{0.000367} = 0.0192 = 1.92\%$$

What we have calculated is the *daily* volatility of the returns on the share. It was based on percentage price changes over a series of trading days. Volatility is normally expressed on an annualized basis in the options market. If we assume that there are 252 trading days in the year, then the annualized volatility is calculated as the daily volatility times the square root of 252.

$$\text{Annual volatility} = \text{Daily volatility} \times \sqrt{\text{Trading days per annum}}$$
$$= 1.92\% \times \sqrt{252} = 30.4\% \text{ p.a.}$$

Intuitively, the reason why annual volatility is much less than daily volatility times the total number of trading days in the year is because it is assumed that the share price moves in a random fashion. Over the course of a year it moves up and down, affected by new pieces of information that change the expected future cash flows. This has the effect of smoothing out some of the extreme volatility that can be experienced over a very short time period such as a day.

Appendix B

Glossary of Terms

Accreting swap   A swap in which the principal increases in each time period.

Accrued interest   Interest on a bond that has accrued since the last coupon date.

American option   An option that can be exercised on any business day during its life.

Amortization   Repayment of the principal on a loan or bond in instalments over a period of time.

Amortizing swap   A swap in which the principal is reduced in each time period.

Arbitrage   A set of transactions in which risk-free profits are achieved because assets are mispriced in the market. More loosely, a strategy that is not entirely risk-free but generates profits in most circumstances.

Arbitrageur   Someone who takes advantage of arbitrage opportunities.

Asian or Asiatic option   Another name for an average price option.

Ask   The offer or sale price of an asset or derivatives contract.

Asset   A physical commodity or a financial asset such as a share or a bond.

Asset-backed securities   Bonds backed by a pool of assets created or 'originated' by a bank or other institution, such as mortgages and credit card loans. The cash flows from the assets are used to repay the bondholders.

Asset-or-nothing option   An option that pays out an amount equal to the price of the underlying if it expires in-the-money, otherwise nothing.

Assignment   Formal notification from an exchange that the writer of a call (put) option must deliver (take delivery of) the underlying asset at the exercise price.

As-you-like option   *See*: Chooser option.

At-best order   An order to a broker to buy or sell a contract at the best price available.

At-the-money option   An option whose strike is equal to the cash price of the underlying. Its intrinsic value is zero.

Automatic exercise   When the clearing house automatically exercises in-the-money options at expiry.

Average price (or rate) option   The payout on a fixed strike contract is based on the difference between the strike and the average price of the underlying during a specified period. In a floating strike contract the strike is based on the average price of the underlying during a specified period, and the payout is based on the difference between this and the price of the underlying at expiry.

Bank for International Settlements (BIS)   The BIS acts to promote international co-operation in financial matters.

Barrier option   An option whose payoff depends on whether the underlying has hit one or more threshold or barrier levels.

Basis   The difference between the cash price of an asset and the forward or futures price. When the futures is above the cash price the basis is negative. This represents the negative cost of carrying a position in the asset to deliver on the future date. When the futures is below the cash the basis is positive.

Basis point   In both the money and the bond markets one basis point equals 0.01%.

Basis risk   The risk that arises because futures prices do not exactly track changes in the underlying asset, because of changes in the basis. This poses problems for those using futures to hedge positions in the underlying.

Basis swap   Both legs are based on floating interest rates but each is calculated on a different basis – e.g. LIBOR versus the rate on commercial paper.

Basket option   The payoff depends on the performance of a portfolio of assets.

BBA   British Bankers' Association, which calculates LIBOR rates each business day for a range of currencies.

Bear   Someone who thinks that a security or sector or market will fall in price.

Bear spread   A combination option strategy with a limited loss if the price of the underlying rises and a limited profit if it falls.

Bermudan option   Can be exercised on specific dates up to expiry, such as one day per week.

Beta   Percentage change in the price of a security for a 1% change in the market.

Bid   The buy price of an asset or derivatives contract.

Bid/offer spread   The difference between the bid price of an asset or derivatives contract and its offer or ask or sale price.

Big figure   In the FX markets, the first decimal places of a currency rate quotation.

Binary or digital option   *See*: Cash-or-nothing option; Asset-or-nothing option.

Binomial tree   A set of prices developed from the current price of the underlying, such that at any 'node' in the tree the asset can either move up or down in price by a set amount and with a set probability. Used to price options and convertible bonds.

Black model   A variant on the Black–Scholes model, used to price European options on forwards and futures.

Black–Scholes model   The European option pricing model developed by Black, Scholes and Merton in the 1970s.

Bond   A debt security issued by a company, a sovereign state and its agencies, or a supra-national body. A straight or 'plain vanilla' bond pays a fixed coupon (interest amount) on regular dates and the par or face value is paid at maturity.

Bond option   A call or put option on a bond.

Bond rating   An assessment of the credit or default risk on a bond issued by an agency such as Moody's or Standard & Poor's.

Bootstrapping   Deriving zero-coupon or spot rates from the prices of coupon bonds or from the par swap curve.

Broker   A person or firm paid a fee or commission to act as an agent in arranging purchases or sales of securities or derivatives contracts.

Bull   Someone who thinks that a particular asset or market will increase in price.

Bull spread   A combination option strategy with a limited profit if the underlying increases in price but a limited loss if it falls.

Bund   Treasury bond issued by the Federal German government.

Butterfly   A long butterfly is a combination option strategy produced by buying a call, selling two calls with a higher strike, and buying a call struck further above that level. All the options are on the same underlying and with the same expiry. It can also be assembled using put options.

Buy–Write   *See*: Covered call.

Calendar or time spread   A strategy that involves buying and selling options on the same underlying with different expiry dates to exploit differences in time value decay.

Call feature   A feature that allows the issuer of a bond to redeem the bond before maturity.

Call option   The right but not the obligation to buy an underlying asset at a fixed strike price.

Caplet   One component of an interest rate cap.

Capped floating rate note (FRN)   The rate of interest on the note cannot exceed a given level.

Cash-and-carry arbitrage   Selling over-priced futures contracts and buying the underlying to achieve a risk-free profit. Or buying under-priced futures and shorting the underlying.

Cash-or-nothing option   Pays out a fixed amount of cash if it expires in-the-money, otherwise nothing.

Cash security   An underlying security rather than a derivative.

Cash settlement   Settling a derivative contract in cash rather than through the physical delivery of the underlying asset.

Cheapest-to-deliver bond (CTD)   The bond that is the cheapest to deliver against a short position in a bond futures contract.

Chicago Board Options Exchange (CBOE)   The major options exchange founded in 1973.

Chicago Board of Trade (CBOT)   Started as a commodity market in the nineteenth century and has now developed major financial futures and options contracts, e.g. on US Treasury bonds.

Chicago Mercantile Exchange (CME)   The Chicago futures and options exchange where the key Eurodollar futures contract trades. Also known as the 'Merc'.

Chooser option   The holder can decide at a preset time whether it is a call or a put option Also known as a U-Choose, as-you-like, call-or-put option.

Clean price   The price of a bond excluding interest accrued since the last coupon date.

Clearing house   The organization that registers, matches, monitors and guarantees trades made on a futures and options exchange.

Clearing member   Not all members of a futures and options exchange are clearing members. All trades must eventually be settled through a clearing member which deals directly with the clearing house.

Cliquet (ratchet) option   The strike is reset on specific dates according to the spot price of the underlying, locking in interim gains.

Collared floating rate note   Has a minimum and a maximum coupon rate.

Collateral   Cash or securities pledged against the performance of some obligation.

Collateralized debt obligations (CDOs)   Debt securities based on the cash flows from a portfolio of bonds or loans. The securities are normally sold in tranches with different risk/return characteristics.

Collateralized mortgage obligations (CMOs)   Debt securities based on the cash flows from a pool of mortgage loans.

Combination   A strategy involving a mixture of options on the same underlying.

Commercial bank   A bank that makes loans to corporations or governments.

Commission   The fee charged by a broker to a customer for completing a purchase or sale.

Commodity   A physical item such as oil, gold or grain. Commodities are traded for spot and for future delivery.

Commodity swap   At least one of the payment legs depends on the price of a commodity.

Common stock   US expression for an ordinary share or equity.

Compound option   An option to buy or sell an option.

Continuously compounded rate   A method of quoting interest rates commonly used in the derivatives market.

Contract size   The unit of trading on a derivatives contract. For example, the 30-year Treasury bond futures contract on the CBOT is on $100 000 par value US Treasury bonds.

Conversion (price) factor   A factor assigned to a bond that is deliverable against a bond futures contract. It adjusts the amount invoiced by the seller to the buyer if that bond is delivered.

Conversion premium   Measures how much more expensive it is to buy a share by buying and converting a convertible bond compared to buying the share in the cash market.

Conversion ratio   The number of shares a convertible bond can be converted into.

Convertible bond   A bond that is convertible (at the option of the holder) into a fixed number of shares of the issuing company.

Cost of carry   The cost of holding or carrying a position in an asset (funding plus storage and other costs) less any income received on the asset.

Counterparty   The other party to a trade or contract.

Counterparty risk   The risk that a trading counterparty might fail to fulfil its contractual obligations.

Coupon   The periodic interest amount payable on a bond.

Coupon rate   The interest rate payable on a bond.

Covered call   The purchase of an underlying asset combined with a sale of a call option on that asset.

Covered warrant   A longer-dated option on a share or a basket of shares issued by a financial institution which trades in the form of a security.

Credit default swap   A contract in which a protection buyer pays a fee to a protection seller. If a defined credit event occurs affecting the referenced asset specified in the contract, the buyer of protection receives a cash compensation payment or delivers the referenced asset to the protection seller in return for cash.

Credit derivative   A derivative whose payoff depends on the credit standing of an organization or group of organizations.

Credit enhancement   Methods used to enhance credit quality in a securitization.

Credit rating   An assessment of the probability that a borrower or an issuer of debt securities will make timely payments on its financial obligations.

Credit risk   The risk of loss resulting from default on a financial transaction.

Credit spread   The additional return on a bond or a loan over some benchmark rate, that is dependent on the credit-worthiness of the borrower and the liquidity of the asset. It is often expressed as a number of basis points over the return on a government bond.

Cross-currency swap   An interest rate swap where the payment legs are made in two different currencies.

Currency option   The right but not the obligation to exchange one currency for another at a fixed exchange rate. Also known as an FX option.

Currency overlay   A strategy used in investment management to divorce decisions made on buying foreign assets from decisions on currency exposures. The manager can hedge the currency risk or take on additional currency exposure.

Currency risk   The risk of losses resulting from movements in currency exchange rates.

Currency translation risk   The risk that results from translating foreign currency earnings back into its home currency when the consolidated accounts of a company with international operations are prepared.

DAX   An index of 30 top German shares traded on the Frankfurt exchange. It is a total return index – dividends on the shares are assumed to be re-invested.

Day-count   The calendar convention applied to a quoted interest rate or yield.

Dealing spread   The difference between a trader's bid and offer (ask) price.

Debt   Money owed to creditors or lenders or to holders of debt securities.

Debt security   A tradable security such as a bond that represents a loan made to the issuer.

Deferred swap   A forward start swap, i.e. one that starts on a future date.

Delivery   The process of delivering assets. Some derivatives contracts involve the physical delivery of the underlying. Others are settled in cash.

Delivery month   When a futures contract expires and delivery or final cash settlement takes place.

Delta   The change in the value of an option for a small change in the value of the underlying asset.

Delta hedging   Protecting against losses on an option or portfolio of options arising from small changes in the price of the underlying.

Delta neutral   An option position that is delta hedged and protected against small changes in the price of the underlying asset.

Derivative   An instrument whose value depends on the value of an underlying asset such as a share or a bond.

Dilution   The reduction in earnings per share caused by the creation of new shares.

Dirty price   The clean price of a bond plus interest accrued since the last coupon payment.

Discount factor   The present value of $1 at the spot or zero-coupon rate for a specific time period.

Discount rate   Generally, the rate used to discount future cash flows to a present value. In the US money markets, the rate charged to banks when borrowing from the Federal Reserve when it acts as lender of last resort.

Dividend   A cash payment a company makes to its shareholders.

Dividend yield   Dividend per share divided by the current market price of a share.

Dow Jones Industrial Average (DJIA)   Index based on 30 leading US industrial shares. In 1997 the CBOT introduced a futures contract on the Dow.

Down-and-in option   Comes into existence if the price of the underlying falls to hit a barrier level.

Down-and-out option   Ceases to exist if the price of the underlying falls to hit a barrier level.

Downside risk   The risk of making a loss on a trading position or an investment.

Dual currency bond   Pays interest in one currency but is denominated in another currency.

Early exercise   Exercising an option before expiry.

Efficient market theory   Theory that asset prices reflect currently available information and fully discount expected future cash flows.

Embedded option   An option that is embedded in a security such as a convertible bond or a structured financial product.

Equity   Share or common stock. An equity holder is a part-owner of the business.

Equity collar   Buying a protective put and selling an out-of-the-money call to protect against losses on the underlying while at the same time reducing (or eliminating) the net premium due. The disadvantage is that profits on the underlying are capped.

Equity swap   An agreement between two parties to make regular exchanges of payments where one payment leg is based on the value of a share or a basket of shares. The other leg is normally based on a fixed or a floating interest rate.

Eurex   The merged German–Swiss electronic derivatives exchange.

Euribor   Reference rate set in Brussels for interbank lending in euros, the European common currency. Its rival is euro-LIBOR, set in London by the BBA.

Eurobond   A bond denominated in a currency other than that of the country in which it is issued, and marketed to international investors via underwriting banks.

Eurocurrency   A currency held on account outside the domestic market and outside the control of its regulatory authorities.

Eurocurrency deposit   Eurocurrency placed on deposit with a bank.

Eurodollar   A dollar held on deposit outside the USA or in an international account in the USA.

Eurodollar futures   A futures contract traded on Chicago Mercantile Exchange based on the interest rate on a notional three-month Eurodollar deposit for a future time period.

Euromarket   The international market for dealings in Eurocurrencies.

European option   An option that can only be exercised at expiry.

Exchange   An organized market in which securities or derivatives are traded.

Exchange option   An option to exchange one asset for another.

Exchangeable bond   Exchangeable (at the option of the holder) for a fixed number of shares of a company other than the issuer of the bond.

Exchange delivery settlement price (EDSP)   The price used to settle a futures contract on the delivery day.

Exchange-traded contract   A derivative contract traded on an organized exchange.

Ex-dividend (xd)   The buyer of a security trading xd is not entitled to the next dividend. It goes to the seller.

Exercise   The action taken by the holder of a call (put) option when he or she takes up the option to buy (sell) the underlying.

Exercise or strike price   The price at which the holder of a call (put) option takes up his or her right to buy (sell) the underlying asset.

Exotic option   A non-standard contract, e.g. a barrier or an average price or a binary option.

Expected value   The expected future value of an asset.

Expiry or expiration date   The last day of a contract.

Extendable swap   A swap which can be extended at the choice of one of the parties to the deal.

Face value   The principal or par value of a debt security such as a bond or a Treasury bill.

Fair value   The theoretical value of a financial asset, often established using a pricing model.

Fill-or-kill (FOK)   An order on an exchange which is either executed in its entirety at the stipulated price or cancelled.

Financial future   An exchange-traded contract in which a commitment is made to deliver a financial asset in the future at a fixed price. In some cases the contract is settled in cash.

Fixed interest (income) security   Literally, a security which pays a fixed income on a regular basis until maturity. Often though it is used as a generic term for bonds.

Flex option   An exchange-traded option that has some flexibility as to its terms, e.g. the strike price can be non-standard.

Floating rate   A rate of interest such as LIBOR that varies over time.

Foreign exchange risk   The risk of losses resulting from changes in foreign exchange rates.

Forward contract   An agreement between two parties to buy and to sell an asset at a fixed price on a future date, or to make a cash settlement based on the difference between a fixed price and the actual market value of the asset on a future date.

Forward exchange rate   The rate to exchange two currencies on a date later than spot.

Forward interest rate (forward-forward rate)   The rate of interest that applies between two dates in the future.

Forward rate agreement (FRA)   A bilateral contract to make compensation payments based on the difference between a contractual interest rate for a future time period and the actual market rate for that period.

Forward start swap   A swap that starts on a date later than spot.

FT-SE 100 Index   An index of the top 100 UK shares weighted by market capitalization.

Futures contract   An agreement transacted through an organized exchange to deliver an asset at a fixed price in the future. Some contracts are cash settled and no actual physical delivery takes place.

Futures option   An option to buy or sell a futures contract.

FX option   Currency option. The right to exchange two currencies at a fixed exchange rate.

Gamma   The change in an option's delta for a small change in the price of the underlying.

Gearing (UK) or Leverage (USA)   In a trading or investment situation, making an enhanced return through a strategy that requires a relatively small initial outlay of capital.

Gilt or gilt-edged security   A bond issued by the UK Government.

Government securities   Bills, notes and bonds issued by governments.

Greeks   The option sensitivity measures: delta, gamma, theta, vega (or kappa) and rho.

Hedge fund   Originally, a fund which takes both long and short positions in securities. Also used to mean a fund that take highly leveraged or speculative positions.

Hedge ratio   The calculation of how much of the hedge instrument (e.g. futures contracts) has to be traded to cover the risk on the asset that is to be hedged.

Hedging   Protecting against potential losses.

Historic volatility   The volatility of an asset over some past time period.

Implied volatility   The volatility assumption implied in an actual option price.

Index   A figure representing the changing value of a basket of securities, e.g. a stock market index.

Index arbitrage   Arbitrage trade assembled by buying and selling index futures and underlying shares.

Index fund or tracker   A fund that seeks to track or match the performance of a market index.

Index futures   A financial futures contract based on a market index, normally settled in cash.

Index option   An option on a market index such as the S&P 500™.

Institutional investor   A firm such as a pension fund which invests money in financial assets.

Instrument   A share or a bond or some other tradeable security or a derivative contract.

Interest rate cap, floor, collar   A cap is an option product typically sold to borrowers, which limits their cost of borrowing. If the interest rate for a given time period covered by the cap is above the strike the buyer receives a compensation payment from the seller. A floor establishes a minimum interest rate level. A borrower who buys a cap and sells a floor establishes an interest rate collar and a maximum and minimum borrowing cost.

Interest rate future   An exchange-traded contract based on the interest rate for a period of time starting in the future. The listed equivalent of the forward rate agreement.

Interest rate option   An option whose value depends on future interest rates.

Interest rate swap   Agreement between two parties to exchange payments on regular dates for a specified time period. One payment is based on a fixed interest rate and the return payment is based on a floating rate, usually LIBOR.

Intermarket spread   Strategy consisting of opposing positions in two different products e.g. a long position in S&P 500™ index futures and a short position in another equity index futures.

International Swaps and Derivatives Association (ISDA)   Trade association chartered in 1985 for dealers in over-the-counter derivatives such as swaps, caps, floors, collars and swaptions.

In-the-money option   One that has positive intrinsic value.

Intrinsic value   For a call the maximum of zero and the spot price of the underlying minus the strike. For a put the maximum of zero and the strike less the spot price of the underlying. Intrinsic value is either zero or positive.

Iron butterfly   A short straddle combined with a long strangle on the same underlying and with the same time to expiry.

Issuer warrant   A warrant (longer-dated option) issued by a company on its own shares.

Kappa   Another name for vega.

Knock-out or knock-in level   The level of the underlying at which a barrier option ceases to exist or comes into existence. Sometimes known as out-strike and in-strike.

Ladder option   Whenever the underlying hits a 'rung' or threshold price level the strike is reset and gains to that point cannot be lost.

LIBOR   London Interbank Offered Rate. The rate at which top-name banks lend money to each other for a specified term in the London market.

LIFFE   The London International Financial Futures & Options Exchange.

Limit order   An order from a client to a broker to buy or sell an asset or derivatives contract with a maximum purchase price or minimum sale price.

Limit price move   Some exchanges only allow price moves within certain limits in the course of a trading session. Trading is stopped if the limit is broken.

Liquidity   There is a liquid market in an asset if it is easy to find a buyer or seller without affecting the price to any significant extent.

Liquidity risk   The risk that trading in an asset dries up and prices cannot be found or are subject to sharp fluctuations.

Local   An independent trader on an exchange.

London Metal Exchange (LME)   The market for trading non-ferrous metals, including futures and options.

Long position or long   The position of a trader who has bought securities or derivatives contracts.

Lookback option   The payoff is based on the maximum or minimum price of the underlying over a specified time period.

Maintenance margin   A system used on some exchanges. A margin call is received if the balance on a trader's account falls below a threshold level.

Mandatorily convertible or exchangeable bond   Must be converted into or exchanged for shares on or by a certain date.

Margin call   When a trader on a derivatives exchange receives a call to make an additional payment because of an adverse movement in the value of a contract.

Market maker   A trader or firm which has agreed to make two-way prices – bid and offer prices – on specific contracts on an exchange.

Market risk   Also known as price or rate risk. The risk that results from changes in the market prices of assets such as shares and bonds.

Mark-to-market   Revaluing investments based on the current market price.

MATIF   The Paris-based electronic futures and options exchange, founded in 1986 and now part of Euronext.

Monte Carlo simulation   A method of valuing a financial asset or portfolio of assets by setting up a simulation based on random changes to the variables that determine the value of the asset or portfolio.

Morgan Stanley Capital International (MSCI) World Index   A closely followed index of share prices from around the developed world.

Mortgage-backed security (MBS)   Bonds and notes backed by a pool of mortgages. The mortgage payments are earmarked to pay interest and principal on the bonds. In a pass-through structure all the investors receive the same pro-rata payments from the mortgage pool. In a collateralized mortgage obligation (CMO) different classes of securities are issued with different payment characteristics.

Naked option   An option position that is not hedged.

Nearby month   A derivative contract with the nearest delivery or expiry date from the date of trading.

Net present value (NPV)   The sum of a set of present values.

Nikkei 225   An index based on the unweighted average of 225 shares traded on the Tokyo Stock Exchange. The Nikkei 300 is weighted by market capitalization.

Nominal interest rate   The stated or quoted rate of interest or return on a loan or debt security.

Normal distribution   The classic bell curve. The Black–Scholes model assumes that the returns on shares follow a normal distribution.

Notional principal   The principal amount used to calculate payments on contracts such as interest rate swaps.

OAT   French government bond.

Off-balance-sheet   An item that does not appear on the assets or liabilities columns on a balance sheet. It can still give rise to contingent liabilities.

Offer price (ask price)   The price at which a trader is prepared to sell an asset or derivative contract.

Off-market swap   A non-par swap where the present values of the fixed and floating legs are not identical. Normally one party will make an initial payment to the other in compensation.

On-the-run bond   The most recently issued and actively traded US Treasury for a given maturity.

Open interest   The number of futures or options contracts for a given delivery month still open.

Open outcry market   A physical market in which trades are conducted by dealers calling out prices.

Open position   A long or a short position in assets or derivatives contracts and which gives rise to market risk until it is closed out or hedged.

Option   The right but not the obligation to buy or sell an asset at a fixed strike price by a set expiry date.

Order-driven market   A market in which client buy and sell orders are directly matched.

Ordinary share   A stake in the equity of a company, carrying an entitlement to participate in the growth of the business and (normally) voting rights. USA: common stock.

Out-of-the-money option   For a call, when the strike is above the price of the underlying. For a put, when the strike is below the price of the underlying.

Outright forward FX   A commitment to exchange two currencies at a fixed rate for a value date later than spot.

Over-the-counter (OTC) transaction   A deal agreed directly between two parties rather than through an exchange.

Par   The face or nominal value of a bond or bill, normally paid out at maturity.

Par bond   A bond that is trading at par.

Parity   Measures the equity value of a convertible bond. It is the bond's conversion ratio (the number of shares it converts into) times the cash price of each share.

Par swap   An interest rate swap where the present values of the fixed and the floating legs are equal.

Physical delivery   The process of delivering the underlying commodity or financial asset specified in a derivatives contract.

Plain vanilla   The most standard form of a financial instrument.

Political risk   The risk of losses arising from exceptional activities by governments, e.g. halting foreign exchange trading in the national currency, or imposing special taxes.

Portfolio insurance   A hedging technique much maligned (probably unjustly) in the aftermath of the 1987 stock market crash. It involves dynamically adjusting a hedge as the market moves by, e.g., trading index futures.

Portfolio management   Managing money by holding a diversified portfolio of assets.

Position   The net total of long and short contracts. A trader who buys 50 September S&P 500 futures and sells 70 of the same contracts is net short 20 contracts. The trader is exposed to market risk unless the position is closed out or hedged.

Premium   In the options market, premium is the price of an option – the sum the buyer pays to the writer.

Present value   The discounted value of a future cash flow or cash flows.

Protective put   Buying a put option to protect against losses on an asset.

Proxy hedge   A hedge that involves using a related financial instrument that is to some extent correlated with changes in the value of the underlying asset to be hedged.

Pull-to-par   The movement in a bond price towards its par value as it approaches maturity.

Putable swap   A swap in which one of the parties can terminate the deal early.

Put–call parity   A fixed relationship between the values of European calls and puts. It shows how long or short forwards can be assembled from a combination of calls and puts on the same underlying.

Put feature   A bond that can be sold back to the issuer before maturity at a fixed price.

Put option   The right but not the obligation to sell the underlying at a fixed strike price.

Quanto option   The payoff depends on an underlying denominated in one currency but paid in another currency.

Quote-driven market   One where market makers quote bid and offer prices.

Rainbow option   The payoff depends on more than one underlying, e.g. the best performing of two equity indices.

Ratings agency   Agencies, such as Moody's and Standard & Poor's and Fitch, which rate the default risk on corporate and sovereign debt.

Real interest rate or yield   An interest rate or rate of return on an investment excluding inflation.

Recovery rate   The amount that can be recovered on a loan or bond that defaults.

Redemption date   The date when the face or redemption value of a security is repaid to the investors.

Reset or refix date   The date when the floating rate on a swap is reset for the next payment period.

Reverse FRN   A special kind of floating rate note. The coupon rate moves inversely with current market interest rates. They can be extremely volatile.

Rho   The change in the value of an option for a given change in interest rates.

Risk-free rate   The return on Treasury securities.

Risk management   Monitoring, evaluating and hedging against potential losses caused by changes in asset prices, interest rates, currency exchange rates, etc.

Rollover   In exchange-traded derivatives, rolling a position from one expiry or delivery month to a later month.

Scalper   Someone who buys and sells derivatives contracts, usually on the same day, attempting to profit from the difference between the bid and the offer price.

Securitization   The process of creating asset-backed securities. Bonds are sold to investors which are backed by the cash flows from underlying assets, e.g. bank loans.

Security   Generic name for a negotiable (tradable) instrument such as a share, bond or bill.

Series   Option contracts on the same underlying with the same strike and expiry.

Settlement date   In the cash market, the date when a security is transferred and payment is made.

Settlement price   The price used by a clearing house to mark-to-market a derivatives contract. Usually an average of the last trades at the end of the trading day.

Short position, short   In derivatives, when more contracts have been sold than purchased.

Shout option   The owner has the right to 'shout' at one time during the life of the contract and lock in a minimum payout.

Sigma   Greek letter used to designate standard deviation. In derivatives used to denote volatility which is measured as the standard deviation of the returns on an asset.

SPAN®   Standard Portfolio Analysis of Risk®. A system developed by CME and used by numerous exchanges and clearing organizations world wide to calculate initial margins for clearing members. It measures the effect of changes in price and volatility on portfolios of derivatives. The initial margin requirement is based on the worst probable loss calculated.

Special purpose vehicle (SPV)   A tax-exempt trust company specially set up to implement a securitization. The SPV issues bonds and buys the title to the ownership of the cash flows which will repay the bonds. It manages the payments to the bondholders.

Spot foreign exchange rate   The rate for exchanging two currencies in (normally) two business days.

Spot interest rate or yield   Zero-coupon interest rate or yield.

Spot price   The price of a security for spot delivery. Also known as the cash or current price.

Spread   The difference between two prices or rates.

Spread trade   A trade involving a combination of options.

Stamp duty   A government tax on share dealings.

S&P 500®   Standard & Poor's 500. An index based on the prices of 500 leading US companies, weighted by market capitalization.

Stock index futures   A futures contract on a stock index such as the FT-SE 100 or the S&P 500.

Stock option   An option to buy or to sell a share at a fixed price.

Stop-loss order   An order to a broker to close out a position and limit the losses whenever a given price level is reached.

Stop-profit order   An order to a broker to close out a position and take the profits to date whenever a given price level is reached.

Straddle   A combination option strategy which involves selling a call and a put (short straddle) or buying a call and a put (long straddle) on the same underlying with the same strike and the same time to expiration.

Straight bond (plain vanilla bond)   Pays fixed coupons on fixed dates and has a fixed maturity date.

Strangle   Like a straddle except the options used in the strategy have different strikes.

Strike price   Another term for the exercise price of an option.

Stripping and strips   Also known as coupon stripping. Separating the principal and the interest payments on a coupon bond and selling off the parts as zero-coupon bonds.

Structured note   A security usually assembled using derivatives that has non-standard features, e.g. payments are linked to a commodity price or an equity index, or the difference between interest rates in two currencies, or the change in the credit rating of a bond or loan.

Swap   A contract between two parties agreeing to make payments to each other on specified future dates over an agreed time period, where the amount that each has to pay is calculated on a different basis.

Swap curve   A yield curve based on the fixed rates on standard par interest rate swaps.

Swap rate   The fixed rate on an interest rate swap.

Swaption   An option to enter into an interest rate swap. A payer swaption is an option to pay fixed and receive floating. A receiver swaption is an option to receive fixed and pay floating.

Term structure of interest rates   Spot or zero-coupon rates on Treasury securities for a range of maturities.

Theta   The change in the value of an option as time elapses, all other factors remaining constant.

Tick size   In theory, the smallest movement allowed in a price quotation, though some exchanges now allow half- or even quarter-tick price changes on some contracts.

Tick value   The value of a one-tick movement in the quoted price on the whole contract size.

Time spread   *See*: Calendar spread.

Time value   The difference between an option's premium and its intrinsic value.

Time value of money   The basis of discounted cash flow valuation. If interest rates are positive then $1 today is worth more than $1 in the future because it can be invested and earn interest.

Trader   An individual or an employee of a financial institution who buys and sells securities or derivatives contracts.

Tranche (Slice)   In a securitization different tranches of bonds are sold with different risk/return characteristics to appeal to specific investor groups.

Transition matrix   A table that helps to predict the probability that the credit rating of a company will change to different levels over a specified period of time.

Treasury bill (T-Bill)   A short-term negotiable debt security issued and fully backed by a government.

Treasury bond   A longer-term debt security issued and fully backed by a government.

Two-way quotation   A dealer's bid (buy) and offer (ask or sell) price.

Ultra vires   Beyond the legal power. Used when an organization enters into a transaction which it is not legally entitled to conduct.

Underlying   The asset that underlies a derivative product. The value of the derivative is based on the value of the underlying.

Up-and-in option   Comes into existence if the underlying rises to reach a barrier or threshold level.

Up-and-out option   Goes out of existence if the underlying rises to reach a barrier or threshold level.

Upside potential   Potential for profits.

Value at Risk (VAR)   A statistical estimate of the maximum loss that can be made on a portfolio of assets to a certain confidence level over a given time period.

Variation margin   Cash paid or received during the life of a derivative contract to reflect the changing value of the contract.

Vega   The change in the value of an option for a given change in volatility.

Volatility   A key component in option pricing. A measure of the variability of the returns on the underlying security. It is based on historic evidence or future projections.

Volatility smile   A graph showing the implied volatilities of options on the same underlying for a range of strikes. Used to pinpoint the correct volatility to price or revalue options. In practice the graph may be a skew rather than a smile.

Volatility surface   A three-dimensional graph showing the implied volatilities of options on the same underlying for a range of different strike prices and expiration dates.

Warrant   A longer-dated option in the form of a security which can be freely traded often on a stock exchange. Issuer warrants are issued by a company on its own shares. Covered warrants are sold by banks and securities houses and are based on another company's shares or on baskets of shares; they may be settled in cash.

Withholding tax   When a proportion of a coupon or dividend payment is withheld from the investor by the issuer and paid over to the government in tax.

Writer   The seller of an option.

Yield   The return on an investment, taking into account the amount invested and the expected future cash flows.

Yield curve   A graph showing the yields on a given class of bonds (e.g. US Treasuries) against time to maturity.

Yield-to-maturity   The total return earned on a bond if it is bought at the current market price and held until maturity with any coupons re-invested at a constant rate.

Zero-cost collar   A collar strategy with zero net premium to pay. The premiums on the calls and puts cancel out.

Zero-coupon bond   A bond that does not pay a coupon and trades at a discount to its par or face value. At maturity the holder of the bond is repaid the face value.

Zero-coupon rate (spot rate)   The rate of interest that applies to a specific future date. Used to price, e.g., interest rate swaps because no re-investment assumptions need be made.

Appendix C
Further Information

SOME SUGGESTED READING

Amran, M. & Kulatilaka, N. (1999) *Real Options*. Oxford University Press.
Bernstein, P.L. (1996) *Against the Gods: The Remarkable Story of Risk*. John Wiley & Sons.
Chisholm, A.M. (2002) *An Introduction to Capital Markets*. John Wiley & Sons.
Dunbar, N. (2000) *Inventing Money: The Story of Long-Term Capital Management*. John Wiley & Sons.
Flavell, R. (2002) *Swaps and Other Derivatives*. John Wiley & Sons.
Hull, J.C. (2003) *Options, Futures and Other Derivatives*. Fifth edition. Prentice Hall.
Kolb, R.W. (2003) *Futures, Options and Swaps*. Fourth edition. Blackwell Publishing.
Marshall, J.F. & Kapner, K.R. (1993) *Understanding Swaps*. John Wiley & Sons.
Partnoy, F. (1997) *F.I.A.S.C.O. Blood in the Water on Wall Street*. Profile Books.
Pickford, J. (ed.) (2001) *Mastering Risk: Part 1: Concepts*. FT Prentice Hall.
Shamah, S. (2003) *A Foreign Exchange Primer*. John Wiley & Sons.
Natenberg, S. (1994) *Option Volatility & Pricing*. Probus.
Walmsley, J. (1998) *New Financial Instruments*. John Wiley & Sons.
Wilmott, P. (2001) *Paul Wilmott Introduces Quantitative Finance*. John Wiley & Sons.

USEFUL WEBSITES

American Stock Exchange	www.amex.com
Australian Stock Exchange	www.asx.com.au
Bank for International Settlements	www.bis.org
Borsa Italiana	www.borsaitalia.it
Chicago Board Options Exchange	www.cboe.com
Chicago Board of Trade	www.cbot.com
Chicago Mercantile Exchange	www.cme.com
Commodity Futures Trading Commission	www.cftc.gov
Eurex	www.eurexchange.com
Euronext	www.euronext.com
Fitch	www.fitchratings.com
Hong Kong Futures Exchange	www.hkex.com.hk
International Securities Market Association	www.isma.org
International Swaps & Derivatives Association	www.isda.org
Kansas City Board of Trade	www.kcbt.com
LIFFE	www.liffe.com
London Clearing House	www.lch.com
London Metal Exchange	www.lme.com
MATIF, Paris	www.matif.fr
MEFF, Spain	www.meff.com
New York Board of Trade	www.nyce.com
New York Mercantile Exchange	www.nymex.com
New York Stock Exchange	www.nyse.com
Osaka Securities Exchange	www.ose.or.jp
Pacific Exchange	www.pacificex.com
Philadelphia Stock Exchange	www.phlx.com

Singapore Exchange	www.sgx.com
Standard & Poor's	www.standardandpoors.com
Sydney Futures Exchange	www.sfe.com.au
Tokyo Grain Exchange	www.tge.or.jp
Tokyo International Financial Futures Exchange	www.tiffe.or.jp
Toronto Stock Exchange	www.tse.com

Index